PENGUIN BOOKS

PAVED PARADISE

Henry Grabar is a staff writer at *Slate* who reports on housing, transportation, and urban policy. He has contributed to *The Atlantic*, *The Guardian* (London), and *The Wall Street Journal* and was the editor of the book *The Future of Transportation*. He received the Richard Rogers Fellowship from Harvard University's Graduate School of Design and was a finalist for the Livingston Award for excellence in national reporting by journalists under thirty-five.

Praise for *PAVED PARADISE*

"Consistently entertaining and often downright funny." —*The New Yorker*

"You might expect a book about parking to be a snore. But I have news to report. . . it's a romp, packed with tales of anger, violence, theft, lust, greed, political chicanery, and transportation policy gone wrong . . . highly entertaining."
—Russ Mitchell, *Los Angeles Times*

"[A] wry and revelatory new book about parking (a combination of words I never thought I would write). . . . The dream of the open road assumes a place to put our cars when we arrive at our destination. This is perhaps why so many Americans expect parking to be 'convenient, available and free'—in other words, 'perfect.' Grabar empathizes with these desires, which is partly what makes *Paved Paradise* so persuasive."
—Jennifer Szalai, *The New York Times Book Review*

"Immensely informative and fascinating account."
—*Pittsburgh Post-Gazette*

"Henry Grabar's *Paved Paradise: How Parking Explains the World* covers a topic most people overlook. . . . The author himself makes the bold claim that 'parking is *the* primary determinant of the way the place you live looks, feels, and functions.' By the end of this compelling and insistent book, you might actually believe it."
—*The Wall Street Journal*

"The parking gods have smiled on Henry Grabar, who has managed to write an engrossing account of the ways in which parking has come to define—and in many cases ruin—the modern American city."
—*Financial Times*

"Henry Grabar analyzes parking in *Paved Paradise: How Parking Explains the World*, taking a topic so quotidian that, when explored with his masterful knowledge of urban history, it becomes almost metaphysical."

—*The New Republic*

"*Paved Paradise*, by *Slate* columnist Henry Grabar, investigates a topic that's somehow simultaneously mundane and radicalizing: our extremely American, almost existential search for a parking spot . . . seeing the country through a 'parking rules everything around me' lens is an eye-opening education."

—*Curbed*

"Grabar presents the overarching story of how the unquenchable infrastructure required by parking has determined nearly every aspect of urban planning. . . . All library shelves will benefit from having this definitive account of an everyday drudgery that deeply affects drivers and nondrivers alike."

—*Booklist* (starred review)

"A deep dive into how the complex rules of parking are affecting us all and what we can do about it . . . [Grabar] proves to be an adept guide to this knotty topic. . . . An engrossing examination of parking and the many other issues that intersect with it."

—*Kirkus Reviews* (starred review)

"Using vivid examples and illustrations . . . Grabar builds a powerful case that making parking a little more scarce will make Americans' lives a lot better. This deep dive into an overlooked aspect of the modern world delivers."

—*Publishers Weekly*

"Grabar offers an intriguing, wide-ranging, readable perspective of the urban American parking scene, its issues, and possible future."

—*Library Journal*

"Henry Grabar has written an excellent book on how badly America has screwed up its parking policies, and in turn ruined many of its cities . . . everyone interested in urban economics (or parking) should pick this one up."

—Tyler Cowen, *Marginal Revolution*

"No one thinks about parking, until they can't find a spot. But the implications of finding room for cars at rest are massive, and Henry Grabar has gifted us with a stunningly eye-opening, wildly engaging survey of a chronically—and wrongly—overlooked phenomenon."

—Tom Vanderbilt, author of *Traffic: Why We Drive the Way We Do*

"Parking—the key to the American landscape, hiding in plain sight. But do you want to read a book about it? Yes, if it's Henry Grabar's lively, entertaining tour of how parking contorts our cities and suburbs into unlivable (or at least unhappy) spaces, and how we can remake them."

—Emily Bazelon, author of *Charged: The New Movement to Transform American Prosecution and End Mass Incarceration*

"From curbside battles to sprawling mall lots, penny-pinching mayors to NIMBY homeowners, Henry Grabar's *Paved Paradise* demonstrates, in rich and at times downright absurdist detail, how parking has come to dominate and frustrate our lives—and how we might save our cities."

—Alexandra Lange, author of *Meet Me by the Fountain: An Inside History of the Mall*

"*Paved Paradise* is a total delight, a tour de force of fantastic reporting. You will never look at parked cars the same way again."

—Clive Thompson, author of *Coders: The Making of a New Tribe and the Remaking of the World*

"When people think of cities and suburbs, they think of housing, office buildings, retail shops, and malls. But few of us ever consider parking. Yet as Henry Grabar tells it, parking actually consumes more space in America than housing. *Paved Paradise* is must reading for mayors, urbanists, and everyone who wants to understand America's parking obsession and what it costs our cities, economies, and society. It is a spectacular achievement."

—Richard Florida, author of *The Rise of the Creative Class*

"Like no one else before, Henry Grabar explains why mismanaged parking is the greatest single cause of many urban ills. Everyone who wants to reduce traffic congestion, clean the air, support public transportation, encourage biking and walking, promote business, increase employment, improve public services, and slow global warming should read *Paved Paradise* and heed Grabar's advice for solving the parking problem."

—Donald Shoup, author of *The High Cost of Free Parking*

"Every American with a driver's license needs to read Henry Grabar's brilliant book on parking. He's interviewed a wonderful cast of characters. His analysis of asphalt disaster is laced with humor to help us process bad news: although parking requirements keep housing costs high and limit new businesses, drivers still can't find a space. Grabar demonstrates why the lively, mixed-use, pedestrian neighborhoods we would all like to live in, or at least drive to, are in very limited supply."

—Dolores Hayden, author of *Building Suburbia: Green Fields and Urban Growth, 1820–2000*

HOW PARKING EXPLAINS THE WORLD

Henry Grabar

PENGUIN BOOKS

PENGUIN BOOKS
An imprint of Penguin Random House LLC
penguinrandomhouse.com

First published in the United States of America by Penguin Press, an imprint of Penguin Random House LLC, 2023
Published in Penguin Books 2024

Illustrations by Alfred Twu

LIBRARY OF CONGRESS CONTROL NUMBER: 2022038827
ISBN 9781984881151 (paperback)
ISBN 9781984881137 (hardcover)
ISBN 9781984881144 (ebook)

Printed in the United States of America
1st Printing

Set in MillerText Roman
Designed by Sabrina Bowers

For Mom and Dad

Contents

PART 3 How to Fix the Parking Problem

Introduction

It was a November afternoon in Queens and Jie Zou was looking for a parking spot. He pulled his white Audi in front of a space on Kissena Boulevard, by Rainbow Bakery, and prepared to back in. But Zong Li drove up behind him, angling for the same opening. It was a typical New York moment, a low-stakes impasse that has its own *Seinfeld* episode, until the men got out of their cars.

The argument escalated quickly. Zou punched Li in the face, and Zou's passenger, Jonathan Zhang, produced a baseball bat, which he swung at Li and his companion. After Li wrested the bat away, Zou and Zhang got back into the Audi and pulled across the street. Li followed, smacking the bat on the hood of the Audi. Then Zou hit the accelerator. When the Audi hit Li, he flipped across the hood of the car. Zou kept driving, jumped the curb, and sent the sedan careening into Rainbow Bakery's plate-glass window. The car ended up six feet into the shop, leaving shoppers lying in the shattered glass. Five people were taken to the hospital; Zou, who left the scene on foot, was later arrested and charged with assault.

John Lo, the owner of Rainbow Bakery, stood forlorn among the smashed display cases, bent wall studs, and Sheetrock dust of his store. "It's just for a parking space," he said in disbelief. It was his opening day.

▮ ▮ ▮ ▮ ▮

You may feel similarly shocked to learn that disputes over parking spaces can and do lead to violence. In a few dozen incidents each year, they even lead to death. Typically, these killings get little discussion beyond a perfunctory spot on the local news, in which a bewildered, siren-lit reporter standing outside a store or an apartment complex asks what is obviously intended as a rhetorical question: How could someone end a life over something so trivial? Over a parking spot?

But since these fights keep happening, it's clear that it's *not* a rhetorical question—nor a very difficult one to answer. Parking-driven psychosis is a regular feature of American life, and these outbursts are more ordinary than we might like to think. Indeed, I have come to see these fits of rage as highly visible eruptions of a common parking urge shared by most nonhomicidal drivers, whether we're behind the wheel or not. They are expressions of the same fear that rises into view anytime our parking comes under threat, whether it's the neighborhood lot or the curb in front of your house. "Thinking about parking seems to take place in the reptilian cortex, the most primitive part of the brain, said to govern instinctive behavior involved in aggression, dominance, territoriality, and ritual display," writes Donald Shoup, the country's foremost parking scholar.

It's not hard to grasp what makes parking a fixation: without a place to park, you can never get out of the car. A parking space is nothing less than the link between driving and life itself, the nine-by-eighteen-foot portal through which lies whatever you got in the car to do in the first place. Whoever said life was about the journey and not the destination never had to look for a place to park. Every trip must begin and end with a parking space, and in no uncertain terms. We expect parking to be immediately available, directly in front of our destination, and most important, free. This is unique. It would be unimaginable to hold any other good or service to the same standard. We expect parking to be perfect. Once, I missed an entire summer afternoon at the beach because I refused to pay for parking and, while I hunted, my passengers (wisely) left on the island ferry without me.

Combine our need for unconditional parking satisfaction with the opaque, contested ownership customs that govern curbs, lots, and shared garages, and you have a recipe for bad behavior. Driving into a new city, I often find street-parking instructions so unintelligible I might as well be trying to read a restaurant menu from twenty feet away, through a window, while steering the car. No aspect of American law is as scorned as parking regulations; no civil servant as despised as the parking agent, which must be the only job whose workers say they cover up their uniforms to eat lunch, out of concern that someone will spit in their food. And those are just the rules on paper. Many communities govern parking by unwritten codes you learn the hard way, or by intricate hierarchies, such as the one at the University of California at Berkeley, where the only way to secure a free, reserved parking space on campus is by winning a Nobel Prize.

Our parking urge doesn't just fuel the occasional dustup. The need for a perfect parking space has also shaped the country's physical landscape. It has become the organizing principle of American architecture, from the parking-first design of the strip mall to office towers that sit like sculptures atop their garage pedestals to the house itself, where the garage is often the largest room and the dominant feature of the facade. In most of the country, it is illegal to build a home without parking. The need for parking determines local politics and the behavioral compact that governs the street in front of your house. At the center of our biggest cities, some of the most valuable public land on Earth has been exclusively reserved for the free storage of private cars. By paving so much ground, the metropolitan parking supply directs the course of floodwaters. Parking determines the size, shape, and cost of new buildings, the fate of old ones, the patterns of traffic, the viability of mass transit, the life of public space, the character of neighborhoods, the state of the city budget, our whole spread-out life in which it is virtually impossible to live without an automobile.

The grayness of a city where it's easy to park is embedded in the word *parking* itself, which once referred to curbside patches of greenery, tiny parks. Now it describes something like the opposite, the lifeless blacktop. Our cities are full of moonscapes for the purpose of storing cars. From the perception of scarcity was born an abundance so great it became the single largest use of land in some cities. Between 1950 and 1980, when Los Angeles was the fastest-growing city in the United States, LA County was adding parking spaces at an almost unimaginable pace—850 new spots every day for thirty years. Parking now occupies two hundred square miles of land in the county. As a single parking lot it would form a square of asphalt stretching from LAX to Sherman Oaks to Pasadena to Downey. Or, for nonlocals, a three-story garage the size of the District of Columbia. And this in a place where people routinely complain about how hard it is to find parking.

Why did we do this to the places we love? Was parking really more important than anything else? In Boston, a woman spoke at a community meeting about a new fourteen-unit apartment building to be built down the street. She objected because of parking. She said she had lost eleven pounds because she was afraid to go to the supermarket, lest she return to find she had forfeited her space on the street. She was starving herself to park. It's a good allegory for the whole American parking picture.

It's not pretty. The "parking shortage" functions as a political cudgel to shut down new business and keep out new neighbors. Laws that require every building to include parking prevent us from creating

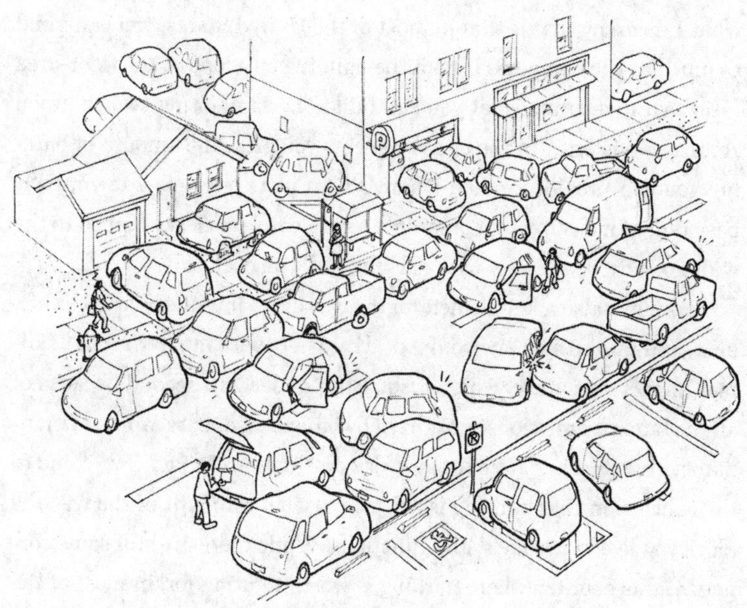

"Hail Mary, full of grace, help me find a parking space."

housing, especially affordable housing, because parking costs so much to construct and takes up so much space. In Seattle, for example, required parking makes up 10 to 20 percent of the cost of construction of multifamily buildings and drives up apartment rents by 15 percent. In California and Arizona, garages increase the cost of affordable housing by 27 percent. The obligation to provide parking makes it impossible to reuse older buildings, compelling needless demolitions, or work with smaller properties, leaving infill parcels fallow. Parking is a mutant strain of yeast in the dough of architecture, making our designs bigger, uglier, and farther apart. If the Empire State Building had been built to the minimum parking requirements of a contemporary American city, for example, its surface parking lot would cover twelve whole blocks. "Parking is power," the architect Andres Duany explained to me. "And what I mean by that is that in most of the United States, you can build as much as you can park. It's not the building envelope or the floor-area ratio that determine what you can build," he said, citing two common zoning provisions. "In the end, what cuts you off is the amount of parking you can provide." When Duany's firm plots out a new town, their base unit of measurement is seventy feet: a whole society planned to the width of a driveway aisle with parking stalls on each side.

Parking is also a key element in the way a city interacts with wildlife, heat, and rain. It's an environmental disaster twice over—first in its direct impact on nature, which it squashes underfoot; second because of all the tailpipe emissions subsidized by billions of dollars' worth of mandatory free parking at virtually every destination. In fact, I've come to the conclusion that parking is *the* primary determinant of the way the place you live looks, feels, and functions. While there are still some corners of this country where parking is worth fighting for, in most of the nation the fight was over decades ago. Parking is plentiful. The country builds more three-car garages than one-bedroom apartments. More square footage is dedicated to parking each car than to housing each person. It is this sea of parking, in which destinations bob like distant buoys, that renders mass transit, biking, and walking difficult or dangerous. "We devote so much land to parking, you really do run out of places to put buildings," Steve Jensen, the former planning director of Omaha, Nebraska, said of his city. By some estimates there are as many as six parking spaces for every car, meaning that our national parking stock is never more than 17 percent occupied. And in spite of all that, somehow, it often seems damn hard to find a space when you need one.

There's a maxim among people who deal with parking professionally that helps explain this situation: Everyone wants parking to be convenient, available, and free. But the forces of time, space, and money conspire in such a way that no thriving place can meet more than two of the three parking needs. Free and convenient but not easily available? That's street parking in Flushing, Queens, or any other big-city neighborhood. Convenient and available but not free? That's the ferryboat parking lot that I left in a huff. Free and available but not convenient? That's where I parked when I missed the boat.

It is the expectation and pursuit of all three parking qualities—convenient, available, and free—for every destination that has led us to require many properties, such as offices, restaurants, and shops, to be more than 50 percent parking by area. Like that woman in Boston, we are wasting away, clinging to the rotten system we know instead of taking a chance on something new and better. In our quest to make it as easy as possible to park, we've made it awfully hard to do anything else.

The "parking problem" is as old as the road itself. In the seventh century BC, the Assyrian king Sennacherib posted signs that read ROYAL ROAD—LET NO MAN DECREASE IT, under penalty of death and public impalement. (And you complain about parking tickets.) Pompeii and Herculaneum have sections of pavement demarcated by raised stones, which may have been early parking regulations. Julius Caesar introduced off-street chariot parking in Rome to reduce traffic. Seventeenth-century New York established a towing service—to clear the streets of animals. You could get your pig back from the pound for a florin, or your horse for two and a half. The terms *dog pound* and *tow pound* both come from this shared history of unclaimed property; a pound was originally an enclosure for animals.

Up until the invention of the automobile, however, the volatile nature of horses was its own form of regulation: you couldn't leave your horse on the street for a week. The advent of the car, especially cars that could be left outside, in all weather, for days or weeks at a time, turned the parking problem into a major dilemma. By the middle of the twentieth century, many experts feared parking—specifically, the lack thereof—was *the* most important issue facing American cities.

Today that seems ridiculous. Amid the crises of racial inequality, widespread pollution, ramshackle housing, job loss, and crime that characterized the urban trajectory after the Second World War, newspaper editorials and conference keynotes were focused on… not enough parking? In the *Los Angeles Times*, "the parking problem" was portrayed as a King Kong–sized gorilla hulking over downtown. Yet we are now living in a world built by the fear of a parking shortage, not just in this country but in many others that have followed America's lead in planning and design.

If driving is freedom, the open road, and limitless space to inhale, parking is its cramped, contested partner, driving's ill-tempered brother, the thing you never see on television because it is simultaneously too boring and too irritating. In the final minutes of *The Sopranos*, Meadow's struggle to park makes a fitting tribute to the series themes of banality and decline. This never would have happened in *Goodfellas*. Driving is the plot of hundreds of movies; parking gets less screen time than using the toilet. Good driving is courteous, but good parking is cutthroat. Driving is the central motif of hundreds of pop songs; if there's a song about finding a parking spot, I haven't heard it. ("Big Yellow Taxi" is the best I could do.)

Yet a big chunk of life happens in and around the parked car: a thousand interstitial moments, scenes of congregation, jubilation, learning, lust, intrigue, horror, and despair. Outside high schools or concerts or convenience stores, parking lots are places of impromptu assembly. The parking lot is where Americans learn to drive. Virtually all of us eat in a parked car from time to time; Sonic opened 3,500 restaurants around the concept. Teenagers in parked cars fondle their way toward paradise by the dashboard light: "Did he try to park?" girls used to be asked. College students assemble in the parking lot to drink themselves into a stupor before football games.

Despite or perhaps because of its growing ubiquity, parking declined from a major field of research and interest to an unloved backwater. Parking is as absent from the training of architects, planners, and engineers as it is from the culture at large. It's overlooked even by the governments and institutions that depend on its good order, marooned between the technical domains of transportation and land use. "Like a bastard child that no one wants," according to one longtime parking executive. The weight we place on good parking in our personal lives is surpassed only by our ignorance of its systemic consequence. I have been reporting on cities for more than a decade, and I have never seen another subject that is simultaneously so integral to the way things work and so overlooked. Car culture, the highways, and the suburbs have been studied to death, but I can count the books about parking on two hands. And yet it comes up in story after story, and it isn't hard to see why: for all the talk about roads and cars, every vehicle spends an estimated 95 percent of its life span parked.

This is in part the story of how we destroyed our cities in search of parking, and the people who helped make it so: the mall builders and the mobsters, the police and the politicians, the garage magnates and the community groups. But it is also a chronicle of those who have begun to repair the damage, waging an unpopular war to take parking down a notch on America's hierarchy of needs, and restore what it took from us.

Not all the way down, mind you. I've read more books about car culture than I care to count, and many have not aged well. Their disdain for the suburbs and the people who live there is condescending at best and, in light of today's urban real estate prices, newly classist. I come to bury that rhetoric, not to praise it. This book proposes an honest reckoning with the subsidies and externalities of cars, but it is not anticar. Parking has made an awful mess of the American city, but drivers are not the architects of this system. In a way they are its victims. In its best moments, driving feels like freedom, but our inability to get around any other way is a kind of prison.

I do, however, take it as a first principle that most people would like to be able to leave the car behind once in a while—to travel on foot, on a bike, with a kid on Rollerblades or a baby in a stroller, on a bus that comes when you need it and goes somewhere you want to be. We are what we build, first because our buildings are an expression of our values, and second because, in time, those buildings come to set the patterns of our lives. This cycle is on full display in this country's long pursuit of free and easy parking.

One reason that Americans retain such nostalgia for college is that it was the only time in our lives so much was within walking distance. We take our vacations to places where we can get out of the car—Charleston, Disneyland, Manhattan, Miami Beach, Rome. Housing prices reflect the desirability of such destinations, making anything but a brief stay off-limits to all but a moneyed few. The promise of this book—the promise of fixing the parking problem—is not to force the reader out of her car but to let her forget it now and then for a moment. In a world with better parking it would be easier, not harder, to find a spot, and much easier to live in a place where you would not need to drive quite so often. In a world with better parking kids could walk to school and grown-ups to the grocery store. In a world with better parking, there might be fewer places to park, but in place of those old parking spots would emerge a city so much richer and fuller and fairer that you would not think twice about what had been lost.

In the last two decades, some people have begun to seek those changes. Architects, activists, planners, builders, researchers, and environmentalists have started to interrogate the country's relationship to parking. How could something so fundamental to our every movement have gone unstudied for so long, missing from textbooks and schools and research journals, even as it became the defining feature of the American urban environment? "The only thing drivers know about parking is the letter *P* on the gearshift lever," a commercial parking expert told me once. "And sometimes they mix that up with the letter *R*." Parking was ready for a revolution. These people have caught on to the central role that parking plays in determining whether we get more places that look like Greenwich Village or another strip mall. Their stories will, I hope, suffuse you with the dawning awareness that parking rules everything around you.

And yet, for most of us, to the extent we think about parking at all, the thought is very simple: Where's my spot?

PART 1

What a Mess We Made

CHAPTER 1

Housing for Cars and Housing for People

> The quality of life in cities has much to do with systems of transport, which are often a source of much suffering for those who use them. Many cars, used by one or more people, circulate in cities, causing traffic congestion, raising the level of pollution, and consuming enormous quantities of non-renewable energy. This makes it necessary to build more roads and parking areas which spoil the urban landscape.
>
> —Pope Francis

In 1991, a generational tale of parking's role in American life began in Solana Beach, California. This story isn't just, or even primarily, about where we should put our cars when we're not driving them. It's about how the need for parking holds an insurmountable power over the decisions we make about the places we live, a claim of such self-evident weight it takes precedence over much else that we say we hold dear. Because it's hard to find a consensus view about whether the parking shortage is real, imagined, or addressable, the need for parking is an evergreen retort, straddling the line between a real right of access and a contrived and disingenuous excuse. One Southern California developer told me that this dual nature was one of the things that made parking such a tricky and emotional trip wire. "It's like a plain pasta that takes on the flavor of whatever sauce you put on it. It's a proxy for *so many other things*, and a real thing in and of itself, and that dance of parking as proxy and parking as parking adds up to a lot of badness and dysfunction." In other words, sometimes people are talking about parking, and sometimes they're talking about something else.

When it came to building affordable housing in Solana Beach, they were definitely talking about something else.

Solana Beach is a posh suburb of San Diego. Time-share condos around pools, houses around cul-de-sac driveways, shops by the highway. Marine layer in the morning, blue skies in the afternoon, and the sound of the Pacific crashing on the beach below the cliffs. Solana Beach, stated *The San Diego Union Tribune*, was "six square miles of sunny coastal ambiance," a place that epitomized the bewildering patterns of postwar suburban development in Southern California.

But there was nothing sunny about the 1928 motor court at 204 South Sierra Avenue, at the heart of the city's down-on-its-heels main drag. The walls were damp; rats and cockroaches roamed the rotten floors at night. Toilets broke and showers lacked hot water. The absentee landlord, Leon Perl, lived in Beverly Hills.

Miguel Zamora, a thirty-nine-year-old tenant from Guadalajara, rented a one-room studio there with his wife and four kids. He fixed things himself and paid for it himself. He repaired the plumbing. Installed a water pump. Put in a new lock.

In January 1991, Solana Beach began inspecting the property, issuing violations to which, the city said, Perl was only minimally responsive. By the fall of 1992, the city had filed an eighty-three-count criminal complaint against the landlord for the illegal conditions. Perl decided it was more trouble than it was worth, so he moved to bulldoze the place. Eviction notices went up on the cracked wooden doors in November.

The tenants were evicted and the building demolished, and the city settled out of court with Perl. The Legal Aid Society, representing the tenants, secured a commitment from Solana Beach to develop replacement housing for the thirteen evicted households by 1999.

By 2005, just three homes had been built. Not until sixteen years after the evictions did Solana Beach, where the median home now costs more than $2 million, put forth a site for developers to house the remaining ten families. The spot the city picked was not quite as good as the site of the original motor court—by then a dirt lot in the middle of a resurgent downtown strip—but it was close to the beach and less than a mile from the commuter rail. It was a city-owned parking lot. A perfect place to build affordable housing.

At least, that's what Ginger Hitzke thought. In 2008, the thirty-three-year-old Hitzke was trying to establish herself as an affordable housing developer. She had started working as a receptionist in a developer's office a decade earlier and, at the start of the recession, was ready to try to build things herself. Hitzke was an improbable figure in the world of Southern California real estate. She grew up poor. Didn't go to college. She was a woman in a male-dominated field. She had just $14,000 in the bank when she went out on her own.

But when a friend scanned and sent her a newspaper clipping about the Solana Beach project, she thought: *This is my model.* A small project in a small city for a good cause. Unlike most affordable housing projects, whose tenants might be granted apartments by lottery, the Solana Beach housing was associated with specific people, kicked out of town almost two decades earlier. People like Miguel Zamora.

Hitzke scraped together $10 million in financing and Solana Beach gave her a shot. She called the project the Pearl, a reference to the slumlord whose evictions had set the process in motion.

There was a reason she had no trouble getting the job: the fixed costs of building things in California are so high that ten affordable units is not an attractive proposition to most developers. In Solana Beach, as it would turn out, the risks were not smaller because the project was small.

I visited Hitzke in October 2020, in a suburb on the other side of San Diego called Lemon Grove, where she worked. She talked fast, swore frequently, and broke up her sentences with a high, staccato laugh. Only when we talked about Solana Beach did her voice sink. "I think people take a bit of joy that I failed so spectacularly," she reflected. "I was in the *LA Times* and now I've got fucking *Slate* on the phone. People call and say, 'Are you okay?' And I say, 'Fuck you. You know I'm not.'"

Her office was on the ground floor of one of her apartment buildings, Citronica Two, and it reflected her boisterous demeanor. Her door was etched with the words BOSS LADY/PATRONA, and her desk sat beneath a bright mural by a local artist named Maxx Moses—a kind of impulse buy. In 2019, stoned at the Warhol exhibit at the San Francisco Museum of Modern Art, Hitzke had experienced a deep longing for art in her life. When she got back to Lemon Grove, Moses was outside her office looking for walls to paint. So she had a mural behind her chair. Nearby, a painting in a gilded frame depicted her as a recumbent, dark-haired Glinda the Good Witch, showering rainbows over an Emerald City modeled after the building. The wand had an *H*, which looked a little like the Hitzke Development logo and also a little like Hillary Clinton's 2016 presidential campaign logo. Ginger loved Hillary. She drove a caravan of teenagers to Iowa to campaign for her. Her Twitter bio read "Fabulous Real Estate Developer + Fat Lady. Proudly race-mixing since 1994. Suburb abolitionist." Hitzke is white; her husband is black; the couple has two sons.

Abolishing the suburbs, well, that was a work in progress. Ginger Hitzke's affordable housing project in Solana Beach was dead. Cause of death: parking.

"Parking has been the number-one topic that surpasses all other things that go along with what you hear when you're trying to develop apartments," Hitzke said. "Crime, property values, community character, parking is an everyday—God, I hate the topic so much." She burst out laughing. "I laugh because I hate this topic so much."

Originally, Hitzke had planned to build eighteen apartments on the site of the Solana Beach municipal parking lot. She would provide thirty-one parking spots to make up for the loss of the public parking, plus add twenty-two spots for residents, inside a fifty-three-space underground garage. Parking fees would help offset construction costs. There would also be a small retail space. She imagined filling it with a little grocery store.

It's worth taking a moment to understand just what compelled the fifty-three-spot underground garage that would drag Ginger down. First, there were twenty-two places for residents—a parking requirement of local zoning here in Solana Beach, like almost everywhere else in the country, to make sure residents wouldn't park in the street. Second, there were the thirty-one spaces in the municipal parking lot, which Hitzke was under pressure to rebuild, underground and at great expense. Because this site sits just one thousand feet from the Pacific Ocean, it falls under the jurisdiction of a group called the California Coastal Commission (CCC). The CCC was born of a virtuous impulse to prevent developers from cordoning off the seaside for the exclusive use of nearby residents. It was created by ballot referendum in the 1970s and later given permanent authority over construction along the state's 1,100-mile coast, including for inland sites.

The CCC was part of a burgeoning, powerful California slow-growth movement, which successfully restricted development in some pristine natural areas, such as Big Sur. But it had a malevolent counterpart: a group of metropolitan homeowners who brought that righteous sense of preservation to urban and suburban neighborhoods. Using tools like parking requirements, single-family zoning, historic preservation, minimum lot sizes, and lawsuits under California environmental law, the state's homeowners wrote the playbook for how to exclude new neighbors—and look righteous while doing it. They were astonishingly effective at keeping new residents out of coastal cities like San Diego, Los Angeles, and San Francisco. Of course, people didn't stop coming to California. Newer, younger, and poorer residents just spilled out away from the coast, into fire-prone forests in the north of the state and scorching deserts in the south. Drive till you qualify for a mortgage, and then spend the rest of your life driving to work.

That was Ginger Hitzke. Though her office was just outside San Diego in Lemon Grove, Ginger lived with her family in Temecula, seventy miles north. There's an inverse correlation between real estate prices and summer temperatures. On a blistering July day, the temperature rises ten degrees from Solana Beach to Lemon Grove, and another ten degrees in Temecula. Before the 2020 coronavirus pandemic, more than half of workers in Temecula spent more than thirty minutes a day getting to work. Some days, Ginger was part of a burgeoning class of California "supercommuters," who spend more than three hours a day commuting. (More than 7 percent of the workforce in her county was in this category, more than three times the rate in San Diego County.)

Which is *why*, ironically enough, Ginger had to rebuild that parking lot in Solana Beach. Because without parking, there's no beach access for the millions of Californians pushed inland by coastal housing restrictions. The fewer people permitted to move to places like Solana Beach, the greater the egalitarian cachet of its free parking. So the California Coastal Commission, charged with preserving the coastline, is also the state's greatest defender of beachfront parking lots. It's an irony that plays out at every national park, at every mountain trailhead, at every beach and boat launch: for most Americans, there is no access to nature without parking. This is why Yellowstone's Old Faithful sits inside a giant horseshoe of parking lots. In Texas, beaches are presumed to be parking lots, and local authorities can keep cars off the sand only if they provide a parking space for every fifteen feet of beach closed to traffic.

Restrict or charge for nonresident parking—as towns in the Hamptons or on Cape Cod do—and wealthy residents can keep the beach to themselves without having to say so. In white neighborhoods along Rockaway Beach in New York City, street curbs that abut the beach are categorized as "fire zones"—a blanket parking prohibition, all down the block, under the spurious logic that fire trucks need the clear curbs to turn around. In a 1995 sketch for Michael Moore's *TV Nation* show, the comedian Janeane Garofalo led a band of multicultural Brooklynites up to the hedge funder enclave of Greenwich, Connecticut, to try to subvert the town's rule restricting park and beach access to residents only. The beach-day crew was barred by police from entering the town parking lot, so they attempted a marine invasion in a flotilla of dinghies, to boos from locals. Three years later, a law student who had been turned away trying to jog in a Greenwich park filed a lawsuit against the town, and in 2001 the Connecticut Supreme Court ruled beaches and parks were public forums and access could not be restricted. But towns like Greenwich simply established hefty parking fees instead: while Greenwich adults can buy a $40 permit for season-long beach access, out-of-town visitors must pay $40 for a single day of beach parking, plus $9 per person in the car. Up the coast in Stamford and Fairfield, nonresidents pay more than ten times as much as residents for a beach parking pass. In Westport, Connecticut, residents pay $50 for a season beach pass, while visitors from New Haven or Bridgeport pay $775. Comparatively, the California Coastal Commission's mission is a noble one. But only because poor people are not allowed to live along the coast in the first place.

While her affordable housing project was shaping up in Solana Beach, Ginger Hitzke was working on the complex in Lemon Grove in which her office now sits: two five-story apartment blocks called Citronica One and Citronica Two. Those names, like Ginger's nearby Citron Court, are both a play on the name of the city and a tribute to Ketel One Citroen vodka, which nursed Hitzke through the debacle in Solana Beach. Both buildings were adjacent to Lemon Grove's commercial center and a light-rail station that went straight to downtown San Diego.

Citronica One survived a close shave with suburban parking requirements. Ginger was sweeping up the crumbs of California's affordable housing tax credits, and she could get only enough money together to build the project with one level of parking. A city politician told her, "We're not going to let parking get in the way of this development." She couldn't believe it. The enduring shock of California politics, for Ginger, was how many people would put their heart and soul into getting elected, only to get cold feet when it came to actually making a call. "Never has a public official who makes the approvals ever said to me, 'How much will your rent increases be?' Never cared about a single thing, but I cannot tell you how many times they ask where everyone will park when they come over for a birthday. No one cares about the quality of life for the tenants. I've never had someone say, 'How tall are your ceilings? Are you doing the minimum?' Ceiling height makes a big difference!" Instead, the focus was always on parking. "We care more about housing for our cars than we care about housing for ourselves. Period."

Not in Lemon Grove, though. Citronica One was built with fifty-six affordable apartments, made possible by the provision of just one parking space per unit. She loved this building: the smooth stucco, the wood-framed windows, the segmented facade that gave the five-story apartment complex the variegated look of an old-fashioned street. And she loved seeing her tenants, some of whom had moved in after living on the streets downtown. When Ginger talked about choosing between housing for people and housing for cars, she was not being metaphorical. She was describing a literal trade-off she makes in every pro forma, the spreadsheet of expenses and revenues that determines how a developer uses her land. Parking costs money and takes up space. More parking means less housing. In a ten-year study of low-income apartments in California, Berkeley's Terner Center concluded that structured parking added $35,945 to the construction cost of every single home. Required parking costs the average American renter household $1,700 a year by one estimate, imposing a half-a-billion-dollar penalty annually on tenants who don't drive. And for every completed building with a bunch of parking included, there was a blueprint for an unbuilt structure that had been sacrificed on that altar.

Across Citronica Lane, Ginger built Citronica Two. This building had eighty apartments reserved for seniors. They were classified as affordable to renters of "very low income," in part because of the savings Ginger had unlocked in her pro forma: only half the apartments had their own parking space.

The tenants didn't always love her back. She may have been providing high-quality, well-maintained affordable housing, but she was also the lord of the public parking here and the keeper of the parking grievances. At a handful of curbside spots reserved for the tenants of her commercial storefronts, Ginger put yellow paint and signs that warned drivers would be towed, but with some storefronts vacant, it was hard to keep parched travelers out of the oasis.

"The perception of available parking makes people insane," Ginger stage-whispered, surveying the curb. "These parking spaces are so coveted. You would not believe the stories people come to the door and tell me about why they have to park right there, they have to, if they don't, their grandmother is going to die, because if they don't park right there, they can't bring her medication, and do I want their grandmother to *die*?" Come on, she would say—if your grandmother lived downtown, you'd expect to pull right up to her door? But that is the nature of parking desire; it is so forceful it obviates, in the moment, any external organizing principle that might separate the car from the curb. There is only the empty spot and the driver that needs it; there is no future occupant, no potential emergency, no set of universal rules. "I am doing emotional damage to people. Open parking spaces to human beings, next to the thing they want to be at, it's like water for a thirsty person. They want to park their car and I'm holding these spaces. 'This *bitch*.'"

I asked if she ever tried to explain to her tenants that it was because they had only one space per apartment, with no guest parking, that they had apartments here at all—instead of a hundred miles away in the desert, or worse, sleeping in a tent under an overpass. "No one gives a fuck!" she exclaimed from an empty spot. "No one cares. Just give me one of *these*!"

Ginger wasn't complaining about the parking obsession because she was some holier-than-thou bicycle commuter. She drove an extended-cab Ford Expedition, one of the biggest cars on the road, because it made her feel safe. "Look at what I drive around in, by myself, like a horrible piece-of-shit human being!" Her house in Temecula had a three-car garage, a driveway that fit three more cars, and two spaces on the street.

This made her a bit of a hypocrite, she reasoned. But also it was not really her fault. Temecula was at the frontier of California sprawl, a place where developers were still cutting the tops off the hills to build those little circuit boards of suburbia. Temecula was where the hot San Diego housing market went to blow off steam, Ginger said. The obstacles to building on the cool California coast were both a professional and a personal thorn in her side.

Everything that went right for Ginger in Lemon Grove went wrong in Solana Beach. Ginger had worked in affordable housing since the nineties, and she thought she had heard it all. You'd propose twenty affordable townhomes and neighbors would ask about the murderous housing projects in Chicago (the city where Ginger grew up, not that anyone at the community meetings knew that). "All these motherfuckers talk about Cabrini-Green, as if they've ever been there in their life," she said. In Fremont, she heard someone freak out that they'd never get their mail again, since postal workers didn't go to low-income neighborhoods.

A cross-section of Ginger Hitzke's design for The Pearl in Solana Beach, California. A 10-year study of low-income apartments in the state concluded that structured parking adds $35,945 to the construction cost of every single new unit.

The discourse in Solana Beach was, somehow, even less guarded. "Low-income people tend to own cars that are in disrepair and ride motorcycles adding to the noise of a 'lights out at 8 p.m. community,'" wrote Marylyn Rinaldi, a neighbor, in a letter to the city council. "Hispanic people typically drop trash wherever they are," wrote Barbara Roemmich, a time-share owner, to the California Coastal Commission.

Several people felt that low-income tenants didn't deserve to live near the beach.

"The development plan calls for ten low-income housing units, but low-income housing should not be at the beach. Low-income housing should be on the other side of the [I-5 freeway] at the closest," wrote Ernest Kurschat, a time-share owner at the nearby Sand Pebbles Resort, in a letter to the California Coastal Commission. He scoffed at the tiny would-be grocery store that Ginger had hopefully presented in her plans. "Is that for the parking lot attendant booth? Or is it a food stamp office for the low-income housing?"

"Back in 1971, I was poor," wrote Jill Hubbard. "I lived in Largo, Fla. No one said to me because I was poor I could live across the street from the beach. I, of course, lived far inland from the beach in an area that was not considered a great part of town."

In an early community meeting, one neighbor told Ginger, "We don't need more diversity in this neighborhood. We already have the Mexican apartments down the street." Another said they shouldn't "comingle" low-income people and million-dollar condos. "Our coastal community is a precious resource that once disturbed its damage is unchangeable," wrote Ray Del Pilar of the ten homes to be built in the parking lot. "I am upset about the low-income housing... behind a place where families with young children stay all summer," wrote Lindsay Hardison. "I am concerned for the safety and quality of our annual vacation spot," wrote Kent Blake.

Several neighbors threatened to move their family reunions elsewhere if the project was built. Others were concerned that Ginger's three-story building would "block the ocean air and cool breezes."

Almost every letter mentioned the sanctity of the parking lot, and the savvier writers made it the center of their argument. Badmouthing the poor was a little unseemly, but complaining about parking was morally unimpeachable. After all, that lot was the staging ground for the junior lifeguard program! Did Ginger expect local teens to learn CPR in a dank garage?

This opposition slowed things down. Hitzke submitted her proposal in March 2009. She won the exclusive right to negotiate with the city the next year and submitted a design. After workshops in 2011, the city convinced her to drop the number of homes from eighteen to ten and make the public garage free (she lost eight units but only one parking space). The cost per unit rose by almost 50 percent, to $664,000 apiece.

It took another *three years* for the city to vote on the project—at a four-hour meeting, standing room only, in April 2014. Annex seating was provided in the lobby of city hall.

Mayor Thomas Campbell asked the crowd to stand and salute the flag, and they dutifully murmured the Pledge of Allegiance. Ginger and her team presented the revised project in the frigid, over-air-conditioned room: smaller, and with a new design. The Prairie-style modernism of the original drawings was replaced by a series of A-frame roofs, like houses on a Monopoly board, in the hope that this traditional form would soften the opposition. It didn't.

Time-share owners unpacked their horror stories of low-income housing. They complained that the project, which had been under way for six years and promised for twenty-two, had been forced upon them with no warning. They said the building, at thirty-five feet high, was towering, physically absurd. And they griped, hour after hour, about the parking. Neighbor Andreas Loeffler told the city that the parking spaces would be too small. Bill Gifford said that the spaces inside the Pearl would be 1.5 feet narrower than the city lot spaces. "That's drastic!" he said. "I go to Whole Foods. If you want to see a small parking space, you want to see a small turning radius—go to Whole Foods in Encinitas. I've been three times, and I'll never go back." Herb Brown said the problem wasn't low-income housing; it was the tight turnaround in the garage. Many residents were concerned about the parking being underground—how would people *find* it? Would surfers have to carry their boards up a one-story ramp, in addition to down the two hundred steps to the beach? "I'm so torn up on it," ruminated Mike Nichols, a city councilman, as the hearing approached hour five. "These parking spaces today, versus those in the future, they won't be the same. It's like watching a baseball game on TV versus at the stadium. It's not the same experience."

Ginger, in a white shirt and black blazer, was perched behind the lectern, biting her lip and taking notes. Not everyone spoke against the project. The town was more restrained, in person and on camera, than it was in writing. Nobody was talking about Mexicans anymore—they were mostly talking about parking. When Ginger rose, at last, she sounded genuinely wounded. "This isn't a fun place to be. I like my job. I like what I do. I'm really proud of it. It's really tough to hear that people don't like what I'm proposing, but I think it's going to be good. I have a very good track record. I take very seriously being a very good developer. Being hands-on. I wouldn't have gotten as far as I have if I didn't care. This is my livelihood and this is my life. Life is short and the world is small and you need to do good things."

And again, ninety minutes later, as the city council pressed her to redesign the parking garage, she gave a final plea: "Can I please ask: please think about housing people more than housing cars. That's all I have to say. Thank you."

The project was approved.

Five and a half years had passed since Hitzke first met with the city. Five and a half years to build ten apartments. Finally she had gotten the go-ahead. Ginger's best friend, who is Mexican American, started to fantasize about the grand opening. They would get low-riders and Norteño music, have some fun with the stereotypes that had been thrown their way...

But the time-share owners weren't done with her yet.

The condo across the street, Seascape Sur, sued Hitzke and the city. Joined by a group of residents under the banner "Save Our Beach Access," they argued that the city had violated a deed restriction requiring the land to be a parking lot in perpetuity. They also said Ginger's ten-unit building ought to require an assessment under the California Environmental Quality Act (CEQA), as if it were a power plant or a freeway. Among the reasons for a CEQA review, they argued, was that the parking spaces would not be visible from the street, so residents, visitors, and employees at the retail space might generate emissions searching for parking at the curb.

Fear of Chicago gangbangers was not grounds for a lawsuit. But the parking shortage? Absolutely. "I think it's very easy for people to look at this and think the neighbors are complaining because it's a low-income project coming in," Seascape's lawyer, Everett DeLano, told the *Del Mar*

Times. "They're not. They would like to see a different city parking lot do this project. It's just that this site is uniquely used for public parking."

The city and Hitzke won the case in 2015, but the plaintiffs appealed, and the matter wasn't settled by the Fourth District Court of Appeals until December 2016—two and a half years after the city's approval. "Seascape does not point to any factual foundation for the testimony of commentators concerning the potential lost parking," the court ruled, and furthermore, there was no deed requiring a surface parking lot on the high bluffs over the Pacific Ocean for all eternity.

By then, Hitzke had been forced to surrender the loans she had earmarked for Solana Beach. She had missed deadlines. And a project begun during the recession, when labor and materials were cheap, was now scheduled for construction during the country's longest run of uninterrupted job growth since the Second World War.

After all that, Hitzke was only a million short—if she hadn't had to replace the surface parking, but only provided spots for the new residents, she could have done it. But that risked starting the process all over again. Solana Beach councilman David Zito, by this point the only remaining elected official in the city who had voted on the original proposal, defended the necessity of the underground garage. They were "ethically, morally obligated" to replace the parking because of "residential harmony," he told the *Los Angeles Times*. (Zito also brought up Cabrini-Green.) Ironically, in the interim, the city had spent $5 million on improvements to make the neighborhood a more pedestrian-friendly walking district.

In 2020, twelve years after she met with the city of Solana Beach for the first time, Hitzke threw in the towel. "They did exactly what they set out to do: stall the project to the point where it stopped making sense anymore." The city-owned parking lot that Solana Beach offered up remained a parking lot. Her project, whose costs had ballooned to $1.1 million per housing unit, had earned a dubious distinction. In a state with the highest housing costs in the country, Hitzke's three-story, ten-unit project, an investigation in the *Los Angeles Times* revealed, was the most expensive affordable housing project in the state—and probably in the country. There were many reasons for that, including the lengthy delays, the state's prevailing wage law, and the surging cost of materials. But the biggest one, the one that broke the pro forma, was that what Hitzke was really building was a fifty-three-space underground garage with a few apartments on top.

The city's sense of its own needs could not have been clearer; the debt to the evicted inhabitants was worthless. Their homes could be permitted only if they could be arranged, geometrically, financially, and politically, around Solana Beach's main concern, which was parking. But even that assurance was at times a moving target. To understand the way that the parking shortage suppresses the production of affordable housing, it is not enough to know that there is a mothballed project like the Pearl in every suburb. You must realize, too, that for every Ginger Hitzke there are ten builders who will not even bother. If you find yourself in her position, negotiating with neighbors over parking spaces, you have already lost. At a time when the country desperately needs more housing, the debate over whether to admit new people into the neighborhood often boils down to a question that's easier to say no to with a clean conscience: Is there enough parking?

The unusual thing about the Solana Beach homes was not the five years it took for city approval, or the subsequent thirty-two-month lawsuit over parking, but the fact that the intended inhabitants of the new project were not anonymous future winners of some affordable housing lottery. They were onetime neighbors, real people with faces and names and homes a little farther inland. Thirty years after the city inspected his run-down apartment, Miguel Zamora was a silver-haired grandfather. He no longer lived a block from the beach. He lived five miles away, longing to return. Others died waiting on Solana Beach to keep up its end of the bargain.

CHAPTER 2

Fighting Over Parking Spaces

The perception of limited parking is a bedrock truth of American community, whether it finds its corporeal form in a baseball bat breaking a windshield or a neighborhood meeting of citizens, standing athwart history yelling, "Parking!" These gripes are part of a hidden, nationwide system through which the parking problem, actual or contrived, controls the production of new homes in this country, especially in the few places where car ownership is optional. Though the country is blanketed in parking codes of dry and technical specificity, and though city budgets have grown fat on parking violation revenue, such institutions are merely a starting point to understanding the real work of day-to-day parking management in this country, most of which is performed by drivers and neighbors themselves. Whether that happens in a letter to the city council or a chair marking a claim to the curb is simply a matter of style.

In reality, lots of high-value parking gets distributed in an extralegal gray zone of pressure, tradition, and theft. Commercial parking is rife with stealing and mismanagement. Regulated street parking is subject to widespread abuse by police, politicians, public-sector workers, diplomats, and disability impostors. Unregulated street parking is a rough business, administered according to local mores and enforced by an implicit threat of violence. And of course, nosy neighbors tell builders what they're *really* allowed to do. Ginger Hitzke is not the only affordable housing developer to have had her ship dashed on the rocks of a "parking shortage."

That is what happened in Boston, in August 2020, when the nonprofit Pine Street Inn found a site for a 202-unit building that would include 140 apartments for formerly homeless people, along with 62 affordable units. Pine Street Inn spent a year negotiating with neighborhood groups, which resulted in the project losing a floor and 23 apartments. Then the owner of a nearby building filed suit to halt the project, arguing that its 39 parking spaces—a special dispensation from the city's zoning board to encourage the production of affordable housing—were not enough and that his tenant, a local brewery, relied on the street parking that the project would jeopardize.

That is also what happened one month earlier in Denver, in the gentrifying African American neighborhood of Five Points, where Eddie Woolfolk had for decades run the Agape Christian Church. Woolfolk, who is black, dreamed of building thirty-six affordable units for people making less than $19,500 a year, especially for those who were formerly homeless and formerly incarcerated, on some land she owned near the church. The required parking would have added to the cost of the $13 million project and reduced the number of apartments, so Woolfolk sought a variance from city planning to provide just six spots. She figured most of her tenants would be too poor to own a car anyway. She had the support of her local councilwoman and the city's zoning administrator. But a dozen neighbors complained about parking to the city's appeals board, which voted three to two to stop the project.

And it was what happened in Buffalo the month before that, when a local nonprofit tried to build nine apartments to serve a waiting list of local families more than six hundred names long. They included two parking spaces. More than fifty neighbors wrote to the city to complain, and Buffalo planners tabled the project.

These stories are not anomalies—they're just three of the stories that got the attention of a local reporter somewhere during the summer of 2020. Neighbors who demand that new projects come with more parking are essentially levying a tax, one that drives up the cost of new homes and stops a countless number from being built at all. This dynamic occurs in distant suburbs and urban cores, but most often it happens in older, midrise, walkable neighborhoods where street parking is hard to come by—in other words, neighborhoods built before parking was required, with a set of nearby amenities to match. Residents who have chosen to live in older buildings in older neighborhoods depend on the public parking supply and do not want to share it. In these places, parking requirements for new buildings function as a protection racket, forcing new neighbors to pay for what old neighbors get for free on the street. This parking anxiety leads the way to Malthusian thinking about neighborhoods and cities: when the impact of new neighbors is measured out in parking spaces, every place starts to look crowded.

This drag from angry neighbors is hard to measure with any confidence, but it is almost impossible to avoid.* In one 2022 survey of twelve thousand U.S. adults, more than half of baby boomers, a group that tends to dominate local politics, said free parking was more important than affordable housing in their neighborhood. (And that was in the abstract!) As in Solana Beach, each of these stories of thwarted

*A 2014 study from Melbourne, Australia (which has similar land use politics to U.S. cities), found that more than half of 325 appeals of new housing lodged over four months of 2012 cited parking as a "significant issue: a reason for objection, refusal or determination." Elizabeth Taylor, "'Fight the Towers! Or Kiss Your C Park Goodbye': How Often Do Residents Assert Car Parking Rights in Melbourne Planning Appeals?," *Planning Theory & Practice* 15, no. 3 (2014): 328–48.

housing production shows the thin line between parking law—nominally, as scientific and impartial a part of a building code as a sprinkler requirement—and the impromptu civic revolts that determine how things actually work.

The parking theorist Sarah Marusek writes about parking as "frontier law," by which she means people feel free to dismiss the impossibly prolix set of rules that govern who can park where, for how long, for how much. The nation's parking supply is also a perpetual frontier in a more real sense, an asphalt territory whose prime plots are seized anew each day. American settlers got to stake their claim only once; American drivers get to put their divining rods to work every few hours.

As a result, it is a distressingly frequent occurrence for someone to be murdered over a parking space in this country. Former NFL safety T. J. Cunningham was a beloved assistant principal at a Denver-area high school when he was killed over a parking space dispute by a neighbor. In Las Vegas, Shane Pacada died of a bullet to the chest over a parking space. In the suburbs of Washington, DC, a man was charged with attempted murder for opening fire on a neighbor who had parked in his spot (the victim was hit but survived). Twenty-eight-year-old Thomas Rodriguez was killed in Dallas after an argument over a parking space.

That was just in February 2019.

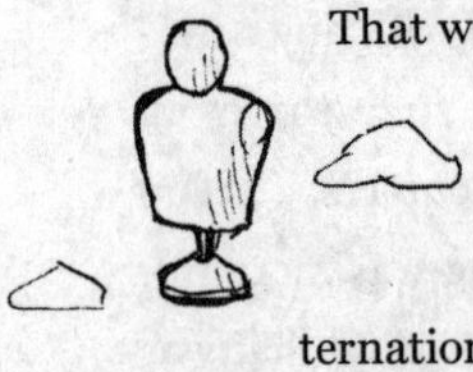

Craig Hicks, the gun-crazy bully who infamously murdered three Muslim American University of North Carolina students in 2015, prompting an international outcry, was someone whose aggressive nature had frightened his neighbors for years. He was also obsessed with parking spots. For nearly a decade, since moving into his wife's second-story apartment, he had left notes on windshields in their condo complex calling attention to parking etiquette. Alternately un- and underemployed, Hicks tinkered with his collection of firearms and surveilled neighbors' parties and parking. Occasionally he would patrol the lot, pistol tucked into a hip holster. The local towing company knew him and stopped responding to his calls; the Finley Forest housing association also told him to stop calling. Police who searched the apartment after his arrest found "pictures and detailed notes on parking activity."

Shortly before she was murdered, Yusor Mohammad Abu-Salha texted a warning to her husband, Deah Shaddy Barakat: "I just got yelled at for it by that crazy neighbor who said we are only allowed two spots." Barakat printed out a map for family and friends, making clear the five unassigned spaces where they could freely park when they visited. It was in one of those free spaces that Barakat had parked when he was killed. On that evening, as the young people sat down to dinner in their apartment, Barakat used his cell phone to record the fatal confrontation that began when Hicks knocked on their door, raving that the lot was full. "You've got three cars in the lot, and I don't have a parking spot," he says shortly before he opens fire.

Hicks is an American archetype. While many parking disputes are one-offs, a good number involve older, heavily armed men who engage in confrontations again and again. They are less self-interested drivers than self-appointed sheriffs of the parking lot. Racism is a recurring feature of these attacks. In October 2019, a Florida man named Paul McClure used a slur before opening fire on two black men parked illegally outside a liquor store. The next month in Milwaukee, Clifton Blackwell spotted a Peruvian American man parked outside a restaurant. "Why did you invade my country?" he yelled. "Why don't you respect my laws?" He threw acid in the man's face. Markeis McGlockton, a twenty-eight-year-old black man, was murdered in a convenience store parking lot in July 2018 for parking in a handicapped space. The shooter, Michael Drejka, tried to invoke Florida's infamous "stand your ground" law. It turned out that he had threatened to shoot another man in the same parking lot just two months earlier. Drejka was sentenced to twenty years in prison.

Those are extreme cases, but many of us have brushed against the threat that undergirds a parking claim (and then driven on). Public officials tolerate this practice uneasily in cities like Boston, Chicago, and Pittsburgh. The chair that marks a freshly shoveled parking spot after a blizzard is not an invitation to sit down. When Boston tried to limit this spot-saving practice to the forty-eight hours after the snowfall, a city councilman protested: "The issue speaks to the basic principle of what it means to be an American.... Like the gold miner and pioneers, residents have a right to stake their claims."

In Hawaii, you might see a spot marked with an upside-down bucket labeled "kapu," a word borrowed from the ancient Hawaiian custom of forbidden acts. Kapu violations are no longer capital offenses, but still worth taking seriously. In Philadelphia, it's "savesies," which is illegal, though that's never stopped Philadelphians before. In Chicago, "dibs" is in effect after a snowstorm, and the implements of dibs (painstakingly recorded by the hundreds on the "Chicago Dibs" Tumblr) might include a piano bench, a wheelchair, a car door, two vacuum cleaners, a chair with a few complimentary beers, a grill, a fully set dining room table, and all manner of Nativity figurines, including a mannequin torso perched on a board between two cinderblocks with the message "The body of Christ compels you not to take my spot" scrawled across the chest in Sharpie. Mostly, Chicagoans save spaces with chairs. In my head I've always imagined the message is that you or your car might be attacked with the object being used to save the space, but sometimes the threat is explicit. "No Parking," read one sign. "I did not spend several predawn hours and risk of cardiac infarction to shovel this space for you. If you are arrogant enough to park here, I hope you are the type of person who can afford a new set of tires." There are threats and pleas in equal measure, and one message that makes clear the solemn territorial understanding. "This is the land for which I fought, These chairs my deed."

Drivers take 21 percent longer to leave a spot if someone is waiting, as if their holding is suddenly worth more once someone else wants it, and that very desire enhances their sense of power and control. They wait 33 percent longer if the arriving driver honks. Is it any wonder parking spaces sell for hundreds of thousands of dollars when even the momentary possession of one can inspire such covetousness?

Every American knows the intense frustration of driving somewhere only to learn the hardest part of the journey still lies ahead, a quest for which there is no map. Commuters often say quickly finding a parking spot is the difference between a good and a bad day. Some couples won't park together, as good relations disintegrate when each beholds the other's parking strategy. Nothing about the car becomes us less than the leaving it. In July 2020, a man in Park City, Utah, called 911 to report that he could not find a parking spot. Employees at Virginia's Newport News Shipbuilding, one of the largest industrial employers in the country, sometimes arrive hours before their shifts and finish sleeping in their cars to procure prime spots. (And this is *after* the city's picture-postcard downtown was leveled to create twenty square blocks of parking.) Where parking can be allocated, no one is above asking for it. In 1987, Mother Teresa used a visit to New York City Hall to finagle two reserved parking spaces for her West Village AIDS hospice.

The headache is particularly acute in the older, denser cities of the Northeast and Midwest, such as Philadelphia and Chicago, and it's no coincidence that American parking homilies tend to have a Catholic flavor, reflecting the social geography of those places. "Little Flower, Little Flower, send me some of your parking power." "Mother Cabrini,

don't be a meanie, please help me park my machiney." "Hail Mary, full of grace, help me find a parking space."

For people who drive in these outmoded environments, finding the perfect parking spot is a pure joy and a source of pride. Julia Hickey, an artist in New York, keeps a Flickr album of her best parking jobs. The technical ability to park has always spurred braggadocio (as its absence invites mockery), although automakers say autonomous technology is coming for it. In Hyundai's 2020 Super Bowl ad, Boston-born actors Rachel Dratch, Chris Evans, and John Krasinski try out the company's new "Smaht Pahk" tech in front of impressed Red Sox slugger David Ortiz. "Just hit the clickah, cah pahks itself." This is a rarity among car commercials, which usually promise the high of the open road but neglect the hangover of parking the car. Pop culture is even worse, since protagonists always seem to find a spot right in front of the restaurant—when parking gets shown at all.

The know-how to wedge a vehicle into a narrow spot is secondary, in any case, to the ineffable awareness of where that spot might be in the first place. In New York, drivers have looked for the clenched fist of a passerby—a sign she is clutching her car keys and about to create an opening. New York and Chicago each have produced their own "parking whisperer," a published expert on navigating street parking. New York parking neurosis even got its own novel, Calvin Trillin's *Tepper Isn't Going Out*, the story of a man who snags great parking spots as a hobby—and then just . . . sits there, reading the newspaper, dispensing advice, and eventually achieving local celebrity. Murray Tepper makes Zen practice out of the city's great annoyance:

> As he moved down the street, looking for a spot that alternate-side parkers call "good for tomorrow," he'd say "Tuesday, Tuesday, Tuesday" over and over, almost as if he were chanting some sort of mantra. He'd listen intently for the sound of an ignition being turned. He'd

glance quickly from side to side, hoping to spot the flicker of a dashboard light that would indicate someone had just opened a car door and might be about to pull out. There were nights when he was totally confident of finding a spot. There were nights when he could almost imagine himself with a large tattoo on his arm that said, BORN TO PARK. There were nights when he knew that it was only a matter of time before he'd slip into a NO PARKING MON-WED-FRI spot, emitting, as the car came to rest against the curb, a final "Tuesday!" loud enough to startle passersby.

But for the most part, in a world where directions, restaurant recommendations, and even finding a cab have all been digitally democratized, there is no substitute for local expertise in street parking.

Parking tactics vary according to need, to the season, and to the driver's personality. In Arizona, parking in the shade and taking a long walk under the sun is considered an investment in your future happiness. Almost everywhere else, people like to search for the closest spot, because they underestimate their time driving and overestimate their time walking. The neuroscientist Andrew Velkey has compared parking lot search strategies to animal behavior. You have either an active or a passive search strategy; you are a condor or a barn owl. One route leads to easier but less nutritious prey (a spot at the corner of the Home Depot lot, near the driveway); the longer, more meticulous hunt yields a more delicious morsel.

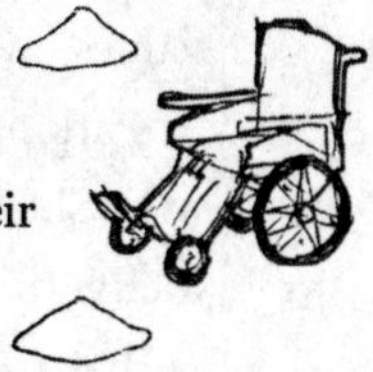

If it seems counterintuitive to think of parking as mostly frontier law—as kapu, beach chairs, gasoline, firearms, the franeleros who ration out curb parking in Mexico City or the parkingeurs who do so in Algiers, the threatening crossed switches I found one morning on my windshield after I parked in someone else's spot in a French ski town—that's because the tiny fraction of parking stays that end in a fee, a ticket, or a tow leave a mistaken impression that parking is a rule-bound affair.

Even residential parking permits, the regulatory project of reserving the curb for people who live nearby, are born from the same kinds of block-by-block uprisings that thwart new affordable housing. Many residential neighborhoods have managed to effectively abolish public curb parking in this way, though the legality of barring visitors from parking has not always been cut-and-dried. When the first residential parking permit programs were established in the 1970s, state courts differed on whether this was allowed. The street was a public right of way, after all, and courts had consistently defended Americans' right to travel. The Virginia Supreme Court held that one such ordinance, in the Washington, DC, suburb of Arlington, violated the Equal Protection Clause of the Fourteenth Amendment by discriminating against nonresidents. But the U.S. Supreme Court overturned that ruling in 1977, reasoning that Arlington's objectives—protecting a residential neighborhood from noise, trash, traffic, and lower property values—were legitimate and nondiscriminatory.

Parking permit zones are parochial. While they may suit the tastes of one block's homeowners, they often don't serve the larger interests of a city. In many cities, for example, permit zones have balkanized the curb parking supply between low-occupancy curbs in single-family neighborhoods and congested curbs on neighboring blocks with apartment buildings. Parking zone gerrymandering can give some residents privileged access to busy neighborhoods. To make matters worse, residential parking permits are sold for peanuts and without regard for the parking supply. It costs just $50 to store your car on the streets of Washington, DC, for the year, and in some neighborhoods the city sells four times as many permits as there are street spaces. To clear up this mess, the District could auction off a fixed number of permits—or, more cynically, it could turn permits into limited, tradable assets whose value would increase, rather than decrease, as the city adds new residents, giving existing permit holders an incentive to say yes to new neighbors.

Or consider South Congress Avenue in Austin, Texas, with its celebrated, walkable strip of small businesses south of the Colorado River. Merchants had long advocated for free street parking as a carrot for customers accustomed to suburban norms. But that free curb parking—which came with a universally ignored time limit—was used up early in the morning by employees of the shops and even downtown workers, who parked and took the bus across the river to save $20 a day in parking fees. Curb parking was jammed by 10:00 a.m., so restaurant and shop customers spilled onto neighboring streets. Neighbors got mad. Then, block by block, they demanded permit parking, which forced visitors to park in an ever-smaller zone of nonregulated residential streets—encouraging further permit adoption. The end result? Curbs almost entirely cleared of cars in residential neighborhoods just a block from the jammed commercial district. Nowhere for gardeners and cleaners to park.

The neighbors around South Congress, a local storefront landlord named Susan Holgren told me conspiratorially, were claiming the curb for themselves because they had turned their garages into Airbnbs—seizing public parking because they'd decided to put their own legally owned space to more lucrative use. Their attitude, she said, was, "'If we give you back the parking, what are *you* going to give *us*?' They speak with forked tongues. And the city council, they're like those little dogs in the shop window, just nodding their heads." The resulting system, which changes from block to block, was totally incomprehensible even to locals, and in all respects representative of the self-interested clusterfuck that is American parking policy. The sense of grievance and suspicion is well earned, and it runs up and down the parking ladder, from the meter on Main Street to the shared driveway to the city meeting. We are a country of drivers and we need our parking and sometimes that means fighting for it.

CHAPTER 3

The Travails of New York's Top Parking Attendant

To the extent that anyone thinks there is order in parking, they think of the parking attendant, that despot whose sentences are handed down beneath the windshield wiper. And yet nothing demonstrates parking's Wild West qualities quite like parking enforcement, a dangerous and degrading job the world over. The work is particularly fraught in New York, the largest and densest American city. Because Manhattan generates such a fever of activity on its streets and sidewalks, the city's culture of advocacy against long-term car storage in the public right-of-way has always been strong: environmentalists and bus riders and bikers and businesses have all worked in concert to make Manhattan one of the most difficult places to park in America. Far from cowing the city's drivers, however, these changes invigorated a fierce counterculture of parking cheats. The first group's righteous resolve was matched only by the second group's wily and brazen resistance. For the drivers, New York's parks, playgrounds, streets, and sidewalks were all places to put your car, if you knew how to break the rules.

I grew up in Lower Manhattan, in a neighborhood of boxy cast-iron buildings cut through with parking lots. Each block was like a grocery store cake with a few slices removed. Residents of the adjacent structures had, over time, poked out lot-line windows from their brick side walls to let the light in. These scatterings of apertures, with the pell-mell pattern of a punched card, overlooked every one of the neighborhood's parking lots.

Those lots were often full of parked cars, but they doubled as public spaces. A long, narrow lot pierced the block between Broadway and Mercer, where the attendant inexplicably permitted my father to teach me to throw a baseball. The north side of Grand Street, a block south, held a huge parking lot that hosted flea markets on Saturdays. Nearby on the Lower East Side, actors performed Shakespeare in the Parking Lot every summer.

Parking on the curb was not such a great option in those days: in 1990, 147,000 cars were stolen in New York City—one theft for every fifty residents. My parents joined the club shortly before Christmas, 1993. Their next car went into a garage, a prewar building with a cable-hauled car elevator serving three floors of parking. Eventually that was torn down for a condo.

The revival of Manhattan around the millennium, which often took the form of apartments replacing parking, and the concurrent decline of car thefts, which fell by an astounding 96 percent between 1990 and 2013, put a lot of pressure on the curb. When he wanted to park on the street, my father would drop us off in front of our building before going hunting. The job was too tedious to share.

New York had been exceptional in this regard since the 1950s. In most of the country, curb parking on busy streets had been banished to increase traffic speeds while parking lots ate away at the buildings "like moths devouring a lace wedding gown." New York City had the good fortune to hold on to many of its older buildings—buildings like the one I grew up in, which was supposed to be demolished for an expressway—and wound up sowing the seeds of downtown's revival instead.

There is always a price gap between free street parking and conventionally priced real estate, but nowhere is the contrast sharper than in Manhattan. On Grove Street, my mom grew up in a rent-controlled apartment building that was, in 2011, converted into a massive single-family home and sold for $11 million. But the 170 square feet in front of the building cost just what they did when she was a kid there in the 1960s: nothing. Land in Manhattan was the most valuable in the world, but it was free if you wanted to use it for just one thing: storing your car on the street.

By the second decade of this century, just 5 percent of parking in New York was metered, and none of it cost money on Sundays. Street parking wasn't just more convenient; even at its most expensive, the curb was always a better deal than the cheapest garage parking. Street parking prices maxed out at $5 an hour, while the median hour in a garage was $19. Cruising around looking for a parking space, in other words, paid more here than anywhere else: an expected return of $14 for every hour you planned to park.

And so New Yorkers embraced the hunt. It wasn't just the price: our prepaid garage space was five blocks away, so my parents often left the car downstairs, in a rare spot that was easy to find, because around the time I became a teenager, the city turned it into commercial parking starting at 8:00 a.m. When the morning routine dragged, it was my job to go and sit behind the wheel in the frigid station wagon, breathing steam in the morning sun and hoping I would not have to move the car when the ticket cop came. I was too young to drive.

❙ ❙ ❙ ❙ ❙

Guarding the thin line between order and chaos in the open, fertile land of the New York City curb is the traffic agent.

For many years, the best of them was a single mother from the Lower East Side named Ana Russi. In 1983, Russi patrolled the Diamond

District, the Midtown block where millions of dollars in precious stones entering the United States change hands each day. She gave out 135 parking tickets a day. The average among the city's other 1,500 traffic agents was just 35. In 1987, Mayor Ed Koch gave her the city's Woman of the Year Award—even after she had shooed the mayor's own chauffeur away from an illegal spot while Koch was having lunch.

It was a rough job, but Russi was the oldest of eight. She had brothers. She knew how to stick up for herself. In Chinatown, a man on the wrong end of a ticket grabbed Russi's radio; she kicked him in the groin and a coworker called the police. Another time, a taxi driver wound up to kick her in the back; a supervisor charged to her defense. "That was a mistake," she reflected. "Never turn your back." Once, a guy with a baseball bat told her he would bash her head in. Russi moved on, but she had his plate number down. He got a ticket in the mail. Another guilty driver tried to frame her for a crack in his windshield. "You're a sick puppy!" she retorted. One more groused that he couldn't get a ticket, he had left his dog in the car. "Can I have his license and registration?" she asked.

"I don't pay any mind to the lip," she said. "I take it from where it comes. They can say anything they want. I just keep writing and walking. Some of them just scream, and some want me to give them a break. 'No breaks,' I say. 'That's against every rule we got.' Sometimes they get mad and they say, 'You people are all alike.' I don't know what they're talking about," she smiled. "You people? Who could they be talking about? A nice Puerto Rican girl like me?"

"You had traffic agents beaten bad, summons books torn, clothing, radio, forget it. They were abused," she recalled when we spoke in 2021. "Abused." There were more than five hundred police reports involving the city's ticket agents every year, including nearly a hundred serious assaults. A traffic agent who ticketed a cop in Long Island City found her tires slashed. Two supervisors drove out to talk with police brass about the incident and left the meeting to find *their* tires slashed. When the city recommended New York State make it a felony to attack a traffic agent, Bronx councilman Rafael Colon objected. "If they're getting beaten up," he reportedly said, "it's because they deserve it."

The work was not taken seriously, and any attempt to perform it with discipline was met with derision and violence. In May 1967, thirty-eight-year-old Esther Neal ticketed a car in the Bronx; the owner broke her nose with a punch. After Neal got out of the hospital, meter maids walked off the job until they won the right to work in pairs. One parking officer was assaulted by a priest in his collar; another went to the hospital only to learn his X-ray technician had been the attacker. Parking officer Dawn Davis had her arm sliced with a razor and required twenty-two stiches. She had also been hit by a car and had her jaw broken on the job. Which she had held for all of three years.

John Van Horn has a theory about why people hate parking tickets. Van Horn is the founder of *Parking Today*, a glossy, ad-rich monthly magazine that serves as the public square of a profession with an inferiority complex. ("Parking Doesn't Have to 'Suck'" was the March 2019 cover story.) Each issue begins with a personal missive from Van Horn. "Why is a parking attendant the most hated person in a city?" the crotchety publisher asked me in 2020. "The parking enforcement officer is judge, jury, and executioner. It's just a piece of dirt! I pay taxes to light it, to put down the asphalt, why the hell should I pay more? I know exactly what people think about parking: they hate it; they believe it should be free, that it's somewhere in the Constitution or the Magna Carta; they believe it's the biggest rip-off that ever hit the planet."

What made Ana Russi the most hated person in the city? She was competitive, smart, and tough. She was ambitious. But she was also a hard-liner who believed in the mission. A minute at a bus stop? Dozens of bus riders would be late for work. A minute at a fire hydrant? A burning building couldn't wait. It helped that she didn't own a car. All this entitlement was alien to her, almost inexplicable.

It had once been so to most New Yorkers. In 1947, Police Commissioner Arthur Wallander was confident that New Yorkers were firmly opposed to "the public streets being used as garages." The sanitation department thought the parked cars made the streets dirty; the police thought they provided cover for creeps and bait for thieves; the firemen wanted to access their hydrants. Kids resented the high-value obstacles on their stickball courts, and the elderly complained that parked cars were making it hard to cross the street. Nevertheless, pressure from automobile owners was eventually too much to withstand, and overnight parking was legalized in New York City at the start of the 1950s.

The meter maids were created at the end of that decade, one hundred women in Dodge sedans. In her wool skirt suit, pillbox hat, and tie, the New York City meter maid looked like an airline stewardess, and she was viewed more as a flirt than as a figure of authority. The moniker *maid* (and the more modern term *parking attendant*, which accompanied the arrival of men to the ranks in 1967) suggested a domestic servant more than an officer of the law. They were paid half as much as the police. Instead of nightsticks they carried tape measures, to record the distance from hydrants. The bag across her shoulder may have made her look a little like a military man, but Lovely Rita was still fair game to ask out on a date.

Police were no help at all. No sooner had the meter maid corps been created than the women began issuing tickets to the personal cars of policemen parked illegally around the station houses, ignoring the union cards that had long functioned as free-parking passes. Police responded with a spree of traffic tickets that sent meter maids to court for supposed moving violations. In 1969, Amelia Lacey was putting a ticket on a car at an expired meter in the Bronx when the owner, Patrolman David Waksman, grabbed her, ripping her uniform, twisted her arms behind her back, and cuffed her. Lacey was arrested on charges of harassment and disorderly conduct; she had made "unreasonable noise," "used abusive and obscene language," and "engaged in a course of conduct which served no legitimate purpose and which alarmed and seriously annoyed" Officer Waksman. It was not the last time a meter maid would be attacked or arrested for annoying a member of the NYPD.

Naturally, morale was low. A rare moment of glory for the profession arrived in 1977, as the Son of Sam serial killer attacked couples necking in parked cars. That August, a parking ticket issued to a car in front of a Brooklyn fire hydrant led to the arrest of David Berkowitz, who confessed to the Son of Sam murders immediately. The ticket had been written by a Staten Island police officer named Mike Cataneo. For the rest of his life, Cataneo received letters of solidarity from parking agents around the world.

In spite of the lack of prestige, the wait for a job *The New York Times* had called the city's "most unpopular civil servant" was long, because parking enforcement was an entry point into the city's civil service—a raft of government jobs that helped lift a generation of black and Puerto Rican New Yorkers into the middle class. When Ana Russi took the civil service exam, she was living with her son in a public housing project that overlooked the Williamsburg Bridge. She had taken night classes to get work as a dental assistant but earned so little that she sewed dresses at night. She fostered a boy, because the payments from the state would help make ends meet. She ended up adopting him.

Russi had seen the ladies in their sharp uniforms on the Lower East Side. Black women, women with skin the color of hers, albeit none yet who talked like she did, with traces of her native Spanish in her voice. She asked one of them how she could get the job, filled out the application, and brought it downtown. It was five years before she was hired as a parking attendant. The uniforms cost a month of her dental wages, money she borrowed from friends and family, but she paid it back quickly. As a meter maid, she doubled her salary overnight, and when Mayor Ed Koch gave the agents a raise in 1980, she was suddenly making three times what she'd made at the dentist's.

Russi was typical of traffic agents in New York, and elsewhere: the work was no longer as gendered as it had once been, but the people who ticketed cars in big cities were often black or Hispanic. (The police force, by contrast, was mostly white—and lived mostly in Staten Island and the suburbs, compared with parking enforcers, who lived mostly in the city.) This helps explain the poor treatment that parking agents received after the honeymoon of the flirty meter maids had passed.

In 1974, in an effort to imbue the agents with more authority, Benjamin Ward, the city's first African American traffic commissioner, had adopted a snazzy brown uniform for the parking enforcers. It didn't reduce incidents of harassment and assault; instead, the attendants became known as the Brownies, a diminutive epithet that agents and later traffic commissioners viewed as downright racist. In 1990, the city changed the uniforms from brown to blue in an attempt to banish the hated "Brownies" nickname.

Around that time, a Queens psychology professor named Elizabeth Brondolo wanted to study how interpersonal conflict affected blood pressure. In parking agents, she found her perfect subject. "They have conflicts in almost lab-like situations," she observed, as opposed to, say, police officers, for whom physical exertion often accompanied stress. "Their arms are down, and then people come up and scream at them. It's a great system for understanding how your cardiovascular responds when you get attacked." Dr. Brondolo studied traffic agents in New York City for almost a decade. She put blood pressure monitors on the agents and gave them diaries to write in, and walked the streets with her subjects. "Positive aspects of traffic enforcement," she wrote in a text for conflict resolution, included "Pride of enforcement, Freedom / Autonomy. Time outdoors. Helping the public. Making the traffic flow. Contact with the public. Seeing the sights in New York City." Effective thoughts: "I am still doing an important job, even if this motorist can't recognize it." The text summed up the insults a parking agent would receive and offered suggestions for how to respond, from muscle relaxation to meditation.

In return for access, Brondolo promised treatment. The agents—mostly women, mostly black—would write down the most demeaning things that had been said to them, and a colleague would read them back. "You're a pig. You're a fat pig." Brondolo was afraid the agents would get sick from holding it all in; instead, she wanted them to practice relaxing in these sessions. It mostly worked, except with racism. "People got so sad and upset we had to stop doing that," she said. "I could not believe the things these people were subjected to."

The people who give the tickets are more conscious than anyone of parking's emotional register, and this is the case far beyond hot-tempered New York City. A 2001 survey of eight hundred traffic and parking agents in the UK found that 90 percent had experienced a violent incident over the past year, and 10 percent had been attacked by someone with a weapon. In New Orleans you can buy meter maid voodoo dolls. During a wave of assaults on officers in the mid-2000s, California pols warned motorists to keep their cool: "Don't beat up the officer. If you do, we're going to prosecute," warned a young San Francisco DA named Kamala Harris. The fallout swept up the thrifty drivers who bought the San Francisco attendants' old three-wheeled Interceptors at auction; not even disco balls, Barbie dolls, and fake fur could hide the stain of parking enforcement. In 2008, a Saint Louis County man driven into madness and debt by parking tickets took a pistol to the local city hall, where he murdered five city officials before being killed by police.

The most thorough documentation of the trials of parking enforcement is *Parking Wars*, a seven-season reality show on A&E whose one-hundred-plus episodes star the workers of the Philadelphia Parking Authority. (The last two seasons focus on Detroit.) The show is classic American reality TV, brimming with raw footage of Philadelphians weeping and wailing. Like *Cops*, it makes hay from the humiliations of low-income people trapped in a cycle of fines and penalties—and the equally low-income workers who must manage their tantrums. The depiction of the City of Brotherly Love was so unflattering that Meryl Levitz, the president of Philadelphia's tourism bureau, said she received more than two hundred notes from viewers who said they would never come back to the city after watching the show. *The Philadelphia Inquirer* called on the mayor and governor to have *Parking Wars* canceled. *Parking Wars,* a parking consultant told me, was "one of the worst things that ever happened to our industry."

As the title implies, *Parking Wars* was not a documentation of parking enforcement's fairness and neutrality. Rather, the inescapable conclusion of the show is that the rules are both overly punitive and haphazardly enforced. Ultimately, it's the inadequacy as much as the rigor of the parking system that roils: the injustice of being punished for something everyone else has gotten away with; the self-loathing knowledge that everyone parks illegally but only you were foolish enough to get caught. (And it only gets worse if you know the first thing about the Philadelphia Parking Authority, an agency set up to fund the city's public schools that instead siphons revenue into lucrative patronage positions for friends and family of elected officials.)

In spite of it all, there was something good in the work. Many years later, discharged from the hospital after a nasty bout with COVID-19, the seventy-six-year-old Ana Russi explained to the doctor how she had stayed in shape. "I walked the streets of New York for many years," she told him. "He probably thought I was a hooker!"

In 1996, New York's agents were transferred back into the NYPD, the end of the four-decade experiment in civilian parking enforcement. (Though traffic agents were not permitted entry to the force's powerful unions.) The job still paid little, but it did not require a college education and retained its appeal for upwardly mobile new arrivals to New York. In 2022, immigrants from Bangladesh made up a plurality in the three-thousand-person traffic police force.

▮ ▮ ▮ ▮ ▮

For New York City's drivers, finding spots and avoiding tickets could become an obsession, more important even than driving the car itself. "We don't use it as much as we would like," a journalist observed of his car in a local tabloid. "Because we don't want to lose our on-street parking space here in Brooklyn. Yes, that's right. Before we drive we ask: Is it worth it to lose our spot? Can we get one when we return?" If smaller cities used chalk on the tires to gauge how long a car had been parked, New York City operated at a different timescale: a windshield caked with pollen, waterlogged autumn leaves, or sooty snow could indicate someone had occupied a curb space for weeks.

That was despite the city's weekly street cleaning, which kept parkers on their toes by enforcing a shuffle for spots. The status of the rules—which were suspended for dozens of obscure holidays corresponding to the city's various ethnic blocs—was read out on the morning radio broadcast alongside the weather, and local elected officials mailed parking calendars to constituents. The city had its parking ticket lawyers, spot-hunting specialists, and an ancient tradition of expertise. "If you're willing to approach the matter methodically," read a typical magazine column from 1969, "you can go on enjoying the masochistic benefits of car ownership in Manhattan for years to come." (Putting the car in the lot was "the ultimate sacrifice.") Mary Norris, a copy editor at *The New Yorker*, chronicled the search for alternate-side parking in more than three hundred posts over nine years on her New York City parking blog. Jerry Seinfeld said of parking in Manhattan, "It's like musical chairs except everybody sat down around 1964."

The most visible way Manhattan drivers tried to beat back the city's parking rules was not by punching meter maids, starting cocaine-fueled baseball-bat brawls, or performing owl-like surveillance of hand-clutched car keys. It was simply by cheating.

Parking-placard corruption in New York was as old as the placards themselves, which began with the sly hint of police union cards but soon expanded to include a whole universe of dashboard gewgaws, from M&M bags (thought to send a secret message to meter maids) to 9/11 paraphernalia (to vouch for one's patriotism and support for cops).

The sociologist William H. Whyte was one of the first to study the issue. On one October morning in 1977 he dispatched a squad of Columbia students to canvass all the parked cars in a square mile of Midtown. The team walked thirty-six miles of curbs and found 4,031 vehicles double-parked—about half cars and taxis and half trucks. The contribution to gridlock was almost incalculable. On every single street and every single avenue, at least one lane was closed to traffic by double-parking, constricting the city's circulatory system. This, the great traffic scientist William Phelps Eno had written, "is about the greatest nuisance and most hazardous practice of motorists." Just one double-parked car was the traffic equivalent of axing the whole lane.

Of the illegally parked cars, half had placards. Many of those belonged to diplomats: the arrival of the United Nations in New York, in 1950, had attracted a population of incorrigible parking scofflaws to Manhattan, concentrated around the Oscar Niemeyer skyscraper on the East River and the consulates and offices that dotted the city's east side. Diplomats could not be held accountable for parking tickets, though that did not stop agents like Ana Russi from ticketing their luxury sedans.

Between March and October 1977, representatives of the Soviet Union in New York received more than 6,500 parking tickets. Israel racked up almost 5,000. Nigeria, Ghana, and Turkey were not far behind. Two diplomats from the West African nation of Guinea had, respectively, 526 and 525 unpaid parking tickets apiece.

A later study, of the period 1997 to 2002, found that the number of parking violations per diplomat was strongly correlated with measures of national corruption—and with less favorable popular views of the United States. Israel and Turkey had really cleaned up their act by that point, and—along with countries such as Burkina Faso, Colombia, Can-

By 2000, New York's city, state, and federal employees had received approximately 100,000 permits exempting their cars from parking restrictions.

ada, Ireland, Japan, and the Netherlands—recorded no parking citations. The leaders this time around were Kuwait, Egypt, Chad, Sudan, and Bulgaria. Violations by diplomats from Muslim countries fell by 80 percent after the September 11 attacks, though they soon rebounded.

In the late 1980s, Ana Russi was promoted and on formal occasions served as a driver for her boss, Traffic Commissioner Sam Schwartz. Schwartz was a cabbie turned traffic czar whose claim to fame was coining the word *gridlock* to describe the way traffic in Midtown ground to a halt every afternoon. Naturally, Schwartz was *obsessed* with illegal parking.

Limos in front of the Plaza and the Regency, town cars in front of Saks Fifth Avenue and the downtown courthouses, film crews, a van of secret service agents, the mayor himself: Schwartz ticketed and towed with a vehemence that had never been exhibited in New York City. He recalled, "Our NO PARKING signs, if you could interpret them, meant no parking for everyone except doctors, newspaper trucks, reporters, policemen, the army, the FBI, the Secret Service, taxis, delivery trucks, Con Ed, the phone company, construction cranes, the post office, handicapped drivers, diplomats, and limousines." He introduced the sign DON'T EVEN THINK OF PARKING HERE and aggressively pursued violators—one reason he took to Ana Russi, parking superstar.

It was not lost on Schwartz that the world's own governing body, theoretically responsible for such lofty tasks as investigating war crimes, was composed of unrepentant rule breakers. So with Mayor Koch's support, he told his tow trucks it was open season on diplomats' DPL plates. Traffic on the east Midtown streets flowed again; the west-side tow pound, stuffed with Mercedes and Jaguars and BMWs, began to resemble the parking lot of a country club. The State Department liaison to the UN called city hall in a huff. "The British say they can't live with your plan because of security needs. The Soviets are outraged. Our diplomats get all sorts of privileges overseas, you know, and already some countries are threatening retaliation."

Flanked by a representative from Foggy Bottom, Schwartz was summoned to the General Assembly to answer for his aggressive towing policies—prompting a rare moment of international harmony. "The Israelis and the Arabs were getting along; Iran and Iraq, which were then at war, were offering each other coffee. All united in attacking me," he recalled. "If someone were taking a tour of the UN at that moment, he might think I had the answer for world peace." Such was the rapt attention in the room.

Diplomacy prevailed. It was not until 2002 that, at the behest of the technocratic mayor Michael Bloomberg, the U.S. Senate passed the

Clinton-Schumer amendment, which allowed the city to tow diplomats' cars and instructed the State Department to deduct the unpaid fines from U.S. government aid. Parking violations plummeted.

The foreign interlopers were subdued, but the city's own workforce was another story. By the turn of the millennium, city, state, and federal employees had received approximately one hundred thousand on-street parking permits exempting their cars from various restrictions. In Calvin Trillin's novel *Tepper Isn't Going Out*, the mayor rages, "Parking is the key to urban order, and I can't seem to get parking under control." A 2006 city study concluded that if government workers drove at the same rate as private-sector employees, nearly twenty thousand fewer cars would enter Manhattan every day. But every public-sector worker had a reason why *he*, as opposed to anyone else who worked in Manhattan, needed to park right in front of the office. When pols tried to slash parking perks, public-sector unions argued it was a benefit they'd earned.

If unlimited New York City street parking was a union benefit, what was it worth? Thieves occasionally smashed windows to steal placards. The union of state troopers issued POLICE SURGEON placards to any doctor who paid a $400 fee. By 2017, there were two thousand "police surgeons" leaving their cars all over Manhattan. We can get a rough dollar estimate by turning to the lively black market for forged placards, counterfeits that relied on the low-paid parking police getting confused by the potpourri of exempt roles. Investigators did occasionally bust fakers, finding that permits sold on the black market for between $500 and $2,600. Even at the high end, it was a bargain—try finding a garage downtown for $2,600 a year; that's just $220 a month! In a 2011 study, one in four permits surveyed was fake, suggesting that there were between ten thousand and twenty-five thousand fake permits in use in the city.

"When someone uses a fraudulent placard like this it's as though they are stealing city resources," the city's chief investigator said in

2017. Still, it was a very unusual type of theft, since it was committed in broad daylight, in front of government buildings, by government employees—and the evidence remained all day long.

Because it was virtually impossible for anyone but a forensic placardologist to tell which permits were real and which were fake, watchdogs focused on illegal uses. Permits could get you out of meters and some restrictions, but you were not supposed to block crosswalks, hydrants, or bus stops. And yet. City employees used a middle school playground as a parking lot until Public Advocate Betsy Gotbaum stopped them in 2004; workers at Brooklyn Borough Hall continued to park their cars along the footpaths in the park in 2021. In a study of the Civic Center area of Lower Manhattan, just 11 of 244 permits were being used properly.

In 2006, the bicycle and pedestrian advocacy group Transportation Alternatives conducted a citywide survey of placard use. Three in four holders were using their permits illegally. Fully half of the cars parked illegally belonged to police officers. When the car was a safety hazard, it was a police officer's personal vehicle 61 percent of the time. Transportation Alternatives had sent out twenty-two researchers on the project; every single one of them was apprehended and asked for ID doing their research, and two were detained. The worst placard abusers were the police, and the police ran the parking enforcement. The days of conflict between Brownies and cops were long gone.

John Kaehny, a former Transportation Alternatives director, went on to run Reinvent Albany, a group dedicated to state government reform. "Parking policy is the perfect way to cut your teeth," he reflected. "It's really about a small number of individuals monopolizing a public resource. That's state government in a nutshell." By conservative estimate, this fraud was costing New York millions in forgone parking tickets, meter payments, garage taxes, and transit fares—not counting the contribution to traffic.

Even if you could accept the idea that cops and court officers somehow had a particular need and right to drive to work, it was harder to defend the back-burner corruption that trailed in the wake of that privilege. Where there were placards you would find them being used illegally; you would also soon find a license plate behind a foggy plastic cover, or folded at the corner, to evade speed cameras and tolls. For the watchdogs who tracked the placards, parking corruption was an ominous sign that police did not think they had to play by the same rules as everyone else.

And watchdogs did see what was going on. In 2007, Transportation Alternatives started a website, Uncivil Servants, where citizens could submit flagrant parking violations by city officials (mostly police). More than 1,600 vigilante parking sheriffs contributed. The NYPD was livid.

Twitter also became a popular platform for pointing out parking corruption. The anonymous Twitter account @PlacardAbuse was particularly fervent in policing the police. When we first spoke in 2018, the account's creator wouldn't tell me his name, but he said his work (posting photos of illegally parked cars on Twitter) had gotten him into several physical altercations as well as earned him complaints to his employer and a menacing visit to his home from the NYPD's internal affairs unit. His best case for taking the issue seriously was not the consequences of the illegal parking, per se, but its implications for the police force. "People given an inordinate amount of public trust to enforce the rules on everyone else effectively cheat and develop a habit of cheating. One of the concerns that we have"—the plural pronoun in reference to the many people who send @PlacardAbuse their own photos—"is that it should be a disciplinary red flag. You should be looking more closely at their behavior. It's an opportunity to weed out the bad apples before they do something really bad."

If diplomat parking violations served as an effective proxy for corruption abroad, what might be suggested by rampant rule-breaking in the city's own law enforcement ranks? Placards, ticket fixing, and fine collection did open a door to more serious criminal behavior. Roy Cohn, the legendary mob lawyer, Trump fixer, and *Angels in America* antihero, got his start making tickets disappear.

In 2011, eleven NYPD officers were indicted on charges of fixing parking tickets for friends and family, a practice that the Bronx DA alleged had robbed the city of $1 million to $2 million. Hundreds of off-duty police officers gathered at the courthouse. They held signs that read JUST FOLLOWING ORDERS and, in what the *Times* called "a stunning show of vitriol," attacked television cameramen to prevent them from filming their colleagues. Police union president Patrick Lynch said the officers were being victimized for something "accepted at all ranks for decades." The prosecutors said the ticket fixing was so widespread they considered charging the union under the New York State racketeering law, as if the NYPD were an organized crime family rather than the law itself.

A couple years later, at the other end of town, a major corruption investigation of city cops featured as a star witness the real estate developer Jona Rechnitz. Rechnitz had noticed one of his firm's clients had "sheriff" plates that allowed him to park anywhere. "When he came to meet me, he would park wherever he wanted," Rechnitz testified, "and that is something I thought was pretty cool." The young developer tracked down the Brooklyn community liaison who procured the placards and made parking tickets go away. That simple favor trading soon escalated into a pattern of bribing the police to do much more than fix parking tickets. By the time he testified in 2017, Rechnitz was funneling gifts to cops that included Super Bowl tickets, diamond jewelry, resort vacations, and a prostitute dressed as a flight attendant who had sex with police officers on a private jet to Las Vegas.

"As we've heard in countless 'broken windows' lectures from the NYPD for decades," the trusted local news anchor Errol Louis wrote in the *New York Daily News* during the trial, "tolerating small crimes fosters a sense of lawlessness, sends a go-ahead signal to crooks and leads to bigger, bolder offenses." Parking corruption had a cost; candidates for public office, Louis wrote, "should present a plan to finally root out the thieves who break the law and steal from the rest of us every single day." As he put it later, "If we knew that public employees were routinely and daily stealing milk from supermarkets and taverns around the city—while cops not only looked the other way, but participated—nobody would shrug and say 'Who cares?' Parking in NYC costs a lot more than a gallon of milk." A common counterargument from rule breakers boiled down to: if I can park illegally, that's one more legal spot for you.

The city's politicians were themselves incorrigible placard abusers. In a representative aside at a Brooklyn Democratic Party breakfast in October 2021, an apparatchik introduced the incoming district attorney by saying, "If you get a parking ticket, don't worry, we'll take care of it." Most of them prized the appearance of reform and announced new initiatives on the subject every few years. It was certainly no longer kosher to endorse beating up parking attendants. But these reforms were always toothless. In truth, the city did not actually want to do a better job with parking enforcement. In 2020, thousands of illegal parking complaints reported to the NYPD were closed in less than five minutes—meaning, without any investigation. In the years since Ana Russi walked the streets, laser plate-reading technology had emerged that allowed a driver adjacent to the curb to scan every license plate on the block in seconds. Theoretically this information could be instantly cross-checked against placard status, against meter payments, and against each block's parking restrictions. But while New York used this technology to track unpaid tickets (to apply the boot or summon the tow truck), officials declined to bring it into the actual business of parking enforcement.

In 2020, a Brooklyn councilman proposed letting citizens report illegal parking. "I tried for years to get the police department to really do some real enforcement," said Councilman Stephen Levin. "At this point, it just seems like the most effective way to address it is to have the public enforce it themselves." One of the city's biggest police unions responded on Twitter: "Imagine if every cop wrote a summons to every vehicle parked illegally or vehicles that are in violation of the vehicle and traffic laws. We could probably bail out NYC, NYS and even feed the homeless." The police were trying to make rigorous parking enforcement seem absurd, beyond belief, as crazy as feeding the homeless. But in a city where fewer than half of all households owned a car, the police seemed to be threatening New Yorkers with a good time.

The biggest problem remained the oldest one, the conflict that had haunted the meter maids since they hit the streets in 1960: the cops. As "Gridlock Sam" Schwartz noted, to protect the parking agents, the city had turned over enforcement to the one group that was most committed to illegal parking as a status symbol and a way of life. The same organization charged with enforcing parking rules was also the one that broke those rules the most often and most openly: the NYPD.

The placard-abuse scandal was in part a story about the intractable challenges of police reform. But the trials of parking enforcement said something more fundamental about parking and the city. The benefits of the placard system were concentrated within an influential bloc of city workers, not least the police themselves. The harms, meanwhile, were more diffuse, spread as they were between the millions of New Yorkers who did not have get-out-of-jail-free parking cards, who were steering strollers around the bumpers of sidewalk-parked SUVs and enduring the traffic that parking chaos begot. This problem recurred in parking enforcement at large: One illegally parked car is a violation with few direct victims, making a $125 ticket seem like an outrageous injustice. But a whole city where illegal parking is a way of life? Together, all those cars obstructed and finally blocked the arteries of the city, bringing its vital functions to a halt.

CHAPTER 4

Destroying the City in Order to Save It

Why do American cities look, feel, and function the way they do? Much of their form can be traced to misguided midcentury efforts to make it easier to park. The question of where to park all these cars consumed American politicians, shop owners, traffic engineers, and urban planners in the 1950s and '60s. In a postwar report on "decentralization"—the flow of business, people, and money to the suburbs—the Urban Land Institute, the national organization of real estate developers, concluded that parking was "the most important single problem facing the central business districts of large cities today." In retrospect, the claim seems laughable. But city planners acted accordingly. Cities sought to emulate the suburban parking model and very nearly destroyed themselves in the process. It was a method that even its biggest evangelist, the mall developer-turned-downtown savior Victor Gruen, would come to bitterly regret. You could draw a direct line from the crowded curbs of the start of the twentieth century to the volcanic wastelands that constituted many American downtowns by its end.

The arrival of Henry Ford's Model T in 1908, along with the subsequent improvements in durability and reliability that permitted year-round outdoor car storage, established parking as a major urban issue. Not only did merchants and country folk quickly abandon horsepower in the first few decades of the century; wealthy commuters could drive themselves, ditching the unwashed, the pickpockets, and the bustle pinchers on the trolleys. Americans' enthusiasm for this new mode of transport was overwhelming and immediate. In 1920s Muncie, Indiana, one woman spoke for a nation when she said she bought a car before she had installed indoor plumbing, because "you can't go to town in a bathtub."

To try to discourage all-day parkers, cities established time limits. Detroit imposed time limits in 1915; Boston in 1920. New York City restricted parking to twenty minutes on Broadway and other big streets. In downtown Los Angeles, it was forty-five minutes. But enforcement was nearly impossible. In Chicago, for example, tickets had to be served to violators in person, which was easy for drivers to avoid. "What can you do?" one sergeant complained. "If they get convicted, they draw a one- or two-dollar fine, and to catch them you have to keep an eight-dollar-a-day cop standing beside the car for maybe five hours. Then they come right back the next day." To track how long cars had been parked, some policemen made chalk marks on the tires. But as often as not, drivers responded not by looking for a new parking space but by rolling the car a few feet forward to hide the chalk. In city after city, the issue was the same: all-day car storage made the curb useless for the hourly comings and goings that nourished local business. "From a survey of the parking situation in the congested area, it was found that violations by persons who park to do shopping are very few," read a report from Ithaca, New York. "The greatest problem has been with the merchants, lawyers, stenographers, clerks and the professional class in general, who are always using the streets for parking as long as they wish."

The resulting problem downtown appeared to be gridlock: cars could barely move. Too many vehicles jammed streets already stressed by the rambunctious mix of streetcars, bicycles, horse-drawn carts, and pedestrians. Cities began to widen roads: Chicago widened 112 miles of street between 1915 and 1930. In New York, planners chopped the stoops off the townhouses on Lexington and Madison Avenues to create more lanes for traffic (they still look strange today) and trimmed the winding garden path that gave Park Avenue its name down to a narrow, decorative median. Countless rows of street trees were felled to widen streets. These curbside patches of greenery had originally been christened "parking."

Contemporary analysts thought the root of the traffic problem was parking. "Aside from the weather," according to the 1928 U.S. Conference of Cities, "there is no question more discussed in our cities today than that of automobile parking." In Washington, DC, parked cars occupied 30 percent of downtown street space by the second decade of the century, and bureaucrats wanted parking on the Mall. In New York, Traffic Commissioner William Phelps Eno wanted to level the park in front of the Plaza Hotel for a parking lot. Widened streets were attempts to seize back traffic lanes that had been taken for double-parking.

With money from the auto industry, the traffic engineer Miller McClintock founded Harvard's Bureau for Street Traffic Research in 1925. Between the double-parking, the cruising for spots, the backing in, and the pulling out, McClintock calculated that curbside parking reduced the capacity of a typical downtown street by 30 to 50 percent. Double-parking was already common at the time of the First World War and, McClintock believed, "the most serious threat to be found in any part of the entire traffic problem." Triple-parking was also practiced, and on some afternoons streetcar operators would call an audible to reroute trolleys from streets so full of wagons, cars, and trucks their vehicles could not pass. "The stored car under such circumstances must follow the peanut wagon, and the sidewalk showcase, into oblivion," McClintock proclaimed. Expressing the conventional wisdom of a generation of traffic engineers, McClintock advised: ban on-street parking.

In 1920, leaders in Los Angeles, which then had the highest rate of car ownership in the world, tried to do just that. They devised a simple solution to the "intolerable conditions brought about by automobile traffic": abolish street parking in the downtown core. The parking ban was enacted on April 10, and traffic sped up by 50 percent. But downtown merchants were apoplectic. Sales were also down 50 percent, they said; the change had, the *Los Angeles Times* wrote, "cast a wet blanket over the business district." Property owners responded immediately by tearing down old buildings for parking lots. There were rumors of a woman who had driven all the way to Pasadena, ten miles away, to buy $23,000 worth of furniture. The ban was scrapped after less than three weeks, though conditions barely improved: in the 1924 comedy *Don't Park There*, the actor Will Rogers has so much trouble looking for a spot at an LA drugstore that he parks in Seattle.

The uproar over the LA parking ban was a sign of how ingrained the right to curbside car parking had become, not two decades after the introduction of the Model T. But the failure of the LA parking ban was in some ways anomalous; in most cities, the trend was toward more, tighter regulation, in the interest of keeping traffic moving. By 1925, Portland, Maine, was painting its curbs in three different patterns to express parking rules. In 1927, Chicago banned downtown parking. Streetcars sped up, to the great approval of retail tenants. The police superintendent thought that Chicagoans of the future would look back at cars parked in the street the same way Chicagoans of the Roaring Twenties regarded pigs in the street: ridiculous! By 1940, more than 80 percent of all traffic signs in American cities had to do with parking.

In the boom that followed the end of the Second World War, the city parking problem went from a traffic hazard to an existential crisis. In a third of two hundred survey cities, merchants believed parking was *the* major problem with their city. "Next to winning the Peace," one journalist quipped in 1955, "America's number one problem seems to be winning the parking problem." In the view of New York City police commissioner Arthur Wallander, "the parking of cars on the public thoroughfares constitutes one of the greatest problems facing the city." By this point, downtown interests had developed a full-fledged fixation on car storage. "Henry Ford probably never foresaw it," the head of the Minneapolis Chamber of Commerce reckoned, "but the mass production of automobiles, while a great boon to foot-sore pedestrians, creates many a headache whenever motorists converge *en masse* on any central point." The Minneapolis Chamber, he wrote, "concluded that erection of a number of multi-story parking garages would save the Minneapolis [downtown] from decentralization." More parking would not just solve the traffic issue—it would also help cities fight suburbs.

This view of off-street parking as an elixir to mend the suburban injury was commonplace. No doubt there was a crisis: The assessed taxable values of Baltimore, Boston, Detroit, and Chicago each fell by double digits between the 1930s and '40s. The proportion of metropolitan Americans living in the suburbs rose from 32 percent in 1940 to 42 percent in 1950 to cross 50 percent shortly after 1960. Workplaces followed shops and homes out to greenfield developments, and by 1970, more Americans were commuting suburb to suburb than suburb to city. Industry followed white-collar work. Between 1948 and 1963, cities' share of metropolitan employment in manufacturing, services, and wholesaling all plummeted. Retail suburbanized fastest of all. In the papers and on TV, cities were frequently characterized as "choking," "rotting," or "decayed," "dying stars, sending out great coronas of flame and energy while swiftly cooling around the central core." "The whole financial structure of cities, as well as the investments of countless individuals and business firms, is in jeopardy because of what is called decentralization," the planner Harland Bartholomew wrote in 1940, ahead of his time. Downtown occupied a tiny portion of the American city but contributed a large percentage of the property tax revenue that paid for schools, police, and other civic functions. Its survival was important not just to department store moguls, property owners, and civic grandees, but for the broader financial health of the city.

William Phelps Eno, who had drawn up the world's first traffic code for New York City forty years earlier, wrote that "premature decentralization" was brought about by the failure to provide "ample parking facilities." "Had adequate parking facilities been available," he wrote, "most of these people would have been glad and willing to patronize their old stores etc. in the central business district. Business has, however, followed the people." Traffic, suburbanization, the rest: parking

The same view of Denver in the 1920s *(below)*, and in the 1970s *(right)*. In the second half of the twentieth century, parking lots ate away at downtowns, in Mark Childs's phrase, "like moths devouring a lace wedding gown."

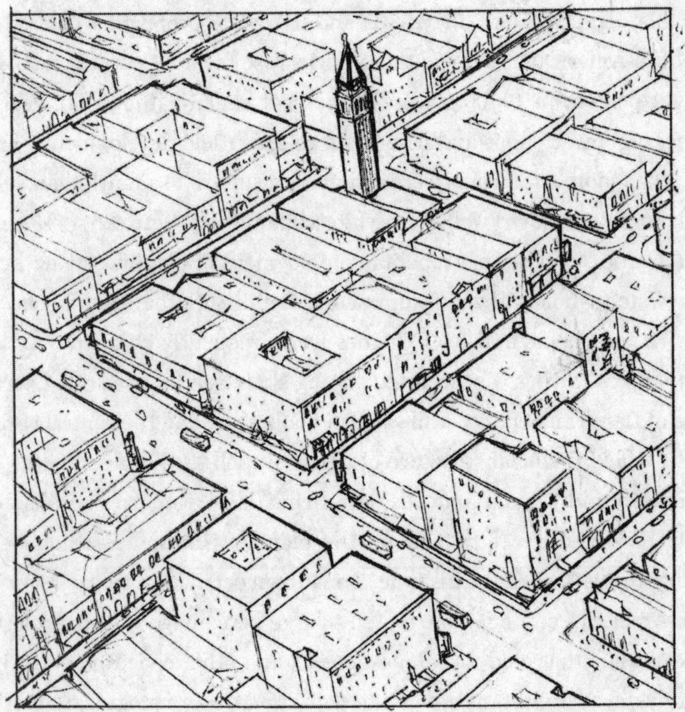

could help, Eno thought. "Lack of adequate parking facilities in central districts has contributed to a great extent in bringing these conditions about." Planners continued to cling to the idea that the downtown revival was just a parking lot away. And they planned accordingly. By focusing on how hard it was to park, they made policy of Yogi Berra's aphorism "Nobody goes there anymore; it's too crowded."

❙ ❙ ❙ ❙❙ ❙

The story of how so many cities sought to imitate the suburbs and regretted it is exemplified by the career of the man called upon to rescue the American city in its time of parking need: Victor Gruen, the

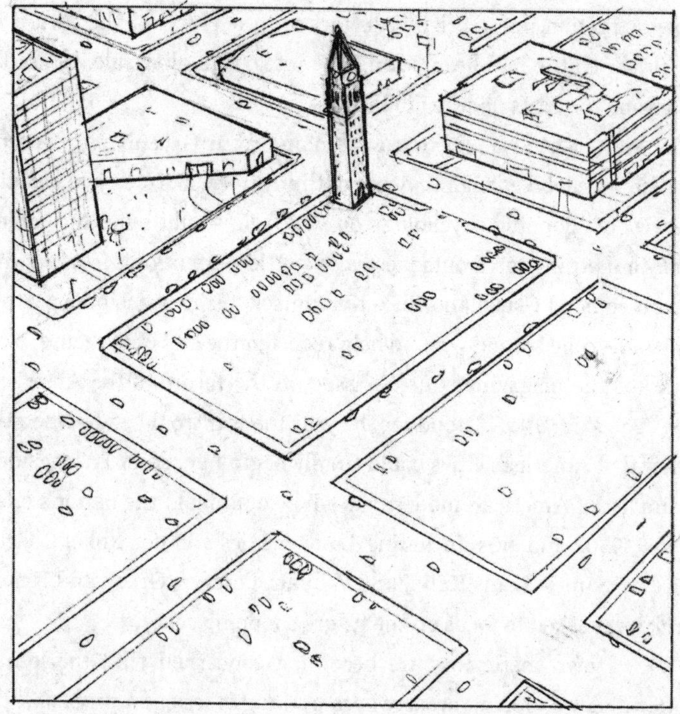

inventor of the mall. Gruen built the model for suburban development and brought it to cities. He never forgave himself.

As a young man in interwar Vienna, Gruen was an architect by day and an actor by night. He spent his evenings in the city's famous coffeehouses running a left-wing theater troupe and performing cabaret routines: slapstick, music, drama. In 1938, he fled from the Nazis to New York, where he founded the Refugee Artists Group. After a personal request from Gruen, Albert Einstein wrote a letter of support for the group's performances; Irving Berlin helped them polish their tunes before two Broadway runs.

Gruen had even more luck in architecture. To pay the bills during his dalliance in musical theater, the Viennese refugee found work in New York on the sensational General Motors "Futurama" exhibit at the 1939 World's Fair. Norman Bel Geddes's model city became the fair's runaway attraction, mesmerizing visitors with a vision of the future in which car traffic had been seamlessly integrated alongside, but separate from, the city's pedestrian life.

By 1941, when he shortened his name from Gruenbaum, Gruen's English was good enough to begin outlining for U.S. trade journals the theories of shopping psychology on which he would build his career. His Manhattan storefronts were also getting attention. *Architectural Record* enlisted Gruen and Elsie Krummeck, his new business partner and soon-to-be second wife, to help redesign the city of Syracuse, New York, for the magazine's "194X" issue on the future of the American city. (The *X* in "194X" stood for the year the war would end—when the renewal of America's cities could finally begin in earnest.) Alongside a dean's list of American modernists who would mold the nation's cities in the 1950s and '60s, including Ludwig Mies van der Rohe, Charles and Ray Eames, Louis Kahn, and William Lescaze, Gruen and Krummeck were asked to focus on the future shopping center.

"Downtown merchants are becoming concerned with the loss of trade to new shopping areas where parking is less of a problem," the editors wrote. The magazine proposed banning cars from a Main Street "mall." At their proposed shopping center nearby, Gruen and Krummeck included a nursery school, a post office, a clubhouse, a library, and a pony stable. It was less a shopping center than a town center—with better parking. Gruen carried this idea forward as he honed his vision for the mall. As downtown's star fell, Gruen's rose.

In 1949, he designed a big-box store for Milliron's on Sepulveda Boulevard in Los Angeles. Three hundred parking spaces on the roof, accessed by eye-catching X-crossing ramps running up the building's sides. Then he convinced the Detroit department store Hudson's to embark on a campaign of suburban expansion, which began with the opening of Northland shopping center in 1954. His partner Larry Smith flew around the country to get the parking arrangement right, culminating in a lot for more than eight thousand cars, color-coded to help drivers navigate what was, at that heady moment, the entirely new experience of losing your car in a giant parking lot. Never one for modesty, Gruen told reporters: "This is not just the opening of a shopping center, but an important milestone for city planners, architects, economists, merchandisers, and the American public at large." He viewed the mall, at the heart of what was probably the largest parking lot in the world, as "an essentially urban environment." The mall was indeed a vibrant civic space for a new generation of Americans, but that luster did not stretch beyond its windowless walls.

As Jeffrey Hardwick argues in his biography *Mall Maker*, Gruen saw his malls and shopping centers, despite their asphalt enclosures, as a step toward the "Europeanization of America." He saw the shopping center not primarily as a rival to downtown but as a replacement for the endless, car-oriented commercial strips that had already emerged, starting in the 1920s, in places like Detroit and Los Angeles, where Gruen had moved during the war. A few years later, living in Beverly Hills and mired in his second divorce, Gruen groused that American retail had made virtually no forward steps since he arrived in New York a decade earlier. "The only progress is that more space for parking has been allowed than was the case before the war," he wrote. The media reception of Northland validated Gruen's vision (the bohemian-intellectual backlash against the suburbs was still a few years away). The German accent didn't hurt. One writer was compelled to gush that "something of the Vienna Waltz pervades Northland." Gruen would compare Northland to the Piazza San Marco. After all, he had gotten Americans—"usually not willing to walk from the garage to the house," he quipped—up on their feet, just as they happily walked on vacation in Paris and Rome. Never mind that it was virtually impossible to walk *to* Northland.

Two years later the architect scored a greater triumph still: Southdale, in Edina, Minnesota, which *Time* called "a pleasure-dome-with-parking." Here, the 5,200-space lot was coded with fifteen animal icons: Goose Lot, Tiger Lot, and so on. An astounding fifty thousand people a day visited Southdale after it opened in 1956. Gruen initially imagined the mall at the center of a little neighborhood of apartment towers and office buildings, with pedestrian paths threading through park space. That never happened, because Dayton's, the department store that built Southdale, sold off all the surrounding land to real estate developers as values rose.

By the mid-1950s, this exuberant exile with sunken eyes and slicked-back black hair had made his name as America's foremost shopping center architect, setting the template for a half century of American social life. His fame and ambition led him to confront the other side of suburban growth and put forth his own answer to the great question of the age: what to do about America's flagging cities.

In April 1956, Gruen arrived in Fort Worth, Texas, to unveil his master plan for the city's revival. Had they known about it, the local movers and shakers would have no doubt found his theatrical background a little silly, and suspiciously socialist. His sponsor, Texas Electric Service Company president J. B. Thomas, had hired Gruen because he saw Fort

Worth plagued by the same condition as many other American cities: middle-class whites were fleeing to the suburbs.

At the Fort Worth Club, Thomas warned the audience gathered in the hall: "It is a plan that will, I am sure, challenge your imagination just as it has challenged mine. It is a plan that, to be properly appraised, must be approached with an open mind." And with that, his punchy guest began the show. Gruen wore his customary suit and tie. Gesticulating wildly or furrowing his brow and tenting his hands in thought, he conveyed equal parts scorn for the American city and hope for its future. His imposing intellectual self-presentation—the accent, the rapid-fire references to Rockefeller Center, the Venetian canals, the Greek agora—was tempered by his repute as a money-minded retail savant whose designs could open women's pocketbooks. Fort Worth's illness was even worse than it seemed, but the architect had the cure. His plan, delivered with the "pomp, drama and fanfare of a Broadway production," would turn Fort Worth into "Dream City America."

Gruen had added other dashes of excitement. His official Fort Worth report began with an eighty-seven-line lyric ode to this "young and vigorous city." He had spent months teasing the American press with promises of his City X plan, without revealing which city it was being prepared for. That was fitting. One of Gruen's big theories about American cities was that they were essentially interchangeable (his traveling slideshow came with a note to self: "INSERT LOCAL DATA HERE") and that urban and suburban problems were also essentially the same. In a City X feature in *BusinessWeek*, Gruen argued downtown "needs a lesson" from the suburbs. It was the right note for a suburban retail architect making the transition to city planning. In Fort Worth, he was trying to bring the mall downtown.

The Gruen Plan had four central elements: The downtown was exclusively for pedestrians, who would navigate via electric trams and air-conditioned passageways. Underground tunnels would carry freight and garbage. Encircling this car-free area was a freeway loop, with connections into six gargantuan parking garages. The idea was to ensure that no place downtown was more than 150 seconds' walk from a parking spot. To swallow up downtown traffic that Gruen predicted would, by 1970, require more street space than the entire built square footage of all Fort Worth's downtown buildings combined, the plan called for sixty thousand parking spots.

This was unheard of. Gruen was telling downtown Fort Worth to build more parking than downtown Los Angeles, a city seven times its size. Gruen was calling to quadruple the existing parking stock in a city that, with its wide, cattle-friendly streets, was already an easy place to drive. In 1956, Fort Worth had twice as many downtown parking spots per person as Atlanta (itself no slouch in the parking department). Still, the out-of-town parking engineers hired by Fort Worth to evaluate Gruen's design were concerned that drivers would have to walk too far. "We know of no situation where this criteria for walking distance has been tested. . . . It is possible that *new walking habits will be formed* under conditions such as those envisioned in the Gruen Plan." If anyone could make Americans walk to the store, it was Victor Gruen—his malls were proof that you could get Americans to shop on foot, under the right circumstances. On the other hand, they wrote, the city might just need to build the garages a little closer.

Thomas, the electricity magnate, need not have worried about the reception: Gruen's presentation was a smash hit. Newspapers around the county applauded Fort Worth's foresight; local leaders were delighted to find themselves the center of attention. The developer James Rouse, who would go on to mastermind downtown renewal projects like Harborplace in Baltimore and Faneuil Hall in Boston, wrote that this "most magic plan" was "the largest, and the boldest, and the most complete dealing with the American city." And even Jane Jacobs, germinating the ideas that would make up her landmark antiplanning book *The Death and Life of Great American Cities*, wrote a self-described "fan letter" to Gruen, saying his Fort Worth plan was of "incalculable value" and would return America to a time of "downtowns for the people."

But Gruen never got his Fort Worth plan: the Texas legislature was not so easily charmed by the vision of the Viennese architect who flew in from Los Angeles, and rejected Gruen's allies' urban renewal bill. Then, in a death blow, the legislature barred Texas cities from building municipal parking garages. In a 1980 appraisal, *The Washington Post* blamed private parking lot operators for spoiling the dream.

But the Fort Worth plan, the newspaper concluded, "is the only unborn child who had hundreds of grandchildren." Gruen succeeded in bringing the mall downtown, as the editors of *Architectural Record* had envisioned in "194X." The city of Kalamazoo, Michigan, hired Gruen to draft a miniature Fort Worth plan for its deteriorating downtown, which he submitted in 1958: a downtown pedestrian zone, coupled with the demolition of warehouses and light industry for parking garages. Kalamazoo leaders did Gruen on a budget: they spent $65,000 on landscaping to open a pedestrianized strip in August 1959. Gruen would try (unsuccessfully) to distance himself from the city's half measures, but the Kalamazoo project was a sensation. Between 1959 and 1985, 140 American cities built pedestrian malls downtown. Some evolved into civic treasures, including the Third Street Promenade in Santa Monica, California, and the Downtown Mall in Charlottesville, Virginia. But most of them failed. Kalamazoo's project has been whittled down to a single car-free block. Fewer than a third of these walkways remain in place.

Gruen's crowning downtown achievement would come a couple years later with Midtown Plaza, an anchor mall for the center of Rochester, New York. It was a city Gruen thought ruined "by parking lots, garages, used-car lots, widened roads and other automotive facilities." Gruen's Midtown Plaza created an indoor civic space at the heart of the city. Many other cities attempted to follow suit by hiring Gruen's firm (San Francisco, Boston) or following through on similar plans (New Haven).

The flaw in Gruen's downtown designs, and indeed most machinations of postwar urban planners, was that they tried to compete with suburbia on its terms: by offering a calm, clean, single-use shopping destination that could be easily accessed by car. At that point, suburbanites might as well have gone to Southdale or Northland. And so they did. The truth was, Gruen never had a historical idea of what an American downtown ought to look like. He invoked Swiss fountains and espressos *en terasse*, but he rarely extolled the charm of Georgetown or Society Hill or the verve of Bourbon Street or Michigan Avenue. Just as Jane Jacobs was mounting her popular and wildly influential defense of the messy, lively American urban neighborhood, Victor Gruen was bitterly on his way to the opposite conclusion: "American cities, with their comparatively short histories and small traditions, offered people little beyond traffic jams."

American car culture, and architects' acquiescence to its demands, was becoming Victor Gruen's bête noire. In 1960, the year after Kalamazoo, he gave a fiery speech to the annual gathering of the National Municipal League on "autocrazity"—the first of several new Gruenisms. "Autocratic fanatics have already succeeded in leveling large parts of downtown cores of our cities, which now resemble the worst bombed-out European cities as they looked after the war. Some of our city cores, in fact, represent only tremendous parking lots and road accumulations, rendered inefficient by the few buildings which have resisted, for some inexplicable reason, the holocaust." The same year, he wrote an op-ed in *The New York Times* proposing a car ban in Midtown and Lower Manhattan. He liked to recount the parable of Motorius, the planet where Motorists demolished everything to spend their entire lives—eating and sleeping—on the road. Then someone got a flat tire, and all the Motorists starved to death in their cars.

Four years later, in his book *The Heart of Our Cities*, Gruen picked a similar target: the traffickist. "He thus proceeds to bring garages and parking lots on sites where people used to live and work and watch theatrical performances, or otherwise engage in urban activities, and thus loosens the fabric of the city," he complained. He was traveling frequently to Europe—to his pied-à-terre in Vienna or on expeditions like the trip to Milan where he personally measured the Galleria, sending the dimensions back in a postcard for the Rochester mall. Again he compared the postwar rebirth of Europe's cities with the apparent disintegration of their American counterparts. Which continent had been bombed, again?

What had prompted this change of heart for the man who had, not a decade earlier, sought to build a Ringstraße of sixty thousand parking spaces around Fort Worth? Gruen was loath to admit any mistakes. He believed mall developers had dishonored his concept, turning their backs on the housing and community facilities he had imagined accompanying the retail. In 1965, he returned to Northland and experienced a "severe emotional shock" from its "wild disorganized growth." "We all should have known better when we planned Northland," he admitted privately. He had two main regrets about his malls. The lack of civic functions was the first. The second: "the ugliness and discomfort of the land-wasting seas of parking." It was the empty car that made the most noise.

In 1968, just before the civil rights movement culminated in a wave of revolts that would expose just how harmful and shortsighted America's philosophy of postwar urban planning had been, Victor Gruen moved back to Vienna. There he met a series of unpleasant surprises. An encounter in the street with the Nazi who had taken over his practice moved the architect to tears. Later, a "gigantic shopping machine" opened south of the city, weakening Vienna's traditional core and stripping the retail from surrounding town centers. The irony was not lost on Gruen. In 1978, shortly before he died, he toyed with crossing the Atlantic again to testify against a suburban mall proposal in Burlington, Vermont, that he said would constitute "premeditated murder of a city by robbing it of practically all its retailing."

"I'm often called the father of the shopping mall," he concluded in one of his last published interviews. "I would like to take this opportunity to disclaim paternity once and for all. I refuse to pay alimony for those bastard developments. They destroyed our cities."

▮ ▮ ▮ ▮ ▮

Not every city had a Gruen project, but all of them tried their hardest to get the downtown core parked to suburban standards. They accomplished this in three ways. First, American city leaders jumped to support highway and Gruen-style urban renewal projects that demolished older neighborhoods. With either intervention, local planners were given great power to rebuild cities according to two tenets of mid-century urbanism: separate residential neighborhoods from commerce and industry and accommodate drivers lest they take their business to the suburbs.

Urban renewal projects targeted dilapidated but lively residential and commercial blocks for demolition. In their stead came car-oriented malls, office towers, and apartments. Some projects succeeded, some failed. All aimed to satisfy the expectation of easy driving and parking at the center of the city. What really stood out about urban renewal, to contemporaries, was its extended time span: the average project lasted twelve years from the moment official planning began (all but ensuring no further neighborhood upkeep would occur) to completion. That lost decade worked to drivers' advantage: cleared land could provide much-needed parking lots. In Buffalo, a chamber of commerce staff member observed that so many buildings had been demolished it looked like the city was paving the way not for cars to park but for airplanes to land. Many architects believed they were planting the seeds of new urban growth. Jack Follett, for example, a partner at John Graham & Co. who worked on Portland's Lloyd Center mall (eight thousand parking spaces), saw the fields of asphalt as a Gruenesque opportunity. "Since the shopping centers of today will eventually become urban centers, the acres we now devote to automobile parking should be supplanted by multilevel structures, so that the land thus freed can be occupied by future buildings." In most cities, that would not come to pass for many decades, if it happened at all.

Meanwhile, the Interstate Highway System, authorized in 1956, was said to be the largest public works project ever undertaken. Expressways destroyed black neighborhoods in cities like Syracuse, Baltimore, and Detroit. To the disappointment of some local officials, the big roads were not accompanied by federally funded parking garages, but they did entrench downtown's dependence on suburban drivers, and the ruined properties alongside freeway trenches were soon torn down to make easy money parking cars. Federal spending subsidized driving, while cities scrambled to raise enough money to operate bankrupt streetcar companies.

Second, cities got into the parking game themselves. In 1951, Houston, Milwaukee, Columbus, Phoenix, Providence, and Sacramento were some of the cities that built their first municipal lots, for example. Pittsburgh, Chicago, and San Francisco all sponsored enormous, expensive underground garages. Public space was requisitioned for parking the world over, from Detroit's Cadillac Square to California beaches to the Place Vendôme in Paris and the Piazza Navona in Rome. Just 5 percent of parking spaces in the country's largest cities were publicly owned in the early 1950s. By 1968, two in three off-street parking lots in big U.S. downtowns were publicly owned; garages were almost 90 percent publicly owned. Private parking operators fought the municipal parking franchise, but their success in Texas was an exception. In 1966, during the debate over public parking in Washington, DC—"the problem of parking automobiles is reaching crisis proportions," the governing Federal City Council stated—garage magnate George Devlin gave a frank reason cities shouldn't get involved: "At the rate we are building automobiles in Detroit, [parking] could well become the single largest use of downtown real estate." It would really be too bad if it were all tax-exempt public property.

Planners conducted isolated studies of how parking boosted real estate values. Not surprisingly, most planners who had supervised demolitions to create lots and garages defended their work.* In 1952, the zeitgeist on parking's amenity value was summed up by J. R. Townsend, city manager of Greensboro, North Carolina: "We have never worked up any data to prove the point. We simply *know* that it is true." ("We ought to obtain this proof," he added.)

Third, cities began requiring new homes, offices, and businesses to be constructed with parking spaces.† Though the entrepreneurial interest in parking had never really abated, it had failed to keep up with Americans' insatiable desire to drive and reluctance to pay for parking. Furthermore, vacant lots tended to be concentrated at the outskirts of downtown. The LA department store Bullock's, a key player in the city's parking story, struck validation deals with local operators. The store subtracted your parking fee from your bill and ran advertisements with a map showing that there were more than eighteen thousand parking spots within five blocks of the store. But five blocks was a long way with full shopping bags. Downtown businessmen believed they had to do better for their clientele, and they got behind laws that required new buildings to include parking on-site. A New York retail executive was blunt: "We are more interested in a single customer who comes to our store by automobile than in 10,000 other people who merely pass by in the street." Just one in five cities zoned for parking in 1950. By 1970,

*In 1953, Fred Tuemmler, a planner in Silver Spring, Maryland, boasted that the DC suburb's nine municipal parking lots had lured DC department store Hecht to open a branch there, sending the assessed value of the area up tenfold. Fred W. Tuemmler, "Boomtown's Parking Bonanza," *American City*, July 1953.

†And old buildings, too—if you planned to change the use from, say, a carpet store to a restaurant, or an office to an apartment building, you needed to bring parking up to code.

95 percent of U.S. cities with over twenty-five thousand people had made the parking spot as legally indispensable as the front door.

And though it is true that parking in America is disorderly, it is not quite true that parking is exclusively grappled over by angry neighbors and drivers with guns. There is a powerful law of parking, too—this third step that virtually every U.S. jurisdiction took in the 1950s and '60s to mandate the provision of parking spaces with every new home, store, school, office, doughnut shop, movie theater, or tennis court. Over time, it was this decision, more than the highways or the malls or the tax-poaching suburbs themselves, that would prove the most influential legacy of the midcentury downtown parking crisis. These so-called parking-minimum laws—which we'll talk more about a little later on—were designed with exactly the amount of study and foresight you might bring to parking your own car at the supermarket: none. As Dad parked the car, so would a nation.

In the end, excess parking harmed cities more than the shortage had. It seems unlikely that anyone in 1945 could even *imagine* a downtown with too much parking—they didn't mean to paint the town gray—but such places were becoming more common by 1960. "The more downtown is broken up and interspersed with parking lots and garages, the duller and deader it becomes in appearance," Jane Jacobs wrote in 1961. Such places weren't just low on tax revenue and sex appeal. They had also lost, to surface lots, many of the older buildings that Jacobs thought so essential to a lively city. In places like New York's SoHo or Chicago's Lincoln Park, such structures would be among the key building blocks of urban population recovery, resettled by recent immigrants, artists, and yuppies. Ironically, many cities *did* finally fulfill the prewar consensus that street parking go the way of the peanut wagon, cutting curb spots by 7 percent each year as lots and garages grew to cover the need. In doing so, traffic engineers deprived local merchants of important curbside access points and left pedestrians exposed to speeding traffic. These wide, fast streets were good for buses, but mostly they helped commuters to race from garages to the suburbs in time for dinner.

In their effort to clear the curb, cities simply moved the parking problem off their streets and into their buildings. Making parking the private and exclusive responsibility of every individual destination had consequences far more destructive than any double-parked car.

CHAPTER 5

Paved Paradise

Most Americans, of course, do not have to fight for parking. On the contrary, the combination of urban renewal, public lots, and parking requirements for private development were astonishingly successful at creating ample space to park. By square footage, there is more housing for each car in the United States than there is housing for each person. All this asphalt constitutes a kind of ecology unto itself, changing the way air and water and animals interact with human civilization. It changes the way we behave, too. "The effect of the cars reaches far beyond the cars themselves," wrote Christopher Alexander in *A Pattern Language*, his landmark study of human landscapes. "They create a maze of driveways, garage doors, asphalt, and concrete surfaces, and building elements which people cannot use. When the density goes beyond the limit, we suspect that people feel the social potential of the environment has disappeared." Perhaps most importantly, making it easier to park did not get rid of the life-draining experience of traffic. On the contrary, it created traffic.

Gruen's distress reflected the dawning regrets of city fathers at large, the start of a half-century planning hangover upon awaking to find yourself surrounded by parking lots. Dude, where's my town? By the end of the 1960s, the emerging consensus was that we would never be able to build enough parking to restore the vigor of the prewar metropolis. In retrospect, the focus on parking as the key to ensuring downtown's survival seems perverse. Downtown business interests and the politicians they supported were delusional. The conventional wisdom in Chicago, for example, had been that the 1954 opening of the record-breaking Grant Park Garage would help ensure that the population of the Windy City was not eclipsed by that of Los Angeles. (It did not.)

In 1957, at a conference in Hartford, the urban historian Lewis Mumford postulated that cities would *never* be able to build their way out of car traffic. It would progress, he said, "until that terminal point when all the business and industry that originally gave rise to the congestion move out of the city, to escape strangulation, leaving a waste of expressways and garages behind them." One planner said the cars coming downtown were like coffee—you had to provide the cups (parking garages). Mumford's metaphor was not so neat. Traffic, he said, was like "dumping a whole orphanage on an overcrowded and bankrupt home."

Even car-friendly engineers never believed that Americans would abandon mass transit the way they did. Frank Turner, the father of the interstate, took the bus to work most days and, as head of the Federal Highway Administration in the late 1960s, would open his meetings at bureau headquarters by asking: "How many of you came by bus today?" In 1953, fewer than half of the fifty-seven thousand people arriving in downtown Atlanta every day came by car, and in their parking assessment that year, city leaders believed that transit ridership would stabilize.

But the more parking lots cities built, the more people drove. Transit executives, whose long-held (and widely despised) monopoly was coming to an end, were some of the first to sound the alarm. The general manager of the Cleveland transit system, D. C. Hyde, argued in 1952 that parking was doing the opposite of what its builders believed: "Destroying buildings and using valuable land for more and more parking lots and garages *hastens decentralization*. . . . It is just as sensible to stop doing things that bring more automobiles into already congested areas as it is to stop buying drinks for a person who is already drunk." Like transit officials in Detroit and elsewhere, Hyde reminded his audience that streetcars and buses were by far the most efficient use of precious street space—and were being rendered useless by automobile traffic. The chairman of the board of transportation in New York went one step further, arguing that *better transit,* not better parking, was the key to halting the suburban ascendance.

In 1965, the chairman of the Boston finance commission slammed the municipal garage program. Boston had built garages for "the bolstering effect they would produce on the city's economy" by pulling in suburban shoppers, George Berkley wrote, even when "no interest was evinced from the private sector." Even assuming a generous boost to retail activity, the city was still spending millions subsidizing its garage operating expenses. By invoking eminent domain to seize properties for parking, Boston had forfeited tax revenue; by subsidizing parking spaces, it had forgone transit revenue. Garages, Berkley added, also caused congestion, detracted from the street's "scenic appeal," and reduced the taxable value of transit-adjacent properties.

Over the course of the 1960s, this view would enter the mainstream. Transit ridership cratered. Residents, stores, factories, and offices abandoned cities. Urban renewal did damage; highways did more. Intellectuals led by Jacobs and Mumford assailed car-centric planning, and local activists in cities like Baltimore and San Francisco organized "freeway revolts" to stop inner-city expressways. Even President Dwight D. Eisenhower seemed to regret what he had wrought with the Interstate Highway Act; ramming the big roads through American neighborhoods had never been his intention. But more than the highways or the slum-clearance projects, it was the need for car storage that ate through American downtowns.

By 1972, the Detroit City Planning Commission made a downbeat assessment of how the Motor City's downtown had wound up dedicating 74 percent of its land to vehicle movement and storage: "The automobile has an insatiable appetite for space. It needs about 300 square feet when stored in its home quarters; 300 square feet when stored at its place of destination; and 600 square feet on its way. It further needs about 200 square feet for those places where it is sold, repaired, and serviced. Thus an automobile needs 1400 square feet of living space. That is equal to the living space of a family unit." A surface parking lot was the lowest-cost use of downtown land, but Detroit had so much parking relative to commercial activity by the millennium that even parking lots were being abandoned.

Parking was just as much of a mess whether you considered it at the scale of your street, your city, or the entire country. Washington paid for the highways, but it did not address the parking. Washington kept track of how many cars were on the road and of how many miles of road we built. But no one kept track of the parking supply, where a car spent almost all its life. Most studies put America's parking supply at a little under a billion spaces. Under the assumption that each space (including egress) takes up 330 square feet, if we were to lay it all flat, the asphalt would cover the entire state of Connecticut—twice. The desert agglomeration of Phoenix has 12.2 million parking spaces, about 3 per person, 4.3 per vehicle, and 6.6 per job, divided more or less evenly between the street, commercial facilities, and home garages. Parking accounts for 10 percent of the manmade landscape in the Valley of the Sun. In Silicon Valley, America's wealthiest and most productive region, parking is 13 percent of the land—not including the curb. According to one estimate, this wasted space cost the region a billion dollars in forgone wages. There are 15 million parking spots in the Bay Area, 2.4 for each car and enough to wrap a parking lane around the planet twice and still have some left over.

The most valuable land in the United States is in New York City, so you might think it would pay for New Yorkers to count the parking spaces. No one has. Estimates range from 1.3 million to 3 million, a staggering degree of uncertainty—and that's just the number of spaces on the street. In any case, New York is exceptional among U.S. cities for its low number of parking spaces. San Francisco, America's second-densest large city, has 441,541 curb spaces, more than one for every household. When estimates include garage space, the numbers go way up. Philadelphia has 2.2 million parking spots, according to a conservative estimate, or 3.7 for every household. Seattle has 1.6 million spaces, or more than 5 per household. And those three cities are among America's most compact; each has robust public transit and schools and shops within walking distance of most homes. Des Moines has the same number of parking spaces as Seattle, though it is less than one third the size. The Iowa capital has almost 20 parking spaces per household. Many American downtowns, such as Little Rock, Newport News, Buffalo, and Topeka, have more land devoted to parking than to buildings.

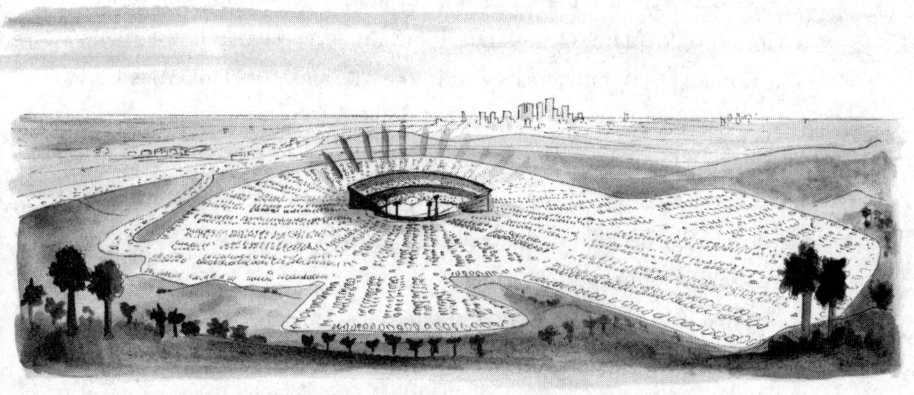

Dodger Stadium, Los Angeles. Ten additional Dodger Stadiums would fit inside the ballpark's parking lot.

In the mid-aughts, when the team of programmers at Maxis were working on the first new *SimCity* in a decade, they studied American municipal architecture, politics, and urban design to try to produce a compelling simulacrum. Lead designer Stone Librande used Google Earth to measure his surroundings. The biggest surprise he found was the size of the parking lots. "When I started measuring out our local grocery store, which I don't think of as being that big, I was blown away by how much more space was parking lot rather than actual store," he said. "That was kind of a problem, because we were originally just going to model real cities, but we quickly realized there were way too many parking lots in the real world and that our game was going to be really boring if it was proportional in terms of parking lots." In the game, he said, they tried to imagine that the parking was underground: "We had to do the best we could do and still make the game look attractive."

All this pavement has direct environmental consequences. One is simply the cost of producing it all: the production of cement is responsible for almost 10 percent of global greenhouse gas emissions, and lots and garages are part of that total, as is all the infrastructure required to serve the sprawl.

A second is the loss of natural land to suburban development. America lost 460,000 acres of wetlands, for example, every year in the 1950s and '60s, and 290,000 acres a year in the '70s and '80s. This transition is associated with steep declines in animal density, especially of birds and bugs. This is happening even in the oldest and slowest-growing parts of the country: Massachusetts, for example, developed more land in the last five decades of the twentieth century than in the three hundred years prior to 1950.

A third is the urban heat island effect. Pavements and roofs absorb energy from the heat-generating elements of urban life, such as buildings and vehicles, which means that cities both warm up faster and cool down slower than natural areas.

A fourth is flooding. A city is, among other things, a complex new hydrological zone, where water collects and flows in unpredictable ways. In sprawling Houston, fifty years of growing faster than any city in America have sealed a Belgium-sized section of Texas grassland beneath asphalt, concrete, and lawn. Flat as a tile and nearly as resistant to water, Houston is the epicenter of the urban flooding epidemic in the United States. When the stronger and more frequent rainstorms caused by climate change pass over this heavily populated region just inland from the Gulf of Mexico, the water has nowhere to go. Various studies have estimated that "impervious" cover such as parking lots may increase runoff and flooding by up to a factor of ten. In the two decades preceding Hurricane Harvey, greater Houston grew by 2.7 million people—the equivalent of adding an entire city of Chicago to the metro area in just twenty years, mostly on former prairie, farmland, and forest. Approximately 770 square miles were developed in this time, with about half of the land becoming impervious. From 1996 to 2011, impervious surface in Harris County increased by a quarter, and from 1992 to 2010, the area lost almost a third of its wetlands—about sixteen thousand acres. In Brays Bayou, one of the city's major creeks, rainfall has increased by 26 percent over the past forty years—but runoff is up 204 percent. Runoff has tripled because the region has paved its way into an unmapped, manmade floodplain. Subdivisions built upstream are causing hundred-year-old houses downstream to flood for the first time.

It's a problem that goes far beyond Houston. Cities like Chicago and Saint Louis have dug huge underground tunnels to hold all the rain. In Philadelphia and Seattle, homeowners have adopted rain barrels and cultivated native plants. Everywhere, architects have installed green roofs and city planners have replaced the desiccated pits of street trees with reedy green swales. Even the engineers of parking lots are doing their best, adapting to stormy weather with porous materials like gravel or crushed clay. If you drive to commune with the spirit of American environmentalism at Walden Pond, Henry Thoreau's retreat near

Boston, you will leave your car on one of America's pioneering permeable parking lots.

A fifth consequence of all this pavement is water pollution. Outside of cities, runoff from roads and parking lots often goes straight into lakes and streams. In the northern part of the country, in the winter and spring, this runoff is contaminated with road salt. In the summer, heated by the smoldering blacktop, it can drain ten to twenty degrees hotter than it fell. In all seasons, it is contaminated by pollutants such as motor oil, rubber dust from tires, animal droppings, pesticides, air pollution residue, and heavy metals. Jurisdictions are frantically trying to slow this phenomenon; by 2020 they had created more than 1,800 stormwater utilities in the United States that try to treat or divert runoff away from sensitive habitats.

A sixth is groundwater absorption, the flip side of flooding. The largest stormwater utility of all is funded by a "driveway tax" in sunny Los Angeles, of all places, which in 2021 put a 2.5-cent annual levy on every square foot of pavement. It is not enough money to encourage greener building practices at scale—but will raise enough across the county to build infrastructure to keep the city's precious rainstorms from being flushed down its concrete river directly into the Pacific Ocean. That will keep the beaches clean. But it will also, crucially, preserve millions of gallons of stormwater that could be used for nonpotable uses like watering lawns and keeping saltwater out of underground aquifers. During difficult times, it could be filtered and put back into the pipes.

The most important environmental consequence of all that pavement is all the driving it incentivizes. Transportation is America's largest source of greenhouse gases, with drivers in Texas alone accounting for half of 1 percent of global carbon emissions. Ground-level air pollution causes hundreds of thousands of deaths every year and is linked to a number of public health problems including lower test scores in children and Alzheimer's disease in older adults. Sprawling settlement patterns are associated with higher levels of obesity. Car crashes are the leading killer of young Americans and injure three million of us every year—including many pedestrians and cyclists, among whom minorities and low-income Americans bear the brunt of the damage. Not surprisingly, car-centric environments lead to the most injuries for both drivers and pedestrians.

Sprawl is built on a foundation of law (redlining, zoning, impunity for vehicular crimes) and government subsidy (highways, tax breaks, cheap oil) too vast and complex to diagram here.* But within that labyrinth of incentives, parking policy is both powerful and easy to reach. If you want lower emissions and fewer car accidents, parking is the place to start. It's not the only way to get fewer people to drive. But because every trip ends with a parking space, it's the easiest. "Control over the availability of parking spaces is a key policy instrument in limiting car trips and for the time being is *the most widely available and readily accepted method of doing so*," states the United Kingdom's Institution of Highways and Transportation. There is some truth to the classic *Onion* headline: URBAN PLANNER SITS IN TRAFFIC OF HIS OWN MAKING. Urban planner should not have required so much parking.

Parking policy may help explain America's status as a global outlier in driving. In 2017, per-capita car ownership in the United States (about 800 vehicles per one thousand inhabitants) was only moderately higher than in Western Europe (about 600 vehicles per one thousand inhabitants) or Canada (about 655). But Americans drove twice as many miles each year as people in peer European countries. This is not because our country is so large—we also drove 60 percent more than Australians and Canadians. It was at least partly because we built a country with exceptional rewards for driving and punishments for

*See Michael Lewyn's book *Government Intervention and Suburban Sprawl* (New York: Palgrave Macmillan, 2017) and Greg Shill's paper "Should Law Subsidize Driving?" *New York University Law Review* 98, no. 2 (2020).

getting around any other way. Top of the list in both those categories is America's approach to parking, which exacerbates this situation in three ways.

First, free parking in busy destinations creates shortages, which compel arriving parkers to cruise for spots, which puts hundreds of millions of miles on the road each year, or double-park, which generates traffic congestion. This traffic is not the product of a lifestyle trade-off. There is no social benefit to be weighed against the lost gasoline and lost time. It's pure waste. One study from 2017 found that U.S. drivers spent, on average, seventeen hours searching for parking every year—$345 per person in wasted time, fuel, and emissions—and the numbers were much higher in big cities.

Second, parking creates sprawl. Because neighbors fear parking shortages and parking laws render urban building sites expensive or simply unworkable, the parking problem acts as a limit on residential and commercial density. This begins site by site, as each restaurant and shop devotes most of its square footage to parking and apartments are stifled by the demands of parking architecture. But it soon expands to define the character of a neighborhood, and even a city, which becomes hard to navigate without a car. This is true for people who cannot afford to live in parking-challenged, close-in neighborhoods and opt instead for far-out suburbs. But it is also true of people in those same inner neighborhoods, because their friends and colleagues, and with them the metropolitan center of gravity, its birthday parties and Apple Stores and pet food shops, are slowly sliding into the car-dependent periphery. According to the U.S. Department of Energy, annual gas usage is much higher in sprawling cities than in their denser peers, even though most workers just about everywhere commute from one suburb to another. Take the country's five most crowded major cities: 2013 gas consumption was 110 gallons per person per year in New York City, 215 in San Francisco, 188 in Boston, 206 in Chicago, and 168 in Philadelphia, well below the national average of 349 gallons a year. The figure was 434 in Charlotte, 520 in Dallas, 556 in Kansas City, 582 in Houston, and 687 in Orlando.

Finally, requiring mandatory parking at all sites doesn't just make the city physically harder to navigate on foot; it also functions as a huge giveaway to drivers. A little bit of every bar tab, the receipt from a child's toy, the price of a pedicure: every dollar you spend out there in the world is paying for the provision of those free, required parking spaces, whether you use them or not. Not surprisingly, all this free or cheap parking—at your house, at your office, on the street, in public lots and garages downtown—induces people to drive. (And exerts a relative financial penalty on those who don't.) As Homer Simpson explains, "If we buy a new car, we get our parking validated for free!" As respondents to travel surveys often make clear, parking in America is free 99 percent of the time. But building it is expensive. Surface parking can cost $5,000 a space. Even in low-cost cities like Phoenix, the median cost of a new structured parking space is more than $19,000. Meeting Phoenix's super-high parking requirements on the lower floors of an office building takes the cost of the project up by 45 percent. The parking scholar Todd Litman estimates it costs $4,400 to supply parking for each vehicle every year, with drivers directly contributing just 20 percent of that—mostly in the form of mortgage payments on a home garage. With about 250 million passenger vehicles in circulation, that amounts to more than a trillion dollars in American parking assets. A different estimate pegs the annual cost of U.S. car storage between $189 and $554 billion, with drivers paying just $5 billion a year.

Parking is not like a cup for the coffee of traffic; it does not just hold a fixed quantity of drivers. Like *The Phantom Tollbooth*'s subtraction stew, parking is a dish that makes you hungry for more parking. Parking forces us to drive more. The more we drive, the more parking we crave. In the early days, certainly, parking facilities arose in response to demand. But later, thwarting the hopes of the planners who decided to require parking in every new building, they began to create it.

In 2015, a group of researchers led by Chris McCahill looked at historical trends in parking supply and commuter behavior for nine cities: Albany, New York; Berkeley, California; the Washington, DC, suburbs of Arlington, Virginia, and Silver Spring, Maryland; Cambridge, Lowell, and Somerville, Massachusetts; and Hartford and New Haven, Connecticut. Using historical aerial photography from three dates to identify and approximate the parking supply, McCahill found that parking growth between 1960 and 1980 was a "powerful predictor" of car use in the following two decades. Every ten spaces added per one hundred residents before 1980 were linked to an 8 percent increase in the share of residents driving to work after 1980. Increase in the parking supply in the study's first two decades was directly correlated with increases in car use in the following two decades. More parking appeared to cause more driving, not the other way around.

Parking built into houses and apartments is a greater predictor of car use than density, transit, or any other neighborhood attribute. In 2009, the parking scholar Rachel Weinberger compared parking and commuting patterns in the New York City neighborhoods of Park Slope and Jackson Heights. Park Slope was an early locus of gentrification in Brooklyn, home to a famous food co-op, a nation-leading density of strollers, and leader of the Senate Democrats Chuck Schumer. Jackson Heights is a central area of Queens known as the "most diverse census tract on earth" for its various immigrant populations. Though Jackson Heights residents make less money, own fewer cars, and have similar public transit access to their counterparts in Park Slope, they were 45 percent more likely to commute by car to transit-accessible destinations in Manhattan. That, Weinberger concluded, was because the midcentury homes of Jackson Heights were six times more likely to have on-site parking than the row houses of brownstone Brooklyn. Later, she expanded the analysis to the entirety of the city's three subway-served outer boroughs. Controlling for income, age, household size, transit service, car ownership, and race, Weinberger found census tracts with more on-site parking had higher levels of car commuting to the Manhattan core. "Anyone who purchases or rents a home that includes an off-street parking space is *de facto* making a pre-payment towards car ownership," she concluded. A separate study found that free on-street parking in New York increased car ownership by 9 percent.

Nationally, people who live in housing with parking included are 60 to 80 percent more likely to own cars than their neighbors without dedicated off-street parking. And not because drivers select apartments with parking. In San Francisco, the lottery for coveted affordable housing attracts scores of applicants of varying income levels for every available unit, whether those units come with parking or not. A team led by the researcher Adam Millard-Ball surveyed lottery winners to compare rates of car ownership to on-site parking provision. Lottery winners who wound up in buildings with one parking space per unit were more than twice as likely to own cars as those who wound up in buildings with no parking.

But the most thorough evidence for parking creating driving comes from offices. Between 80 and 95 percent of American workers get free parking at the office. When workers are forced to pay for parking themselves, the share of employees driving to work alone falls on average by 25 percent. Along with jobs, expensive parking is the key determinant of whether American transit projects attract new riders. When employers with subsidized parking offered a cash equivalent to workers who didn't drive, drive-alone rates fell by 17 percent.

A particularly dramatic example of the nudge of free parking comes from the Bill & Melinda Gates Foundation, which in 2011 moved 1,200 employees into a new headquarters in Seattle. At the time, 90 percent of employees drove to work. Where the city would once have *required* Gates to build parking for its employees to reduce traffic, Seattle instead asked the foundation to charge its employees for parking to reduce traffic. The foundation still provided more than seven hundred reserved spaces on-site and nearby. But employees had to pay to park, $12 a day, with a maximum fee of $120 a month. Bike lockers and transit cards were free. The fees and the fee structure, which made driving a day-by-day added cost, rather than a prepaid monthly expense, seemed to affect employees' choices. In 2012, just 42 percent of employees drove to work. By 2017, it was down to 34 percent. Monthly parking functioned like a gym membership, one of those sunk costs workers felt guilty for not making the most of every day.

Even if parking is a kind of narcotic that creates its own demand, we mostly managed to build enough parking. So why does parking feel scarce? Part of the explanation may be what psychologists call the availability heuristic: It's easy to recall the anxiety of being unable to park. It's a terrible feeling to be trapped behind the wheel, especially when you have to pee. It's also easy to remember finding a *great* spot on a crowded block. But when parking is easy, it is as thoughtless an experience as you can have behind the wheel.

Part of the explanation is that Americans don't like to walk. Victor Gruen's Fort Worth plan set the limit an American driver would walk at two and a half minutes. In 1966, worried planners in Atlanta recorded average walking distance from a parking spot in peer cities: 501 feet in Nashville, 555 feet in Dallas, 478 feet in New Orleans. In other words, the average walking distance from parking spot to destination—the expectation of a walk downtown—was less than two city blocks. The implication was that lots and garages would be needed on every other block. Ironically, the proliferation of parking facilities was not helping this metric; studies have since demonstrated that pedestrians overestimate walking times when they find themselves exposed to a parking crater. A walk down a leafy street of houses and shops isn't so bad. A walk past six parking garages to run a single errand is less appealing. Taught to expect "rock star" parking in front of every destination, American drivers groused when they were given anything else.

And part of it is just bad management. In truth, even in American neighborhoods that claim to toil under a parking shortage, there really *is* enough parking. Really! "Usually when I do a study, they tell us parking is jammed, and you find out maximum peak occupancy is 60 percent," says Richard Willson, a professor at Cal Poly Pomona. In a study of ten Southern California cities, he found peak parking occupancy was just 56 percent, but lots and garages looked full because the most visible spaces filled first.

"Almost every place I've ever worked has started by telling me there's a parking problem," says David Fields, a consultant at Nelson\Nygaard, a firm that helps cities address parking and other issues. "What they mean is that the parking space in front of the place I want to go is not available when I arrive." This demand for immediate, unconditional satisfaction distinguishes the provision of parking from most other goods—a seat at the bar, or a cab at the airport. In 2015, Fields, Weinberger, and Joshua Karlin-Resnick analyzed parking studies of twenty-seven mixed-use American neighborhoods and found "parking was universally oversupplied, in many cases quite significantly." Assuming that a district with sufficient parking would have 15 percent of its spots available at the busiest times, they found that the oversupply ranged from 6 percent to 253 percent. In the third of their cases where there was talk of a "parking shortage" in newspaper articles or community meetings, the oversupply was on average 45 percent. Concord, Massachusetts, where residents yearned for "much-needed parking," had 1,688 open spots on the busiest days of the year where 927 would have sufficed to create 15 percent vacancy. One study of 42 stores with dedicated parking found peak occupancy rates between 24 and 58 percent. Near hip South Congress Avenue in Austin, the parking supply is never more than 60 percent occupied. In Albany, New York, parking is never more than 50 percent full. In Paducah, Kentucky, occupancy never goes above 38 percent.

And that is true of apartment buildings as well, despite whatever the self-appointed sheriffs of the condo lot may believe. At housing complexes in suburban Redmond, Washington, maximum parking occupancy was 65 percent. In Seattle, residential lots and garages were only 63 percent occupied at night, probably because approximately 20 percent of occupants did not own cars. A study of more than two hundred multifamily properties across Washington, DC, concluded that parking was oversupplied by 40 percent. In Chicago, builders supply two spaces for every three units, but they need only one. In Boston and its suburbs, a survey of almost twenty thousand housing units built since 2000 found that the mandatory garages were 30 percent empty at peak times—almost $100 million had been spent on forty-one acres of obligatory but unused parking. When the housing was built near transit, or the housing was affordable, garage occupancy fell even lower. And because free parking encourages car ownership, these occupancy numbers are higher than they would have been had these buildings constructed smaller garages.

It is difficult to turn back the clock and pinpoint, spot by spot, how the postwar parking hunger created the cities we know today. Surveying the moonscapes of American downtowns around their 1990 nadir, it was awfully hard to separate parking that was created by policy—by laws that compelled private builders or by public authorities—from that which emerged as a result of market demand, through disinvestment or the agency of individual owners who decided that surface parking was the most lucrative use of their land. Consider the parking-rich city of Hartford, Connecticut, which went from having 180,000 people, sixteen thousand parking spaces, and four department stores in 1957 to 120,000 people, forty-seven thousand parking spaces, and zero department stores in 2009—with the exact same number of jobs. This trajectory suggests a chicken-and-egg question. Is Hartford in a rut because parking lots have consumed the cityscape? Or did the cityscape fall apart into parking lots because Hartford was struggling? You can pose the inverse question about thriving, parking-challenged cities like New York, Boston, Portland, and San Francisco: Are real estate values high because they are dense, vibrant environments? Or are they dense, vibrant environments because real estate values are too high to sustain surface parking lots?

We can't be sure, but there are clues. New York, Boston, Portland, and San Francisco have something in common: they all designed downtown parking caps under pressure from the Environmental Protection Agency in the 1970s. It's hard to separate the effect of these parking limits themselves from the ongoing influence of the political culture that created them. But if these limits did lead to more walkable, prosperous cities, that would be in line with a large body of research that suggests the parking supply shapes driving patterns.

No city of any size could have permitted everyone to come by car and retained a vibrant downtown. To take an extreme example: in 1966, one transportation scholar calculated that if everyone who commuted to Manhattan every day drove alone in a car, storing those vehicles would require a five-story garage the size of Manhattan below Fifty-Second Street. That was one point where Gruen was right: sooner or later, the commuter would have to get out of his car. He could leave it at home and take the bus. He could do it on the edge of a pedestrian downtown, though not without a handful of enormous public garages. Or he could do it in a privately held lot, right in front of his destination. In most American cities, that last option is more or less how things worked out.

PART 2

Charging for Something Everyone Expects to Be Free

CHAPTER 6

How to Use Parking for Money Laundering, Tax Evasion, and Theft

> Why should I pay when if I apply myself, maybe I could get it for free?
>
> —George Costanza, "The Parking Space," *Seinfeld*

Despite city fathers' best efforts, there remained some places in America so lively that parking could not be convenient, immediately available, and free. In such place arose a breed of men, and they were mostly men, whose prime assets could compel visitors to pay for parking. Big downtowns, professional sports stadiums, hospitals, and airports are all in this category. At airports, parking sometimes brings in more money than aviation itself. (Not having a proper mass transit connection can be good business.) Paid lots and garages make up a small fraction of the American parking picture, but they loom large in the collective imagination. The reason most people hate paying for parking is the same reason the parking industry has thrown off so much cash. "Guys love parking," one parking vendor reasoned. "They put a car there, it sits there doing nothing, and they make money." With that cash came trouble. The history of commercial parking in the United States is in part a history of theft: workers stealing from bosses, bosses stealing from the government, politicians stealing from the people.

In the 1950s, architects dreamed garages might assume the psychic role of Europe's great train stations, luminous halls of stone statues and Latin inscriptions beneath which commuters, tourists, soldiers, and immigrants rubbed shoulders. A few garages did become beloved civic totems, such as the Parkade in Spokane, Washington, or the Temple Street Garage in New Haven; some attractive public spaces were appropriated as parking lots, including for several decades the plaza in front of Notre Dame in Paris. But most parking structures fail to match the grandeur of a train station bathroom. Lots and garages rank among society's least-loved establishments, the domain of roosting pigeons, flickering fluorescent lights, and a sense of lurking danger. For a guarantee of secrecy and solitude, Mark Felt and Bob Woodward chose an underground parking garage to transmit the secrets that brought down Richard Nixon.

When a parking garage got attention for its good looks, as Herzog & de Meuron's Lincoln Road garage in Miami Beach did when it opened in 2011 ("All muscle without clothing," Jacques Herzog said, like the scene on the beach itself), it was the exception that proved the rule. Since 1990, the American Society of Landscape Architects has recognized only one parking lot. "Architects write me about parking lots, because they're interested in seeing parking lot patterns and things like that," the artist Ed Ruscha said of his parking lot photographs. "I'll tell you what is more interesting: the oil droppings on the ground." That low opinion is shared by parking attendants, only 5 percent of whom found their job meaningful in a 2015 survey. No other profession in America scored below 20 percent.

In one of precious few movies made about parking, *The Parking Lot Movie*, Meghan Eckman follows the trials of the beatniks and goofballs who run a lot next to the campus of the University of Virginia in Charlottesville. The attendants are mostly graduate students, with future careers in academia and the arts, a self-described "ragtag group of fractured poets" who wax philosophical about justice, anger, income inequality, and parking.

"You could almost see the truncated syllogism in their head," one attendant says of drivers' sense of entitlement. "Like: 'I bought the car; how could there not be a place to park it? Surely it comes with a parking space.'"

Customers treat them badly, but the scorn builds solidarity. "On the rung of employment, it's beneath taxidermy, it's beneath bellhop—bellhops get uniforms," one attendant says. "'I hope you're proud of yourself, you're a parking lot attendant,'" another former attendant, James McNew, reflects, imitating a driver talking down to him. "I am proud! I hope you're proud, driving your father's car and trying to beat out a forty-cent parking fee. Who's come further?" But the job is also exhilarating: "In the parking lot we were dynamos, whirlwinds, rulers; we had complete autonomy. We had it all in a world that had nothing to offer us."

John Van Horn, the publisher of *Parking Today*, got his start selling equipment to garages and started the magazine when he couldn't find anywhere to advertise his products. *Parking Today*, he thought, could be a real, independent trade magazine—in contrast to the house organs of the industry groups. Still, it is largely a positive take on the trade.

Not that Van Horn has no tales of scandal. On the contrary, he will freely hold forth on various rumors of theft and murder in the business. It's just that they don't go into *Parking Today*, he said, because what would be the use? Instead, he channeled his taste for the macabre into a three-part noir, *Death by Parking*, in which a hard-boiled PI runs afoul of various parking magnates—and finds love along the way. Here's how one of Van Horn's characters explains the temptations of commercial parking: "Parking is a cash business. No one will ever make you account for all the money. There's no inventory to list and track, so unless you are knowledgeable about the parking business, there is no way to prove just how much money is collected on any given day. In parking, you are renting space by time. Who knows how many cars come and go and how long they stay? So although you actually collect, say, $225 on a given day, who says you can't put $750 or $1000 in the bank. At that moment, the additional $525 or $775, which may be the result of a bank robbery or numbers running, becomes perfectly legitimate. You pay your taxes, and buy your house, or limo, or whatever." That's the beauty of an all-cash business: you can pocket the cash and underreport to the IRS, or money launder and overreport to the IRS.

Garages get robbed, too. "People never understood: You could steal more money from a parking garage than from a bank," said Dennis Cunning, an industry vet turned auditor. In the eighties, Cunning ran the garage at Boston's Prudential Center, where one Bruins playoff game could bring in $50,000 to $70,000 in cash. They'd hire security details with shotguns to man the door. Operators in New York at that time would get calls saying, "There's no attendant here." Someone had stolen the nice cars, stolen the money, and locked the attendant in the trunk of a car. The union contract had a special provision for workers to receive compensation for lost pocket money in the event of a robbery.

Mostly, however, the theft came from inside the house. This was the "cigar box" era, where employees making minimum wage were charged with stuffing vast amounts of cash into a box every night. For those who chose to line their pockets, the scheme was simple: the attendants could report half the cars to the manager; the manager could report half of those to the owner; the owner could report half of those to the IRS. Everybody won except the taxman. One possibly apocryphal story parking auditors tell, to illustrate the shamelessness of the people they investigate, concerns a visit to a Manhattan garage shortly after the attacks of September 11. Hundreds of cars are parked, but they aren't in the books. Upon confrontation, the attendant says, "Well, yes—it's a real tragedy. Those people lost their lives on that day. . . . God bless America." The auditor, running his hands over the clean, still-warm hoods, knows better.

One outsider who works with parking companies explained the laid-back management style that allows this chicanery to persist: "Imagine if you were the executive in charge of a one-fleet airline, and I asked how many people were on the airline? I don't know. Is Joey on the plane? I don't know. How much did Joey pay? I don't know. That's parking."

Every so often, a parking lot bandit hits the news. Freweyni Mebrahtu was a lot attendant at the Smithsonian's Air and Space Museum annex in Chantilly, Virginia, outside of Washington, DC. Mebrahtu worked for Parking Management, Inc., collecting $15 parking fees from arriving visitors. For three years, she gamed the system, collecting cash but withholding stubs, with the electronic car counter unplugged. The FBI found she had pocketed the fees of nearly sixty thousand thousand cars, for a total take of nearly $900,000. Some days she went home with more than $4,000 cash. The money paid, among other things, for her kids to go to college and one of her daughters to have surgery. Mebrahtu shared her secrets with a colleague, Meseret Terefe, who took home almost $500,000 in a red duffel bag. Both attendants were sentenced to long prison terms.

That was child's play compared with the conspiracy Anthony Gricco executed at Philadelphia International Airport, which a district attorney later called "one of the largest rip-offs ever to hit the city." Between 1990 and 1994, Gricco was the regional manager with Ampco System Parking in charge of garages at the Philly airport. His brother-in-law, William McCardell, supervised the day-to-day work at the toll booths and collected money from the cashiers. A third collaborator, Michael Flannery, was a technician at the company that printed the tickets.

Fliers returning from vacations and business trips would rack up high multiday parking fees, which they dutifully paid upon exiting the airport. Participating cashiers collected the money but used a separate stack of short-stay tickets to record the exits and open the gate. Long-term parkers were getting counted as short-term parkers, and the difference between the two fares went directly into the cashiers' pockets. Flannery disabled the fare displays so that customers didn't realize their $100 payments didn't match up with the $10 charges recorded on the official record. McCardell would drive by at the end of the shift, stuffing a brown paper bag with cash and Philadelphians' unscanned long-term parking tickets. Four days. Seven days. Ten days. They'd paid their full fare, but as far as the airport could tell, they'd each stayed only a few hours. In this way, hundreds and hundreds of parking hours could be erased from the ledger every day—and from the cash register.

The key to this scheme was the fake short-term parking tickets to transform overnight stays, in the books, into simple pickups and drop-offs. In the beginning, Flannery assembled these in the most basic way possible: pushing the button on a ticket machine over and over, then resetting the counter so the audit wouldn't record dozens of missing cars. Each cashier would use these tickets to steal cash from thirty cars. Together, the men could bank about $600 to $900 a day this way.

Gradually, manager Anthony Gricco recruited more and more cashiers, asking if they were interested in making a little extra money. One cashier, Carol Eller, who served nearly a year in state prison after her conviction, testified that Gricco would hand her $700 a week for her trouble, and sometimes more.

To scale up, in 1990 Flannery started printing the counterfeit day-tripper tickets himself—thirty tickets a night, three nights a week. By the end of the year, two hundred fake tickets a week. In 1991, another airport garage was brought in on the scam, and Flannery cranked up his printer to produce eight hundred fake tickets a week. Eventually fifteen cashiers were cooking the books. "We were always stepping it up, more, more, and more," Flannery said. "Gricco told me at one time,

The history of commercial parking in the United States is in part a history of theft: workers stealing from bosses, bosses stealing from the government, politicians stealing from the people.

there were twenty-five hands in the till." In 1993, 1,100 tickets a week; 1,400 tickets a week by 1994.

That summer of 1994, an alarm bell went off for cashiers swapping out real tickets for fake ones: the Philadelphia Parking Authority suddenly decided to install smoke detectors in the booths. Flannery realized the "smoke detectors" contained tiny cameras, and called a meeting at Gricco's house to discuss pulling the plug. The men decided to keep going. On September 22, the Philadelphia DA pounced, arresting cashiers after the night shift with cash and unrecorded long-term tickets stuffed into their clothes. The investigators concluded the cashiers had pocketed more than $3.4 million in airport revenue, but unofficial estimates were much higher. In 1995, the year after the bust, airport parking revenues jumped by $7 million!

Most cashiers pled guilty but kept their mouths shut. It took almost two years for the police to gather enough evidence to indict Gricco on charges of conspiracy, theft, and forgery. One cashier testified that an official at the Philadelphia Parking Authority had been on the take, too. But though eleven cashiers had been convicted and some were already in prison, a Philadelphia jury found insufficient evidence and cleared Gricco and McCardell on all charges. This verdict was a testament to how hard it was to conclusively demonstrate organized theft in the parking business, short of finding someone with their pockets stuffed with cash and ticket stubs.

Gricco did do time eventually, after he was convicted of tax fraud in 2001. In that trial, Flannery, the ticket printer, broke ranks and testified for the prosecution, revealing the inner workings of the operation. Gricco struggled to explain how he had come up with $735,000 to buy houses, jewelry, and cars. "I was raised not to believe in banks," he told the jury, arguing that he had saved up money by working several jobs during the 1980s, a story corroborated by his mother. Unfortunately for him, his annual tax returns between 1983 and 1990 showed average annual income of less than $12,000 a year. Gricco was found guilty. Afterward, he would throw the whole profession under the bus, arguing for a shorter sentence on the grounds that managing the airport parking lot did not constitute a "position of public or private trust."

It was hard to argue with that.

❙ ❙ ❙ ❙

Naturally, all this loose cash attracted the attention of organized crime. Among the most famous examples of parking's rough history is Kinney Parking, which was founded on Newark's Kinney Street in 1945 by Manny Kimmel. Kimmel had owned a handful of garages in the city; he had also run the numbers game in Newark in the twenties and thirties, along with the mobster Abner "Longie" Zwillman, who used Kimmel's car parks to store bootleg hooch during Prohibition and later became a part owner of Kinney, according to the FBI. By 1970, parking profits had enabled Kinney to expand into a holding company called Kinney National Service Inc., which owned (among other things) *Mad* magazine and the film studio Warner Bros. You could make Hollywood money parking cars.

But the old business was unreformed. Judd Richheimer, a friend and college roommate of Kinney president Steve Ross who worked at the company in the sixties, remembered a garage foreman named Butchie. One day a man came in and tried to steal a car. Butchie turned the air compressor on so there would be a lot of noise; then he took the guy downstairs and broke both his arms and both his legs and threw him out on the street. "I had said, you know, that I could call the cops and have him arrested; but Butchie said, 'No, he'll be out in a day and he'll be back. This way, the message goes out to his friends, too.'" Richheimer also said the company had a million-dollar slush fund, skimmed from parking lot cigar boxes, to pay bribes. In a 1970 feature, *Forbes* magazine ran an inset on the rumors that Kinney had mafia connections, which Manny's son Caesar doggedly denied. Steve Ross, seeking legitimacy in his new role as a Hollywood mogul, spun off the company's more prosaic holdings, including parking, into a smaller company run by a young garage industry heir named Daniel Katz.

It was a great time to run parking garages in New York City. In 1973, Mayor John Lindsay and Governor Nelson Rockefeller had drafted a "transportation control plan" to meet the air pollution standards of the newly formed Environmental Protection Agency, which included an initiative to ban most on-street parking in Manhattan south of Fifty-Ninth Street and eventually prohibited the development of new off-street lots and garages in that area. Mayor Abe Beame, who succeeded Lindsay, thought the plan would "make a ghost town" of Manhattan, but was forced by the U.S. Supreme Court to begin "hooding" parking meters in 1977. By 1981, the parking industry estimated that more than twenty-five thousand spaces had been eliminated in the Manhattan Central Business District as lots and garages gradually gave way to new buildings. Meanwhile, the city's economy rebounded, and the number of arriving drivers grew higher every year, up 33 percent between 1975 and 1985.

One result of this was that garage owners were getting rich enough to get into the development business. Kinney's Dan Katz was among them: when a young lawyer and wannabe developer named Leonard Boxer approached him in the early 1980s about buying a lot on Second Avenue and Twenty-Sixth Street, Katz saw an opportunity to get in on the action. "Rather than just pay me and you build this," Boxer remembered him saying, "Let's do something together." Boxer did the legal work. Katz, who had taken Kinney public, brought the money. In 1984, a third partner, Norman Segal, pestered Stanley Zabar (of the famous delicatessen) into selling the trio a cluster of low-rise commercial buildings on Broadway and Eighty-Seventh Street. Segal wanted to call it the Minsk: "If the Anglo-Saxons could come over here and name their buildings for their ancestral home, so could I." Katz and Boxer overruled him, and they called their 150-unit tower the Montana, because it was west of the famous Dakota building.

New York City garages had been grandfathered into a densifying city and protected from potential competition, and they were swimming in cash. At Kinney's location across from the Plaza Hotel and Central Park, monthly rates rose from $213 in 1978 to $425 in 1984 (in 1984 dollars). Between 1982 and 1983, according to a city study, the cost of parking in Manhattan rose by five times the rate of the consumer price index. While only half of Kinney's two hundred locations were in Manhattan, they accounted for 80 percent of the firm's profits.

The cost of parking in Manhattan was the subject of a popular joke that went something like this:

> A man walks into a bank in New York City and asks to borrow $5,000. The loan officer says, "We're going to need some collateral." So the man hands him the keys to his Ferrari. The bank accepts the Ferrari and gives the man his money. Two weeks later, he returns the $5,000 plus $15 in interest. The banker says, "It's been great doing business with you, but we checked you out and learned you're a rich man. You've got a good salary, a big house on Long Island, and no debt. Why did you need to borrow five thousand dollars?" The man responds, "Where else can I park in Manhattan for two weeks for fifteen dollars?" (Sometimes the man is Jewish, Indian, Chinese, Italian, Jamaican, or a blonde.)

Still, there was more money to be made in apartment buildings and condos. By 1986, Kinney was the largest publicly held parking company in the United States, and Katz and his partners were looking east, where they'd bought the site of an old Woolworth store on Eighty-Sixth Street and Third Avenue. This building would be even bigger, with 256 apartments. Keeping with the theme, they called it the Colorado.

But trouble was brewing, in the form of an FBI crackdown that would eventually ensnare Dan Katz. The bureau was in the midst of its war on organized crime, and one of its targets was the Palma Boys Social Club in Manhattan's East Harlem neighborhood. Bugging the small storefront, which Martin Scorsese would later re-create for *The Irishman*, complete with wiseguys at a folding table outside, led to the indictment and imprisonment of Anthony "Tony" Salerno, a boss of the Genovese crime family. The bureau also uncovered scores of incriminating details about the Teamsters Local 272, the city's powerful Garage Employees Union, which was run by Tony Salerno's brother Cirino "Charlie" Salerno, also known as "Speed."

The Teamsters had represented Manhattan garage workers for decades and periodically organized strikes that sent commuters scampering for the subway. Speed Salerno had been an officer of Local 272 since 1972, except in 1979, when he was kept from the position by a labor law conviction for accepting $1,000 from a city garage owner. But he was reelected in 1981, and the practice of extracting payments from garages continued.

"I was running the garage when the owners called and said, 'Put a thousand dollars in a paper bag,'" the auditor Dennis Cunning recalled in 2020, of his days working in Manhattan, "and a little later Charlie showed up and I handed the bag to the owner, then Charlie had the bag. I had no idea what went down in that basement, but I do know, after that, that none of the cashiers would go into the union. I was also told, 'Watch what you say or you'll sleep with the fishes.'" In short, if a garage owner wanted to hire nonunion workers such as cashiers, that was just fine with the union, as long as Charlie Salerno got his payoff. Another industry vet joked, "There was a time in this country when there was a shortage of brown paper bags."

Later on, Salerno and other Local 272 officers would be charged with using the union as a "racketeering enterprise," padding their pockets with bribes to the tune of $300,000, not including gifts and vacations. Garage owners complained their employees had been threatened with guns or told they could expect "wet cement poured down [their] throat." Victor Alfieri, the Local 272 vice president convicted for failing to investigate Salerno's conduct, told the judge they had been warned (at another La Cosa Nostra social club uptown) no one was to "ever go near Charlie Salerno." Alfieri also implied he would have been killed if he had tried to blow the whistle on Salerno's behavior: "I can't say nothing to them. When I got the job, [Salerno] was there, I can't throw the boss out, I wouldn't be here talking to anybody."

But the most damning testimony about the corruption in Manhattan garages came from a made man named Vincent Cafaro, who delivered electrifying testimony before the U.S. Senate on the influence of the Genovese crime family on affairs in New York City. Cafaro's betrayal was considered so serious that his own son offered to take on a contract to whack his dad, though the son was arrested and Cafaro senior, if he is still alive, remains in witness protection.

Cafaro's Senate testimony was wide-ranging: About half of new buildings in New York City, Cafaro said, put money in the hands of wiseguys in one way or another. Kennedy Airport was controlled by the Lucchese mob, Cafaro said. The Genovese family controlled the docks, the brand-new Javits Convention Center, and the hotel and restaurant workers, he said.

And the family controlled the parking union, thanks to Charlie "Speed" Salerno. Local 272 "is ours," Cafaro said in an affidavit. "It belongs to our brugad.... In order to run a garage or parking lot in New York City, you have to make a deal with 'Speed.'" "Speed collects money from garage and parking lot owners and delivers this money to East Harlem," Cafaro told the FBI. Every month, he said, Charlie Salerno would bring a few thousand dollars to the Palma Boys Social Club for Cafaro and Fat Tony—"shakedown" funds from the local.

Dan Katz, the president of Kinney and developer of the Montana, learned he was under investigation in 1987. At first his lawyer, Judge Tyler, thought the feds might have Katz on tape talking to Charlie "Speed" Salerno about a "sweetheart contract." But Tyler later told *The New Yorker*'s Connie Bruck that he thought there might have been something more to it than that. Sure enough, in another statement, newly minted government witness Vincent Cafaro described helping a contractor named Leon Morono obtain a building contract for a residential skyscraper on Eighty-Sixth Street and Third Avenue, across from Papaya King—the site of the future Colorado building that Katz and his partners were putting up. Here's Cafaro: "Katz told Speed that [Morono] had bid too high and that if he lowered the bid by about $1,000,000 that Morono would obtain the contract." Cafaro relayed this information to Morono, and got a $100,000 finder's fee for his role in the bid rigging. Later, Cafaro said an owner of Kinney named Katz worked with Speed Salerno to arrange construction bids.

Dan Katz was found on the morning of August 12, 1987, parked in his Cadillac near his Great Neck, Long Island, home with a shotgun wound to the chest. He died at the hospital later that morning. The shotgun, between his legs, had belonged to his grandfather. He left no note, but police determined he had died by suicide. Detectives told local reporters the 48-year-old was depressed about "bad business deals." Tyler, the lawyer, told Bruck that Katz's death left him puzzled. "He wasn't happy, of course. But, from the case the prosecutor had described, even if Katz had gone to trial and been convicted, he might have gotten a sentence of a couple years—not really reason to kill himself."

"It's hard to believe now. You can have affairs, get caught doing the most incredible things, have no embarrassment," observed Doug Sarini, another parking executive, who was shocked by Katz's death and said the Kinney president had offered a helping hand when he was getting started. "Here you had a guy whose reputation was impeccable. Some people can take the embarrassment of a scandal, no matter how insignificant. He was one of those people who couldn't handle any negative impact to his reputation."

Most guys in the parking business, of course, didn't much care about such things. The reputation of parking as a sketchy, duplicitous, and occasionally dangerous business persisted even after the widespread adoption of credit card payments around the millennium. These days, guys mostly reminisce about the bad old days. "Have we had a poor reputation? Yes. Did we deserve it? Yes," the garage consultant Clyde Wilson wrote in 2021 in *Parking Today*. "Do we need to try and hide what we are and who we are? NO." As in many fields, whatever inefficiencies once made this forgotten industry a good target for robbers or gangsters had left it, by the start of the twenty-first century, slow-moving prey for innovators, start-ups, and private equity.

CHAPTER 7

A Trip to the Heart of the Commercial Parking Industry

There is one place in the United States where Victor Gruen's ambitions were realized.* A metropolis ringed by huge parking lots, where tourists and commuters leave their cars in the morning and hit the streets on foot, reliant on a fast and frequent transit system. It is a place the Austrian émigré surely would have hated. In 2019, I visited Disney World—not the park but the parking lot and associated transportation command center—with a group of guests from the National Parking Association, whose conference was meeting nearby. These were the people dragging the parking business into the twenty-first century. They were small-time operators, university administrators, equipment vendors, city planners, techies, and executives

*According to Disney historian Sam Gennawey, Walt had just one book on urban planning on hand when he died: Gruen's *The Heart of Our Cities*. See Sam Gennawey, "E.P.C.O.T. and the Heart of Our Cities," The Original E.P.C.O.T., sites.google.com/site/theoriginalepcot/essays/epcot-and-the-heart-of-our-cities.

at the conglomerates that controlled a larger and larger share of the nation's paid parking supply. Like everyone who does boring, unloved work, they reveled in each other's company.

There are about forty-five thousand parking spaces at Disney World, about as many as in a major American downtown. Ten to twenty families lose their cars here every day. The five hundred employees who manage these lots are, like all Disney employees, known as "cast members," and the standard for their behavior is high: "Preserve the magic. Model the Disney look." They must wave at the courtesy trams, which shuttle families from their parking spots to the park gates (what would otherwise be a walk of thirty to forty-five minutes with small children). They must "create surprises and magical moments," which seems like a tall order for managing a gargantuan parking lot under the fickle Florida sky.

The inside of the park is a car-free city whose transportation options include twelve monorail trains, thirty boats, twenty-nine trams, sixty-one vans, and 304 elevated cabins on an aerial gondola. Mostly, though, Disney World moves the masses on a fleet of four hundred diesel buses, which clock 175,000 rides a day, making the resort's transit system roughly on par with that of Atlanta or Minneapolis.

Just as Main Street revivalists drew inspiration from Walt Disney's small-town facsimile in Anaheim, California, so the parking people had come to Orlando to soak in the Disney way. Two visitors were from Newport News Shipbuilding. Another was from Seaside, Florida, an architectural experiment in tightly knit urbanism that had grown so popular as a tourist destination that some visitors had to park their cars miles away and ride a shuttle bus downtown.

At the NPA conference, parking people didn't have to explain themselves. Men in oxford shirts milled about in the hallways of the Loews Sapphire Falls Resort, the colossal hotel on the edge of Universal Studios that served as our home base, ducking in and out of the day's many panels until the drinking could finally begin. "We're doing it from behind in Ohio!" a man yelled, to laughter, at the Universal Orlando Margaritaville. He meant license-plate reading.

The NPA says 581,000 people work in parking, making the industry about the size of the United States Postal Service. The parkers who could afford three nights at the Loews Sapphire, the conference admission fee, and the surrounding ticketed events were the cream of the crop. "Anyone who gets in this business stays in this business," said one parking executive, over a beer. "Because they're not qualified to do anything else!" retorted another. It was like that scene in *Ferris Bueller's Day Off* when the kids hand the Ferrari keys to a valet, who says, "Don't worry, I'm a professional." Cam responds: "A professional *what*?" "Nobody plans to get into parking," conceded another exec. A fourth described his life story as "my life and times of sucking on carbon monoxide."

"You're the first person they see," said another exec, straining for philosophy but sounding like a killer doorman, "and the last person they see."

One night at the bar I met Carl DePinto, a tall, bony man who ran parking at Duke University. DePinto was ragging on one of his old colleagues: "This guy used to raise his gates at five p.m.!" (Raising the gates means forfeiting the day's revenue to let frustrated and impatient drivers out of your garage; later, a vendor gave me a T-shirt that said, "Keep Calm and Don't Raise the Gates.") "I wouldn't raise my gates except on Christmas Day," DePinto crowed. Growing up in Hoboken, Carl DePinto's favorite thing about Hot Wheels was getting the last car back in the box. Later, he ran the garages at New York–Presbyterian Healthcare System, which a rival told me takes in about $3 million a month in parking revenue (as much in thirty days as a baseball team might generate from parking all season). DePinto talked about parking at a Manhattan hospital the way other city kids might talk about Fashion Week or the New York Stock Exchange. "Manhattan's crazy, but it's an animal, bro. You're going to pay in because you're making it. I was there during the recession and my business didn't hiccup. Didn't go down a damn penny." He also designed the garage for Frank Gehry's first residential skyscraper downtown.

The mood at the conference in Orlando in 2019 was one of gentle defiance: Christine Banning, the president of the sixty-eight-year-old trade group, set the tone in an early address: "There is so much in the media 'Parking is dead,'" she cried. "If I see one more report, I don't know what I'm going to do." In fact, as Banning spelled out, things were looking pretty sunny for parking that fall: autonomous cars had failed to materialize, Uber and Lyft were still pouring billions of dollars down the drain, millennials were finally buying cars. The pandemic was still six months away. "That normal human life pattern is taking shape," Banning observed of millennial car buying, "and there's a bright future ahead of us."

Despite America's surplus of free parking and Americans' related hatred for paying for it, commercial parking is a lucrative business because parkers receive a great deal of help on both sides of the ball. Supply of parking is subsidized because developers are required to build lots and garages but rarely consider them sources of revenue. As a result, parking companies—most of which do not own the properties they operate—aren't obligated to recoup the capital costs of garage construction ($30,000 to $40,000 a stall, a line item long since dissolved into the developer's pro forma) and are free to print cash from a lease that requires little in the way of supplies, labor, upkeep, or advertising. Those who *do* own their lots tend to be real estate speculators first and foremost, but long before they flip their parcels for condo construction, they benefit from a property tax system that looks kindly on underdeveloped land, no matter its potential.

On the demand side, the subsidy is vast. The entire American built environment is virtually impossible to navigate any other way than in a car, ensuring a never-ending stream of people who need to park. But garage operators benefit from more direct support: many of their customers don't actually pay to park. Those fees are instead paid by their employers, subsidized by federal tax exemptions, "validated" by the offices or shops they visit, or bundled into the cost of their rental apartments or football tickets.

The core concept here is not rocket science. Parking professionals, who once said they were in the hospitality business and now claim to work in "mobility," dispute the categorization, but the fact is their product is a commodity: like a barrel of oil or a bushel of wheat, the most important characteristic of a parking space is that it is right in front of you when you need it.

Which gets to the real reason parking can be so lucrative: because no one wants to walk more than two blocks for a parking space, parking operators are granted an oligopoly by default, with only a few choices available at a given location. "We'd never admit this," admitted Jim Huger, the impresario of Premium Parking who claimed to run about half the commercial parking supply in New Orleans, "but we like monopolies."* Huger's strategy is clever: premium rents and management of the lots… by a separate LLC run by Huger himself.

"Doesn't that create a conflict of interest?" I asked.

"It's good to play both sides," he responded.

---

*There's more than one way to a parking monopoly. After Dan Snyder bought the Washington football team in 1999, the front office successfully persuaded their suburban Maryland county to forbid fans from walking to football games. Then they raised the parking rate from $10 to $25. Shortly afterward, a lawyer named J. P. Szymkowicz parked ten minutes away at the Landover Mall (for free) and was turned away from the stadium. Szymkowicz sued; he learned that the team was trying to police parking at the mall after they found that more than 1,500 cars had used the (free) mall lot during a Monday-night game. The county repealed the ban. Later, Snyder took over the amusement chain Six Flags and tried to execute a similar scheme in Agawam, Massachusetts, ending entry into Six Flags on foot. One of the owners whose lots had served as auxiliary, unofficial parking for the theme park learned about what had happened in Washington and mounted a campaign to unseat the mayor. The mayor lost the election and Agawam repealed the ban. Ten years after that, the Atlanta Braves got Cobb County, Georgia, to bar property owners from charging for parking during baseball games, concerts, or other events at the team's new SunTrust Park stadium. After an investigation by *The Atlanta Journal-Constitution*, commissioners repealed the law.

"Like Adam Neumann," I said, referring to the self-dealing WeWork founder.

"Yeah, but I don't have a board of directors."

To some extent, a guy like Jim Huger has it easy compared with Duke's Carl DePinto. When you manage parking for a hospital or a university, your obligations are not only to the almighty dollar but also to institutional demands and social hierarchies. At Duke, DePinto is routinely vilified in the student newspaper. "Of the expansive list of evils at Duke . . . few are more malicious and loathsome than Duke Parking & Transportation," wrote senior Bella Miller in her column, Make Duke Weird. Art Champagne, the director of the nuclear laboratory shared between Duke, UNC, and other institutions, told the paper DePinto was "making it really hard for us to do our work." "There's no way to win against parking," he added. The price of a daily parking pass had doubled from $5 to $10.

"We are in a business, unfortunately, where we are mostly hated," DePinto said. "Even nuclear physicists pay for parking." Attaining high rank at a university rarely comes with an assigned spot. Instead, the pass is known as a "hunting license."

University of California head Clark Kerr used to say a college president's job was "providing parking for faculty, sex for students, and athletics for the alumni." A modern university, he went on, could be thought of as "a series of individual faculty entrepreneurs held together by a common grievance over parking." And reward: it's at Berkeley that Nobel Prize winners get reserved parking spots.

Increasingly, the reality is that students, too, demand parking in ever-greater numbers. Students say parking rates are second only to quality of teaching in their satisfaction with a university. Kiriana Cowansage, as a neuroscience postdoc at the University of California at San Diego (and my cousin), found herself caught up in what she described as an "institutional caste system" so fine toothed it makes airline boarding look like a kibbutz. After five years of experience, UCSD reclassifies senior postdocs as "research staff"—which for Cowansage meant her "A" permit was downgraded to a "B" permit. A scarlet letter. She was no longer able to freely check in on her lab, despite her professor's best efforts to reinstate her parking status, and was forced to park nearly a mile away. "I ended up working mostly at night, and eventually switched to working entirely at home in order to avoid parking purgatory," she recalled. "I'm fairly confident the situation actually delayed my career." Bob Hope used to joke, "It takes four years to get through UCLA, or five if you park in Lot 32."

For every employee like my cousin there's one like Ben Thomas. At the Mayo Clinic in Rochester, Minnesota, the anesthesiologist assistant went viral filming himself arriving at an on-site parking garage after his parking privileges were upgraded. "On-site parking I got!" Thomas shrieks as the gate lifts, giddy as Daffy Duck atop a mound of gold bullion. "Just like you guys. I'm with all of you guys now, I park downtown! Oh, this is amazing. I feel rich! On-site parking! Thirteen years for this! Thirteen years for this! It's a dream come true! I love it—I don't know if I love this ramp—but I love it. Thirteen years, you too can have this. On-site parking."

Institutions like these, from Disney World to Duke, have reached a rarefied tier of insight about parking: garages are so expensive to build, and drivers' willingness to pay so low, that giving everyone drive-in, one-minute-walk access to your amusement park, hospital complex, university, or shipyard is impossible. You cannot build your way out of a true parking shortage. Especially when you consider the opportunity cost of the land, which for many institutions is huge. They are speculators too, and most central parking lots are, in the eyes of administrators at a top-tier university, vacant sites for new buildings. Like many people who try to manage parking for an institution, Carl DePinto wanted to see fewer people drive to work alone. So he used parking revenue to subsidize transportation alternatives. At Duke, the share of people driving alone was just 74 percent (compared with 90 percent in Durham). "We're proud of that," he said.

The NPA says parking is a $131 billion industry, which can be a little hard to visualize until you visit the equipment fair. All the anonymous furniture of the parking garage? Somebody makes that. Somebody travels around the country selling it, fighting to get it installed. Parking deck expansion joints you can count on, to protect concrete from changing temperatures. Wheel locks. Custom cone stencils. Valet tech. Robotic arms. Rolling garage doors. "Signal Tech: We Do More Than You Think." Start-ups with the same gibberish names as all the other startups: Oobeo, Sparx, Survision, Orbility, Meypar, Designa. Brett Marsden, an exterminator with a law degree, was hawking his own invention, a sloped attachment for ledges and rafters to keep the birds away. The Aviangle. "This garage was obliterated with birds," said Marsden, a fit man with a gold watch, a bead bracelet, and salt-and-pepper hair. He was showing me a video of pigeons nesting in a White Plains, New York, parking structure. "Now the birds have nowhere to go. The acidity of the bird droppings will eat through the concrete—there was a dealer on the sixth floor, his cars were obliterated." Obliterated! He warned of slip risks, fecal spores.

Most of all, what was being sold at the NPA was competing technology to finally kill the parking industry's white whale: correctly counting the number of cars that enter a garage.

I I I I I

Most garages are not owned by people who know anything about parking. They are built, begrudgingly, by developers whose real expertise is in office buildings or condominiums, or by local governments under pressure from nearby businesses. The design is a throwaway from an architect who resents the assignment. The equipment is the cheapest thing around. The operator—SP+ or QuikPark or Inter-

Park or LAZ, or more likely some local outfit—is brought in on a fixed-rate contract that puts the onus to maximize revenue on an owner whose interests lie upstairs.

And then there was Chicago's Poetry Garage, a quarter block of downtown between the creaking rails of the Loop and the Chicago River. Ten posttensioned concrete floors of pure car storage, with room for 1,168 vehicles and more with a team of valets. Whoever the typical absentee garage owner is, the owner of this garage, John Hammerschlag, was the opposite.

Hammerschlag had worked in parking in Chicago for four decades; he knew the story of every garage. That one, which once belonged to Dan Katz. That other one, with the trees on the roof, which he helped design. This one over here, which paid him a pretty penny for a small adjacent lot because they needed a street outlet for their ramps. In 1989, he became the chief of General Parking and the largest provider of parking in downtown Chicago, with nineteen thousand spaces. With his thick black mustache, the forty-year-old Hammerschlag was one of the *Chicago Tribune*'s "89 to Watch." He joined the posh East Bank Club, where the staff knew him by name.

In 2020, Hammerschlag ran an eponymous consulting service, and while he could have retired if he wanted to, he couldn't seem to stop collecting parking assets: a cruise ship terminal in Galveston, two big garages in downtown Chicago, surface lots that comprised half of downtown Roanoke, Virginia. He couldn't turn down a deal. And: he really loved parking.

In October 2020, in a stuffy room in the bowels of the Poetry Garage ("There's Poetry in Parking," says the website), Hammerschlag chatted with Ali Naqvi and Hasan Jafri, two SP+ employees who managed this facility. Ali was here every day; Hasan supervised a portfolio of a dozen garages around the city. Hammerschlag said he sometimes talks to college students about parking. "Half of them come up to me or send me emails: 'Can I work for you?' I say, 'You're not as good as Ali.'"

"What about me?" said Hasan.

"You're hamburger meat."

Ali had been working in parking since he lost his job at Met Life after 9/11. He'd been working at the Poetry Garage for three years, but, he admitted, it felt like forever.

Hasan: "John will make you feel like it's been forever." They laughed.

"John wants to see what we make today, what we made last week, same day last month, last eight days," Ali complained.

"And we get the numbers the next day," John said, "and because he's late and now he's talking to us, the numbers are going to be late."

If a stereotypical garage owner won't know who's in the garage, or for how long, or what they paid, John is the opposite. You better believe John's garages use credit cards.

Twenty years ago, when this garage was built, John was a consultant on its design. Later, he bought it. He knew it inside and out: Why the elevators were split between two lobbies—to keep the commercial storefront at the corner intact. Why one elevator lobby had three shafts and the other two—because one sat outside the building's core, so the extra elevator didn't cost him a spot on every floor. Why the checkout gate was on the incline—to keep it away from the booth, so that irate drivers were that much less likely to leave the car to holler at Ali face to face. Why the temperature in the elevator lobbies was set to forty degrees each winter—any higher and the homeless would sleep there. Why one side of the second floor needed a pigeon net and the other didn't—because that side faced the El, where crazies came to throw out bird seed, and he didn't want to be running a shitbox.

To hear John tell it, he was a man with attention to detail in a world of goofery. The NPA: "The early guys got involved because it was a cash business, and they could steal. They're operators, and you turn around, they'll stick a knife in your back." Developers: "I've got a lot of opinions about how ignorant they are." Architects: "I won't work for the architect. They'll neuter me. Who gets assigned the garage? The most junior architect who doesn't know a fucking thing." City politicians, taxing his business into oblivion with rates between 30 and 40 percent. Online aggregators putting pressure on his prices. He had a chip on his shoulder about being a garage guy. "Parking guys get looked at with disdain. We screw up every project, and there's this image of a short, fat guy with a stogie hanging out of his mouth and a flannel shirt buttoned up to here." John said the *a* in *fat* nasally like *eh*, in the midwestern style.

Clean-shaven, hair gone white, Hammerschlag sported a leather jacket over a pink button-down shirt. He was gruff and he cursed like a mechanic, but he also listened to NPR in the car and liked to vacation in France. After talking to a friend with an MFA in poetry, he assigned each floor of this building to a poet, as a mnemonic device to help returning drivers find their cars. In the elevator lobby, poems played on repeat on the loudspeakers. Unfortunately, those rooms were not sealed, and sound leaked from above and below, creating a cacophony of looping, overlapping recitations. "People hated it. I hated it. Did it bring any business? No. Does it help you remember? A little . . . We did a study once and the thing people most remember is the floor number." Nevertheless, the poems persisted on the walls: Auden, Dickinson, Langston Hughes. Billy Collins, funnily enough, with "Forgetfulness."

Hammerschlag usually took his bankers up to the roof of the garage, an alpine lake of slab between the skyscrapers, and on one fall day in 2020 he took me. Structurally speaking, a garage is a bridge, Hammerschlag explained. Its concrete decks are threaded with stretched, taut steel cables. He grabbed an empty bottle of Rémy Martin from against the wall and dropped it in the trash. It's a reminder that garages, while privately owned, are also wound-up bits of street that rise into public viewpoints, helix-shaped bows tying up the asphalt ribbons of the city. In Chicago, garage roofs offer some of the best free views of the city. In smaller cities, some garage roofs have been transformed into public spaces, but here in Chicago, they are too profitable for that. So the garage roof remains a do-it-yourself vista.

It's here, John said, that you can really give a lender a sense of this place's potential: eleven million square feet of office space within one block. John's client roll was a Yellow Pages for this little corner of downtown: he had prepaid validation contracts with BMO Harris Bank, the Jewish United Federation, the office tower at 181 Monroe, nearby hotels like La Quinta and Kimpton Gray, and a special contract to provide low rates for the Lyric Opera, Chicago's magnificent opera house abutting the river. He had a contract with Enterprise Rent-a-Car and four dozen "reserved" places on the second floor, which cost as much as $500 a month—or got awarded, as a thank-you gift, to the employees at nearby firms who cut big parking deals with him.

The challenge of the garage business is striking the right balance between "monthlies" and "transients." Monthlies were a reliable source of income, and sometimes they didn't show up and you could sell their spaces twice, but here at the Poetry Garage, they added up to just $2,400 per stall per year, after taxes, or barely more than $6 of revenue per stall a day. That was still more than $2.5 million in after-tax revenue for an open-air block of concrete with lights, elevators, and a handful of full-time employees, but John could do better. Transients, on the other hand, were charged $11 for their first twenty minutes (a bullshit price, John said, since no one would park there for just twenty minutes) and $49 when they hit the eighty-one-minute mark. Plus, you might get two or three of them a day.

But John Hammerschlag had a problem. Thirty-two bucks an hour may have been the listed price, but you'd have been a fool to pay it, because in 2020, you could go online and buy a full day in the Poetry Garage for $21, using the parking aggregator SpotHero. "Online resellers are devastating me," John groaned. He said he was the last of the bigger players to go along with SpotHero, realizing he had no choice but to fold. "We had a great business because there was no transparency."

Commercial parking thrived in a world where harried drivers scanned sandwich boards and did multiplication in their heads. Guys with nice corner real estate, guys like John, would have an easy time with schmos from Naperville who came to see a show. That was not really true anymore, thanks to aggregators like SpotHero. SpotHero's CEO, Mark Lawrence, argued his company was good for parking operators, because while it lowered prices, it drove traffic.

"Oh, that's bullshit!" John scoffed to the sheer walls of the downtown skyscrapers. "He's an asshole. He believes his own propaganda. And I say he's an asshole because he affects my business and he tells lies. He's the Trump of the parking business. It's the same cars, he's not bringing any more cars downtown, we're all just competing with each other. How would Lawrence know? He doesn't have a garage. He doesn't know what the numbers are before he showed up. He doesn't have a clue."

❚ ❚ ❚ ❚ ❚

Mark Lawrence was barely born when John Hammerschlag was the king of Chicago parking. He graduated from college into the Great Recession, took an entry-level banking job, got laid off, and moved in with his parents outside of Chicago. There, Mark tooled around with a familiar start-up formula: find a successful new company, and apply its model to a field that hasn't yet been disrupted. Uber of X, Amazon of Y. Mark wanted to start the Airbnb of parking.

Initially, as a kid from the suburbs accustomed to stress-cruising snowy streets before a Bulls game and going home with a parking ticket, Mark assumed there was not enough parking in Chicago. His company would bring all this new parking to market and alleviate traffic and congestion. Ten years later, with tens of thousands of spots in his portfolio, he had experienced an epiphany. "It's not that there's not enough parking," he said. "It's that there's too much, and you don't realize where it is."

Mark started the company at a place where overwhelming demand from outsiders was already drawing locals into a black market. If his software was to be Airbnb, this place was his Dubrovnik, teeming with pent-up demand. The place was Wrigley Field, the Cubs' beloved bandbox ballpark on Chicago's North Side. What makes Wrigley special is not really its small size, irregular dimensions, or ivy-crawled brick outfield wall, but that it is nestled snugly inside a neighborhood. It was precisely the shortage of parking that distinguished Wrigley from the little-loved generation of postwar stadiums epitomized by the White Sox's facility on the South Side. In the 1980s, the Sox bulldozed a beloved local bar, to which it is said Babe Ruth once ran for a beer between innings, in order to ensure their new ballpark could be properly flanked by parking lots. The Cubs, on the other hand, suffered from a bona fide parking shortage.

For years, at Wrigley like at other prewar stadiums (Louisville, Kentucky's Churchill Downs, the Big House in Ann Arbor, Michigan), private parking had been sublet for big events the old-fashioned way: with a cardboard sign in the driveway. The city had special North Side parking rules for Cubs games. The team was the last in the majors to play most of its home games in the afternoon, a tradition that dated to the era before high-powered floodlights but one the owners would have happily abandoned for nighttime television ratings if they could have. But they couldn't, because night games, it was thought, would overlap with the commute home, create a parking nightmare, and hurt local businesses by discouraging other activity.

In the spring of 2011, Mark went door-to-door around Wrigleyville and asked the neighborhood's commuters to let him manage their parking spaces. While they were at work, Mark would rent out their spaces on Craigslist. He'd take 15 percent, and they wouldn't have to lift a finger. Unless the game went fourteen innings, they'd never even know anyone had parked in their spot.

If you were going to the game, meanwhile, you'd suddenly find a cheap and reliable option you could arrange before you'd even left work.

If the spot was a hike from the ballpark, a free shuttle was provided. (That was Mark, in his '91 Nissan Sentra.)

By summer, he had a website. He googled "How do you get customers?" He watched teenagers explain SEO on YouTube. And he managed to create a viral blog post on the site, mapping the free parking around the United Center, the West Side arena where the Bulls and Blackhawks played. He made it in Microsoft Paint.

That such a post could draw tens of thousands of clicks was evidence of how opaque the parking market remained. Roads were mapped online and rerouted drivers according to live traffic reports. Restaurants were mapped, photographed, and competing for customer approval. Virtually every product, from sneakers to airline tickets, could be comparison-shopped within seconds. But the parkingscape was as shrouded as the surface of Venus, and what you could glean through the windshield, crawling along at a cruiser's pace of fifteen miles per hour—the shape of the lot, the fullness of the curb, the fine print on the street sign, the price on the sandwich board—was all you could hope to know.

Eventually Mark got his break: an agreement with a major firm, Central Parking (the predecessor of SP+). "Let's start with something small," an executive told the stunned founder—"a couple thousand spots." SpotHero got under way near Soldier Field, home of the Chicago Bears, and expanded into the fringes of downtown Chicago. Soon, SpotHero was adding parking spots in places that no one knew were on the market: a historic building by the Board of Trade, for example, that wasn't allowed to put signs up. Residential buildings with spots available during the day; businesses with spots available at night. The city, in reality, had more parking than drivers could possibly use—but carved into proprietary fiefdoms, it wasn't being efficiently put to use.

Mark Lawrence was an interloper, but he maintained garage guys made deals with him because he brought them business. "Garages may be getting less per spot, but they're getting more cars parked, and that's what matters. It's a low-marginal-cost business, so incremental dollars drop straight to the bottom line. I ask them, 'Are you making more money?' And that's when they get quiet." It could have been even more, of course, if SpotHero's comparison shopping didn't drive down prices. But Lawrence made no apologies for that; he wasn't raised in a valet lot. "I started this company as a driver."

Once he had a critical mass of garages signed on, SpotHero managed to pull in the doubters. Men like John Hammerschlag. "The Hammer," Lawrence reflected. "One of my least favorite fans. A very old-school parking guy. Hammerschlag can knock us, but what's he relying on? Old-school parking validations. That's annoying, and they have a cost—handing out tickets to doctors' offices and dentists' offices, cutting deals with thousands of businesses. It felt good because he had full control. Hammerschlag can say whatever he wants, but it's like, 'Hammer! You're empty at this time.'"

The existing system, Mark concluded, was insane. "If the aliens were looking down on us, they'd think we're nuts. You're going somewhere and you don't know where you're going to leave your means of transportation? You're going to drive around in circles?" With SpotHero, one study projected, thousands of miles driven vanished from Chicago roads every day, just because drivers *knew* where they were going to park.

At the time Mark was thinking up the idea of SpotHero, Chicagoans would drive to the Loop and meander through the canyons looking for parking. Most considered the cavernous, ten-story garages to be the option of last resort. This was the way things worked in most American towns and cities, and it was partly because, as Mark observed, the commercial parking garages were expensive and unpleasant.

But it was also because, until 2008, street parking in most Chicago neighborhoods cost just a quarter an hour. No wonder so many drivers opted to cruise instead of patronizing the Poetry Garage. If you found an open meter, you could park all afternoon at the center of the country's third-largest city for the price of a cup of coffee.

CHAPTER 8

When Wall Street Bought Chicago's Parking Meters

One winter day in 2009, Chicago alderman Scott Waguespack got a call about trash blocking an alley in his North Side district. The rookie alderman called the sanitation department and then drove over to see for himself. In a remarkable coincidence, the alley happened to be behind the offices of LAZ Parking, the company that managed the city's parking meters. The ground was strewn with papers, some shredded, some intact, concerning the sale, a few months prior, of thirty-six thousand Chicago parking meters to a group of investors led by Morgan Stanley. In the depths of the financial crisis, the City of Chicago had received an offer that seemed too good to be true: $1.156 billion to lease thirty-six thousand curbside parking spaces for seventy-five years. The city barely took in more than $20 million a year from its parking meters; now Chicago was going to get a ten-figure check in a time of need. Waguespack had been the loudest of only five Chicago aldermen to oppose the parking meter sale, arguing in vain that the city was rushing a valuable asset out the door. Even a billion dollars, Waguespack thought, might not be enough for nearly a century of revenue from thirty-six thousand parking meters. Now, for the first time, picking paper off the ground in an alley full of garbage in the freezing cold, he learned that for the next seventy-five years, Chicago had handed over its streets to... the emir of Abu Dhabi?

Yes, indeed: through 2084, Chicago had leased its parking meters to (among others) the tiny emirate of Abu Dhabi, a hidden 25 percent partner in the Morgan Stanley group. This confirmed Waguespack's suspicions that the city had not been on the level about the calculations concealed behind the parking meter deal. What kind of promised ROI had brought parking meters in the American Midwest to the attention of a country halfway around the world? Waguespack gathered up the papers and brought them to the Chicago inspector general.

No city had sold its parking meters before, but when Mayor Richard M. Daley put Windy City curbs up for auction at the start of 2008, it felt like the most natural thing in the world. It was Daley's father, Democratic kingmaker Richard J. Daley, who had been Chicago's first "mayor for life," but the younger Daley was entering his third decade in office and all but guaranteed to eclipse his father's record twenty-one years in city hall. Daley junior had steered Chicago into a new era. His great achievement was the revival of the city's downtown, whose skyline had grown robust on his watch. Even as the lawyer son of a mayor, Daley managed to telegraph a kind of white-ethnic, blue-collar demeanor—he was "just a guy from Bridgeport," the city's South Side Irish American enclave, as one adviser put it. At sixty, he had the jowly face of his old man and thinning black hair combed back on his head. But Daley was not an old-school boss like his dad. He was at ease in the city's corporate boardrooms, and no action better exemplified his faith in the private sector's power to help the public than his quest to sell off city assets.

The icon of Richard M. Daley's Chicago was Millennium Park, a jewel box that had opened above the downtown railyards in 2004. With features that bore the names of the city's first corporate citizens—BP

Pedestrian Bridge, Bank One Promenade, McCormick Tribune Plaza—the park symbolized Daley's mission to vault Chicago out of its industrial past (the trains below) and into the ranks of global cities, represented here by yet another Frank Gehry concert venue and Anish Kapoor's *Cloud Gate* sculpture, better known as the Bean. Millennium Park was Chicago's new public square, and it had been built with over $100 million in donations from the city's business titans and $208 million from selling off the city's garages.

Getting the private sector to take public responsibilities off his hands was one of Daley's trademark strategies. "It was more than in the air," Paul Volpe, then the city's CFO, said later. "I mean, we were the leaders in it.... You couldn't go anywhere without Mayor Daley's reputation for being a leader in this industry being brought up to you." Volpe was, like Daley, a Chicago lifer; a retail banker-turned-bureaucrat who had worked his way up through city departments and still lived in the same Northwest Side neighborhood where he grew up. When Daley offered him the job running the budget, Volpe felt it was like asking a ten-year-old if he wanted to play second base for the Cubs.

Daley had engineered the nation's first toll road privatization, selling the highway that connected Chicago to Indiana. He privatized janitorial services, street resurfacing, and delinquent tax collection. He was working on selling Midway Airport, which would have been the country's first privatized airport, and considered selling the city's treasured Lake Michigan water system. He had sold off those four city-owned parking garages at the heart of the downtown. At the time the New York–based investment bank Morgan Stanley won the bid for the parking meters, the Chicago City Council had already passed its 2009 budget—with $150 million in meter-deal money included. When the meter deal came before the council that December, its approval was a foregone conclusion.

Part of the problem for aldermen like Scott Waguespack trying to assess Morgan Stanley's bid with a back-of-the-napkin calculation was that no one really knew how much parking *should* cost. While parking experts viewed meters as a tool to manage contested curb space, most residents had rightly come to see them as a sneaky, punishment-oriented moneymaking device. In 2016, for example, the country's twenty-five largest cities collected $1.3 billion from illegal parking citations—about as much as they collected from meters and lucrative garage taxes put together! Chicago raked in $264 million from parking tickets in 2016—more than *ten times* as much as the city was able to wring from the meters themselves. More than thirty thousand of the meters covered by the Morgan Stanley lease were set at either 25 or 50 cents an hour—the same price as at the start of Daley's mayoralty a generation earlier. Only about nine hundred meters, mostly in the Loop, cost more than $1 an hour.

In other words, Chicago's meters had been underpriced for so long they no longer freed up any parking spaces or raised much money, except insofar as they justified parking patrols, which led to reams of tickets that often didn't relate to the meters at all (expired registration, etc.). The last citywide meter study had been conducted in 1985, but the city and the company that led the study had not even agreed on the number of meters in Chicago (the two surveys were off by more than a thousand). It may have been beyond the Chicago finance department to even *imagine* a system that charged drivers a market price for curbside real estate adjacent to downtown offices or neighborhood movie theaters. It was not, however, beyond the dealmakers at Morgan Stanley.

On Tuesday, December 8, Mayor Daley announced the bank's winning bid, which he said would "strengthen our city finances for the long-term." Paul Volpe, the budget guy, raced to get the parking meter deal through the city council. The finance committee looked first, on December 9. Why are we rushing? asked one alderman. "We've been working on this for the better part of a year, so we haven't been hasty," Volpe told them. "You had a year, but you're giving us two days," another alderman retorted. One of the city's lawyers read some of the lease out loud, which hardly helped. "What does that all mean?" a third alderman wailed. An intricate chart was passed around, which some aldermen turned upside down in hopes of making sense of it. The mayor's office had shown the aldermen a ten-slide PowerPoint deck the previous day, but they didn't get to see the leasing agreement until the morning of the committee meeting. Alderman Toni Preckwinkle, one of the few dissenting voices in the room, wanted to bring in an outside analyst to provide an independent evaluation. There was no time, she was told.

Scott Waguespack did his best to do just that. He was something of an outsider in Chicago politics, a transplant from Colorado who had served in the Peace Corps. He was also brand new to the job, having won his seat just the year before on a council where many aldermen served for decades. His staff put together a hasty analysis of the proposal that came up with a radically different value for seventy-five years of feeding Chicago's meters: $4 billion. (A later analysis prepared with his office put it at $5 billion.) The city had received only two bids, nearly identical, and both of them seemed to short Chicago taxpayers by more than a billion dollars. "You know, I got the thing at the last minute, just like everybody else," Waguespack told Volpe. "I sat down with some people. I ran some numbers and frankly I just don't think the numbers added up. If we can quadruple the rates in 2009, and we bring in $20 million a year, we're quadrupling that.... When you project that out, we're talking about a lot more money than $1.1 billion for a quick shot in the arm to last us through 2012 and maybe 2013.... That's the problem with this thing. I think—if I'm wrong, show me the numbers—but if it is so simple for a company to come in here and quadruple the rates, and we know they're going to do it, and we know they're going to have a high profit margin because this isn't a difficult business to deal with, then show me the numbers." Waguespack wanted to see the city's own valuation of the meters. How had Daley's office come to the conclusion that this bid was, as Volpe assured them, on the high end of what the city could expect? If the city council was about to vote to turn meters into a powerful revenue stream—and no one had any doubt that they were—why weren't they thinking twice about giving up control?

Volpe was curt. "To delay it puts our budget at risk," he said. "This is the deal. Either we accept it or we don't." The sale of the parking meters passed the finance committee and arrived in the full council the next day.

This session of debate would be remembered as one of the city council's more embarrassing episodes. "This money is not going to be spent like a drunken sailor," said Alderman Bernard Stone. (In reality, the $400 million portion of the payment Volpe promised to keep for a rainy day would be almost entirely spent before Mayor Daley's term expired.) "We'll all support aldermen who need to adjust their rates [to please constituents]," argued Alderman Bob Fioretti. (In reality, the city would find itself paying millions of dollars to Morgan Stanley every time it adjusted parking meter rates, hours, or locations.) Finance committee chair Ed Burke extolled the city's advisers, including the consulting firm William Blair: "These are people we can have faith and trust and confidence in." (It was William Blair that provided the secret, miscalculated valuation that led Chicago to accept the bid.) Alderman Brian Doherty told his colleagues, "If anyone cannot figure out the simple math... then they really need to take an economics class because this is sound fiscal management any way you look at it." (Multiple independent analyses would conclude Chicago left, at minimum, a billion dollars on the table.) Alderman Richard Mell summed up the oversight role of the city council: "How many of us read the stuff we do get, OK? I try to. I try to. I try to. But being realistic, being realistic, it's like getting your insurance policy. It's small print, OK."

The 150-page contract was approved by a vote of forty to five, after twenty-four hours of review. Daley felt he had scored a coup. While the city had sought bids months before the stock market crashed, the onset of the Great Recession made the extra billion dollars particularly welcome. Now the mayor could avoid a property tax hike. He traveled the country to lecture mayors and CEOs about privatization. He suggested President Barack Obama "think outside the box" just as he had. "If they start leasing public assets—every city, every county, every state, and the federal government—you would not have to raise any taxes whatsoever," he said. "You would have more infrastructure money that way than any other way in the nation." When the newly created entity Chicago Parking Meters LLC inevitably raised meter rates, forcing drivers who had once paid the meter with a stash of change in the ashtray to keep a jug of quarters in the passenger seat (two hours of parking in the Loop now required twenty-eight quarters), Daley took responsibility for the technical issues. But, he added, "in the long run this is the best thing." As layoffs decimated the newspaper industry, he told reporters who asked about the meter deal that their bosses should be looking for similar opportunities.

They say Chicago is the most American of American cities, and that is certainly true of its architecture, which offers an à la carte menu of domestic building styles from 1880 to the present, often all on the same block. The big divide in the architecture of Chicago is not between prewar and postwar, or downtown and the neighborhoods, or residential and commercial. It is between those structures built BP (before parking) and AP (after parking). Before parking, stables were so loathed that the city required builders to get the permission of *every property owner* within six hundred feet to build one in a residential neighborhood. Chicago BP is the metropolis of the imagination: Art Deco skyscrapers, elevated trains, corner bars nestled inside neighborhoods of three-flats and Victorians, low-slung corridors of uninterrupted commercial storefronts stretching halfway to the state line. Chicago AP looks like run-of-the-mill suburban sprawl: chain stores lurking behind salt-crusted parking lots.

It took nearly four decades for Chicago to begin to revise its white flight–era aim to create more parking wherever possible, a shift that came in part thanks to Richard M. Daley's old-fashioned aesthetics. He liked flower boxes, wrought-iron fences, and historic buildings. (Martha Stewart, he said, was an influence.) Daley tried to reform the building code to make Chicago pretty again. In 1998, faced with new clusters of attached houses whose ground-floor garages required laying great combs of driveways over the sidewalk, the city decreed that townhouse garages must be accessed through alleys or shared driveways. Chicago struck a special deal with Walgreens to try to make its stores look better. The city established a design review for strip malls in residential

Marina City, Chicago. Bertrand Goldberg's "corn cob" towers, completed in 1963, offer a handsome early example of the "parking podium" model that would come to define high-rise residential and commercial architecture in the United States.

neighborhoods. And planners decided that parking must be on the side of retail buildings—not in front, separating the windows and the door from the sidewalk. This not only brought the entrance closer to pedestrians; it also left open the possibility that the side parking lot (unlike a front lot) could one day become a building of its own. Owners of lots and garages were instructed to build or landscape to keep parked cars hidden from the street. In 2004, Chicago established its first parking *maximums* for new development—hard limits on the parking narcotic.

Still, Chicago seemed to have a split personality. Not only did residents invoke parking as an excuse to block new housing, as they did everywhere. The city's own planners, committed to fighting climate change and encouraging biking, walking, and transit with one hand, were still trying to coax new parking out of builders with the other.

Right around the time Mayor Daley was trumpeting Chicago's downtown resurgence—the mayor was one of many new arrivals who boosted Chicago's downtown population from 18,000 in 1980 to 110,000 in 2020, even as outer neighborhoods suffered mass departures—the city caught the eye of young Baptist pastor named Nathan Carter. A self-described Indiana farm boy, Carter had come to Chicago for school and then gotten hired by a small church in the city's Lincoln Park neighborhood. It was more than a little different from home. Carter had grown up in the house his father grew up in, and his father before him. It was a place with a sense of permanence, and that was an idea that Carter wanted to bring to Chicago. He wanted to build a neighborhood church.

For Nathan Carter, this was what church was supposed to be about, even in the big city: Knowing your neighbors. Getting involved in community institutions. Children growing up together. This had once been the model of the city church, and it persisted to some extent in Chicago's black neighborhoods, immigrant enclaves, and geographically defined, dwindling Catholic parishes. But it is not a mainstream Protestant idea now. It's the antithesis, in a way, of the Evangelical megachurch, which draws congregants from many miles away and re-creates bygone civic institutions like swimming pools or after-school programs within its walls. It was also incompatible with the small Lincoln Park church where Carter had wound up preaching—a commuter church only one of whose members lived in the neighborhood (with his parents). The rest drove an hour from the suburbs on Sundays. Pastor Nathan outlined his vision to them: the church would begin again, as a local institution on Chicago's West Side. Move to the city, he said. Fight against the coming and going that makes city congregations as changeable as college classrooms. Twenty families agreed. Pastor Nathan paraphrased from Jeremiah: "We are exiles from Jerusalem living in Babylon—we should put down roots; seek the welfare of the city."

But Carter did not think Chicago was an unredeemable Babylon; in fact, he quite loved it. Russiaville, Indiana, where Carter had grown up, was not Winesburg, Ohio. Its small-town charm was as ragged as an old coat of paint. People grew up to leave. Carter's idea of community was an imagined one; an amalgamation of what he knew about his grandparents' Russiaville and what he read in the books of Wendell Berry, the Kentucky writer whose chronicles of the fictitious Port William sparkled with the threads of strong social ties. When Carter read Berry, his heart ached for a sense of place. He had traveled to Chicago as a kid—charter buses to Cubs games, field trips to the Art Institute—and later went to college at Wheaton, in the suburbs. As the Jews could find in Babylon both the big, bad, idolatrous city and the glimmers of the new Jerusalem, Carter found what he sought in Chicago. "How do I love thee, let me count the ways," he said of his adopted hometown. "Walking to my dentist and my grocery, and everything I need in one place. I love the old lady that sits on the stoop two doors down and keeps her eyes on the street and talks your ear off as you pass that way."

Carter was not the first person to think critically about the role of neighborhood churches in big cities. Tim Keller, a prominent advocate for urban ministry in New York, argued churches were not keeping up with the way young people wanted to live. Eric Jacobsen, a pastor in Tacoma, Washington, had developed a theory of an "embedded church" that was rooted in the concepts of New Urbanism, the school of anti-sprawl architecture. An embedded church, Jacobsen said, should be in a neighborhood with homes and businesses. It should have a direct connection to the street. It should deemphasize the parking lot.

Those visions meshed with Carter's own. It was with Berry on his mind that he stumbled upon a faded storefront church on Roosevelt Road. To the south was a vast, open green space where once had stood the Chicago Housing Authority's ABLA Homes, before most of them were demolished in the mid-2000s. (The Keanu Reeves movie *Hardball* was filmed and set here.) To the north were Little Italy and the Illinois Medical District. The stretch of Roosevelt Road seemed so forgotten by time that an adjacent building still had a sign for George McGovern's 1972 presidential campaign. His building wasn't much either. But it would fit a congregation of the size Carter wanted, a group of about 120 people. Having bounced from a YMCA to a school to a storefront, he looked at this old building and saw stability. Plus, it was a short bike ride from Pilsen, the Mexican neighborhood where Carter lived with his wife and daughters.

In any case, Carter wanted Immanuel Baptist Church to grow outward. Instead of building a gym at the church, he would encourage his congregants to join a neighborhood gym. Instead of having a church book club, they would join book clubs in the neighborhood. He was constantly trying to move the church beyond its walls; onto the sidewalk, into the park, into the unscripted rites of Sunday lunches and evening football games. Another writer he admired was Jane Jacobs. "Jacobs would say a neighborhood is like a small town when it's working well," Carter said. "And there are megaforces in play in our society that make that hard. But it's still possible, and I'm trying to live that out." In 2016, Carter's church struck a deal with its landlord to buy the dilapidated storefront on Roosevelt Road.

Then everything fell apart. Chicago told Carter he needed one parking spot for every eight seats. Without the parking, his lender wouldn't give Carter the loan. The pastor looked everywhere. There was nothing to buy. There were some lots they could share, but these were not in good enough shape to pass muster with the city. And, he was told, if the church was renting parking, it needed a ten-year lease. The irony was not lost on him; he'd tried to build a church that the faithful could get to by walking or biking. And now he was being done in by the very car culture he'd tried to escape. He felt hopeless. "We turned over every stone we could, and we exhausted all our options," he said.

A friend in the congregation gently suggested the Chicago parking code might be a sign from God. Pastor Nathan should look west. Find a new church, and a new neighborhood for his family.

❙ ❙ ❙ ❙ ❙

The 2009 arrival of Chicago Parking Meters LLC (CPM) had ruffled some feathers, mostly due to faulty equipment and rising rates, which angered Chicago drivers. Then, six months after the deal was signed, the city's inspector general, a Daley-appointed lawyer named David Hoffman, dropped a bombshell report. The parking meters the city had leased to Morgan Stanley, Hoffman found, were worth between \$2.13 and \$3.53 billion. The city had been ripped off by a billion dollars, maybe two. Morgan Stanley, which moved quickly to securitize its meter debt, told its investors the profits over the lifetime of the deal would amount to \$9.58 billion, before interest, taxes, and depreciation.*

*This figure should not be read as an exact parallel to the \$1.156 billion Morgan Stanley paid Chicago, since it does not discount for the lower value of future meter revenue—according to Chicago inspector general David Hoffman's 2009 report (at page 18), the last thirty-seven years of the meter deal would account for just 7

Hoffman went on: Chicago city hall had not even tried to figure out what the meters could be worth if they remained public. In December, when Alderman Scott Waguespack had asked CFO Paul Volpe for the city's data that showed the bid was fair, Volpe had told him the bid spoke for itself: "These assets are only as valuable as the free market will bear." Volpe's confidence was fueled by a secret report the city had commissioned, which suggested a lease value between $650 million and $1.2 billion—a dramatic miscalculation that seems to have stemmed from the fact that William Blair & Co., the firm that had come up with the meter-sale idea in the first place, had used an unreasonably high "discount rate," undervaluing the future meter revenue had the city retained the asset. No one outside the mayor's office had reviewed the merits of the lease. There had been no public report from the financial analyst hired by the city, no public comment, no testimony from experts, no presentation of current research on privatization, and no discussion of safeguards, such as a shorter lease, a revenue-sharing system, or limits on rate increases.*

As foreclosures exploded across the city's South and West Sides, and the extent of Wall Street's unpunished culpability for the financial crisis

---

percent of the present deal value. Money now is worth more than money in the future, because it can be invested for greater yields—the present-day value of $1 million in 2100, for example, is just $25,000, because by investing $25,000 now, you can expect $1 million in return by 2100. This makes the up-front dollar amount look slightly more reasonable (in light of Morgan Stanley's $9.58 billion figure) but the seventy-five-year term of the lease look especially bewildering. Why seventy-five years? Probably to enable the Morgan Stanley consortium to qualify for a favorable tax depreciation associated with "ownership."

*What Daley had effectively done was take out a very cumbersome, high-interest loan. But instead of trying Chicago's luck in the robust and competitive municipal debt market, he had packaged this transaction as something that had no comparables and few interested bidders, increasing the odds of a serious misfire in the bidding. Do two bidders a "market" make? See Julie A. Roin, "Privatization and the Sales of Tax Revenues," *Minnesota Law Review* 85 (2011): 1965. Chicago was penalized by ratings agencies for forfeiting future parking revenue just as it would have been for taking on future debt service.

became apparent, the city had let Morgan Stanley walk away with a billion dollars in quarters. Alderman Joe Moore later said it was the vote he regretted most in twenty-five years on the council.

Mayor Daley blustered: "Like anything else, you can issue any type of report. I can criticize anything." The deal was a good one, he insisted. Some of his allies on the city council, whose forgone oversight was implicated by the inspector general's report, backed him up. Bernard Stone slammed Hoffman's credentials: "He's not an MBA. He's not even a CPA." Finance committee head Ed Burke said, "It's easy to be a Monday-morning quarterback." (A decade later, Burke would be indicted for extortion, after the FBI caught him on tape soliciting bribes in exchange for permitting the remodeling of a Burger King parking lot in his ward.)

The city made two classic pro-privatization arguments to refute Hoffman's thesis. First was the "inferiority" argument: the city would never have operated the meters as well as a private company could. Hoffman thought this argument was weak on its face; these were parking meters, after all, not a power plant or even a recycling service. Moreover, he wrote, this argument was undermined by the chaos that had accompanied the takeover. "We botched the transition," Volpe admitted later. "There was no question. We botched that transition." Chicago Parking Meters LLC depended on Chicago's meter expertise in that first winter after the deal, paying city mechanics and other employees $1.2 million to smooth over their own ineptitude.

The other, more interesting justification was the "impossibility" argument: only an independent group like CPM would be able to withstand the political pressure to lower parking rates. Volpe's office noted that "neighborhood rates at thousands of meters have remained at an extremely low rate of 25 cents per hour for more than 20 years." Chicago had done a bad job running parking meters in the past; why should it have been expected to do a good job in the future? Hoffman argued that didn't check out, since by leasing the meters the city *had* in effect raised rates. Aldermen were explicit about this—there was no mystery about how Morgan Stanley would be making the meters more profitable. Furthermore, other cities had demonstrated the political willpower to raise parking prices and keep them high. Journalists at the *Chicago Reader* found something even more damning: In 2007, Daley's administration had proposed a number of taxes and fees to fill the budget, including raising parking meter rates. City officials had projected, just two years earlier, that they could nearly triple their annual income from meters, from $22 million to $56 million. Other cities that wanted cash on hand for future meter revenue successfully sold bonds tied to future parking receipts.

The lease seemed to take a toll on the mayor. He owned it. Two weeks after the hubbub of the IG's report, the *Tribune* ran a Daley parking meter cutout with a hole for quarters atop the mayor's scrunched face. A subsequent poll showed that 90 percent of Chicagoans disapproved of the meter deal. It was the biggest mistake of his twenty-two-year mayoralty, said Marilyn Katz, one of his public relations advisers. "It's one thing to give away and sell your airports, or a tollway, because you know, some people take it, and they pay tolls," she said later. "But the parking meters were an insult every day that said 'Fuck you' every time you parked your car." In a column, "Daley Dynasty Teeters on Pyramid of Meters," the *Tribune* columnist John Kass compared Daley unfavorably with Denver mayor (and future Colorado governor and senator) John Hickenlooper. In 2003, the rangy brewery owner had run for mayor of Denver promising to lower parking prices, and filmed an ad in which he prowled the streets in a suit with a change belt, a meter fairy feeding expired meters.

It must have shocked Daley, who inspired such confidence his aides thought he was practically infallible. Here's Volpe again, who was demoted after the meter-deal fallout, talking about his old boss: "There were times he would direct you to do something, and you'd kind of sit there in the back of your mind and go, 'Is that really the right thing to do?' And months later, after you saw how it all played out, you'd sit there and think, 'My God, this man had—he was right again.' And right again, and right again. And he just had amazing instincts."

In the summer of 2010, Daley shocked the city by announcing he would not run again for mayor. His wife was sick; his approval rating was near 35 percent. He had failed to win Chicago the Olympics. And then there was that damn meter deal. "Daley's legacy," said the city's next transportation commissioner, Gabe Klein. "He was hated for it." The meter deal made an easy punching bag on the campaign trail. One of the candidates vying to succeed Daley was Carol Moseley Braun, who had been the first black woman to serve in the U.S. Senate. "We got scammed and snookered and held up by people with ballpoint pens," she said. Even Daley's little brother, who ran unsuccessfully for mayor a decade later, said it was a mistake. When the deal was passed, Volpe told the city council that the Daley administration would bank some $400 million, letting the interest alone cover the city's old meter income of $20 million a year. By the time Daley left office, just $76 million of the billion-dollar meter deal remained in Chicago's coffers.

In other ways, too, the Daley administration's role came to look worse and worse. Daley left office and went to work at one of the firms that had negotiated the deal, along with a handful of his top advisers. Daley's cousin was a top figure in Morgan Stanley's Chicago office. The firms that advised the city on the meters received more than $7 million for their work when the contract was signed. The chief financial consultant, William Blair & Co.—the firm that claimed to have brought the idea to Chicago in the first place, back in 2007, and produced the lone estimate of the deal's value to the city—turned out to be working on other deals with Morgan Stanley at the same time. A couple of years later, Felipe Oropesa, an executive at the garage company that ran the Chicago system, was found to have taken bribes to deliver contracts for the installation of the meters themselves on Chicago streets.

It took just four years for the meter deal to change the reputation of public-private partnerships in the United States. The meter deal would go down, wrote the *Chicago Tribune* op-ed board, as "one of the dumbest and most despised decisions in the council's history." And this from a city council that had sent two dozen members to prison over the past thirty years.

❚ ❚ ❚ ❚ ❚

In February 2009, Scott Waguespack heard that Chicago Parking Meters LLC would be extending the metered hours in his North Side neighborhood from 9:00 a.m. to 6:00 p.m. Monday through Saturday to 8:00 a.m. to 9:00 p.m. seven days a week—thirty-seven new meter-hours each week. He had been working with residents and businesses on a congestion plan for the area, and that month, he tried to switch 270 of the neighborhood meters back to the old schedule. The city's revenue department told him this would cost hundreds of thousands of dollars a year in payments to CPM.

It was like picking those papers out of the trash all over again. Waguespack suddenly realized: When the Chicago City Council signed off on the meter deal, they didn't just trade away parking revenue. They traded away Chicago's streets themselves. They lost control over rates but also control over the curbs—how they could be used, and by whom. Wall Street ran the streets now, and if Chicago didn't keep its parking meters right where CPM wanted them, the city would have to pay up.

Gabe Klein, who took over the Chicago Department of Transportation under Daley's successor, Rahm Emanuel, arrived from Washington, DC, with fashionable ideas about twenty-first-century cities. Klein wanted to take the streets back from cars. Chicago has endless, broad thoroughfares that intersect every quarter mile to form that familiar, Jeffersonian checkerboard that characterizes the American Midwest. Klein wanted to adorn them with parklets—little pockets of seating and greenery in curbside parking spaces. If that spot had a meter, however, building a parklet would mean renting the spot *back* from CPM. Unsurprisingly, the cost was highest in Chicago's downtown, where sidewalks were busy and outdoor seating in short supply: $12,000 a year. Klein wanted Open Streets, a periodic event to shut streets to cars and open them for joggers, kids on bikes, ball games, and more. It was impossible, he said, because of the cost. It went on and on. Bus lanes. Bike lanes. (And later, curbside seating for restaurants to weather the pandemic.)

The city's first car-free lanes for bus commuters were implemented in 2012 and 2013 and required planners to remove more than one hundred parking spaces. That meant undertaking a study of parking usage to figure out how full the curbs were, and then finding comparable spaces (comps) to meter and allocate to CPM in exchange. This wasn't just a lot of extra work; it also got harder and harder as the obvious "comps" were traded away. And as the low-hanging fruit got metered on CPM's behalf, planners found it harder and harder to remove spaces for other uses: Bike parking. Pickup and drop-off zones for restaurants and stores. No-parking zones near intersections that would make pedestrians entering the crosswalk more visible to oncoming traffic. Rush-hour parking bans that took meter hours out of commission were reversed, slowing down traffic. Lower-cost city-owned meters could not be installed near CPM meters, since that kind of competition was forbidden in the contract. Parking ticket fines had to be at least ten times meter rates, and unpaid tickets had to be sent to a collection agency. Chicago could not, like London or New York City, enact a congestion pricing plan. Block party? Festival? Parade? Expect an invoice from CPM.

Chicago had leased a product it was still responsible for taking care of, and now the city's long neglect of the parking situation would start to really cost Chicagoans. The Loop, the downtown area where the city's L trains converge in a ring of shrieking elevated track, had been known for its corrupt parking practices for decades. In Studs Terkel's 1974 book *Working*, the legendary Chicago radio host interviewed a parking officer who told him he was ordered not to enforce parking violations—not around city hall especially. "If you violate that rule, they stick you on some abandoned corner where you can't write tickets."

By 2009, this situation had scarcely evolved. Motorists parking in the Loop just used disabled placards, passed through families like Cubs season tickets, which exempted them from meter payments under state law. The City of Chicago had long tolerated this practice; Chicago Parking Meters LLC did not.

The dealmakers at Morgan Stanley had made an allowance for a small amount of disabled parking in the contract. But as it turned out, the portion of parked cars in the Loop with disabled placards under their windshields was closer to 90 percent. In this, Chicago was not alone: Baltimore had some blocks where two in three cars used placards, to such an extent that the documents had acquired street value and the police clocked two dozen placard thefts each month. San Francisco estimated it lost $22 million a year to disabled placard use—on $55 million collected, suggesting that nearly one in three parking meter users in the city was claiming a disability.

But only Chicago was suddenly on the hook for the practice. Over the first four years of the deal, CPM charged the city $73 million to make up the difference. To put it in perspective, the city was now paying CPM almost as much for apparent disabled parking fraud in one neighborhood, every year, as it had generated just a few years earlier from all thirty-six thousand parking meters.

There was another problem: in 2009, CPM had instituted a new two-hour parking limit, which merchants soon discovered made it nearly impossible to legally park on the street and catch a movie, a show, or a concert. Theaters lobbied to have the city change the time limit to three hours in some places, and the Daley administration obliged. Now CPM was telling Chicago those changes to the system had reduced revenue by $20 million a year for the lifetime of the deal—and sent the city an invoice. At this rate, Chicago would wind up paying more than a billion dollars *back* to CPM long before the end of the concession. Technically, Chicago could change its parking meter rates. But it would pay dearly for the privilege.

In 2011, Chicago elected its first new mayor in more than two decades: Rahm Emanuel, a fiery former congressman fresh off a spell as President Obama's chief of staff. In a cartoon in the *Chicago Tribune*, Emanuel was a ballet dancer preparing to catch four airborne ballerinas: the schools, the police, and the deficit—three daunting issues he probably had in common with every other big-city mayor at the time—and one he didn't: parking.

The city had to plead its case in the state capital to get the disabled placard fraud fixed. A new state law restricted meter exemptions to drivers who physically could not reach or use parking payment boxes. The number of placards in Illinois fell from three hundred thousand to thirty thousand, and a city survey showed that disabled placard use in the Loop was down to 17 percent.

Parking was front and center in Rahm's first meeting with Lois Scott, his new CFO. Scott told city departments to speed things up: if a construction project didn't need a dumpster for two months, they shouldn't have one sitting on the curb for two months. The city's Department of Transportation held off on the kinds of projects that peer cities were undertaking. But more than anything, the administration needed to get Morgan Stanley back to the table. Scott, whom Emanuel had lured from the private sector, would go to municipal finance forums and badmouth Morgan Stanley. She wanted to guilt-trip the company for treating a major American city like that. Not only did Morgan Stanley regularly do business with Chicago and its peers; the bank had hundreds of employees who worked downtown. In Chicago's steak houses and taverns, the bank's name was as bruised by the parking meter scandal as Daley's own.

In January 2012, Chicago leaders decided the city would not pay the fees for changes to meters and streets including loading zones, bus lanes, street fairs, and the like—what CPM called "true-up" payments—going back to the spring of 2011. With $25 million in the balance, CPM and the city headed to arbitration. Daley had been content to let CPM calculate its own invoices, but that approach quickly became untenable as the bills mounted. The true-up was not a hard science: Who could say if a parking spot's usage had declined as a result of the city's new time-limit extension for theaters or because CPM had quadrupled the rates? Making street parking really expensive had in fact discouraged many people from parking in CPM spots: by 2018, the average systemwide occupancy was just 25 percent. With the block half empty, how much did it really cost Morgan Stanley when Chicago took back a parking space?

The following year, Emanuel revealed a new contract, saying he was trying to "make a little lemonade out of a big lemon." The original deal, he stressed, could not be undone—the money had been spent anyway. The city had lost in its attempt to dispute the disabled parking charges. At issue in the revised deal were the invoices CPM sent every year. CPM had blamed Chicago for all decreased meter usage—as if the company hadn't raised some rates tenfold in that time frame. The city said the new math would save Chicagoans a billion dollars in payments to CPM over the life span of the deal. For the prior two years of street fairs and other closings, for example, CPM had asked for $49 million; the city would now pay $9 million.

Critics like Scott Waguespack felt it was Chicago's last chance to get out of the deal—that CPM's overbilling wasn't just a disagreement, it was fraud. Waguespack quoted his colleague John Arena: "CPM was like a vendor contracted to perform work for one price who then sends a bill for ten times that amount. As anyone would, the Mayor sent that bill back and said that we wouldn't pay it. Good for him, and good for the city he serves. But just as I could not call a client and say, 'See how much money I have saved you,' we can't call that [$1 billion] 'savings.' It was never due and payable."

Remarkably, this renegotiation did not touch the original scandal of the deal: that Mayor Daley and the Chicago City Council had signed away an extra billion dollars in future revenue to Morgan Stanley. The whole arrangement had become such a fiasco that Emanuel could take credit for lowering the city's future payments to the bank, a situation that was the opposite of how things were supposed to go. (Chicago was supposed to be *getting* paid!) Even under Emanuel's deal revision, according to one calculation, the city would still be paying $500 million in true-up fees to CPM over the life of the lease. Indeed, by 2018 the annual true-up payments had rebounded back to the $20 million range. Worse yet, for deal opponents, the city defended the revised contract in court, scuttling a public-interest lawsuit that had sought to undo the whole thing.

Emanuel did one thing more. Knowing that the day-to-day outrage in Chicago was less about the initial swindle, or even the subsequent hundreds of millions the city would have to pay the meter company, but simply about the fact that it cost more to park now than it used to, Emanuel sought a sweetener: free Sunday parking in the neighborhoods.

Two dozen aldermen quickly signed on in support. Others were not sure it was a good idea. Arena, representing suburban neighborhoods on the city's Northwest Side, was one of those not in favor. "It's bad parking policy," he said. "It's going to hurt the business community." (Later, Arena got in trouble for demanding a parking spot at a police precinct so he could attend a Cubs–White Sox game.) Alderman Michele Smith, from Lincoln Park, said local businesses had reached out immediately to reject free Sunday parking. Emanuel said the aldermen could have paid parking back if they wanted it; Ameya Pawar, another North Side alderman, did not seem excited about making that choice. "What it ends up setting up is a situation where, 'Well whose side are you on? The business or the constituents?' It's problematic." In April 2014, the city council did restore free Sunday parking on some retail corridors.

The great irony of the Chicago parking meter deal, some Chicagoans were coming to realize, was that the part that made everyone the most angry—higher parking rates—was not all bad. "It's a boon for transit, for bikeshare," said Klein, the transportation commissioner. "The raising of the rates is very positive. It's just that the taxpayer didn't benefit." Local businesses found that parking spots were suddenly available for customers and deliveries. Restaurant workers used free parking on side streets instead of parking right in front of their workplaces. Downtown parkers found it easier to swallow garage prices, instead of blocking traffic by searching endlessly for openings at the curb. And the scrutiny on parking in the Loop forced the Illinois statehouse to end the disability fraud that defined the Chicago downtown parking experience.

The meter saga was a story of political incompetence and financial-industry profiteering, but more than anything, it showed how little anyone—politicians, drivers, the press—had seriously considered the price of parking. Even Morgan Stanley could not have imagined it would make back its billion-dollar investment by 2019—with sixty-four years of parking meter receipts still to come. On the eve of the pandemic, its parking profits had topped $100 million for six straight years, not including penalty payments from Chicago that would total $80 million by 2022. In private, CPM still saw the opportunity to make much more. Fewer than 10 percent of meter violations were caught, it believed, and a hiring spree on enforcement would help with that. By 2024, CPM projected, annual revenues from Chicago parking meters would cross the $200 million mark.

When Pastor Nathan Carter heard the city wouldn't let him buy the storefront church on Roosevelt Road, he did not take it as a sign from God. Instead, he got a lawyer, learned about parking requirements, and sued the city of Chicago.

What Carter learned was that Chicago's rules that required parking according to each land use made no sense. Theaters that seated fewer than 150 people required no parking, yet here was his church, seating 146 and frantically searching for eighteen parking spots. Libraries needed no parking for their first 4,000 square feet, but Carter's 3,900-square-foot church needed eighteen spots. The lawsuit alleged the city was violating the First Amendment by treating the church differently.

It took two years for Carter to close on the church building. During the litigation, the city twice extended the maximum distance for the required parking lot, until finally Carter inked a ten-year lease on a Park District parking lot a half mile away. None of his parishioners ever parked there, but that was the price to pay for opening a church in the city. Another price to pay: the seller, who had previously agreed to sell the church two buildings, had raised the price, and now Carter could only buy the one.

One Sunday in the summer of 2020, I went to the service; it was the first outdoor service of the year, and the first full-scale gathering since the pandemic had shut down religious gatherings in Illinois that spring. Families gathered on the grass to sing hymns, and toddlers waddled away from their blankets. Carter gave his sermon under a clearing sky, and a Chicago policewoman pulled up to listen. Afterward, we milled about in the shade behind the newly renovated church. It is hard to believe the city had tried so hard to shut it down. There was on-street parking right in front. And on Sundays, it was all free anyway.

PART 3

How to Fix the Parking Problem

CHAPTER 9

The Professor of Parking Starts a Cult

Once there were parking lots
Now it's a peaceful oasis.

—Talking Heads, "(Nothing but) Flowers"

One man knew more about parking than the city planners and cared more about cities than the parking guys. In 2005, an economist at the University of California at Los Angeles named Donald Shoup published *The High Cost of Free Parking*. It was a sensation, and not just for a 733-page doorstop about car storage. Shoup got a feature story in *USA Today* and hooked famous people on parking. He became an urban planning celebrity overnight. "I believe it's a wake-up call to change the way we think about parking," said Paul Farmer, the executive director of the thirty-thousand-member American Planning Association (APA). UCLA let Shoup teach an entire course on parking, where every year new students would be converted into parking-policy apostles before fanning out into the offices of local governments, university faculties, real estate developers, and architecture firms. Everywhere they went, they preached Shoup's radical doctrine: there is too much parking, and it's too cheap.

One student set Shoup up with a Twitter account, @ShoupDogg. A former student named Kevin Holliday started the Shoupistas Facebook group in 2008. Holliday had earned $15 an hour to read drafts of *High Cost* and give his professor notes, before going on to a career as a parking planner, a position that consists mostly of people rejecting your expertise for their own. In Davis, California, home of the Bicycling Hall of Fame, Holliday watched as the city council spent a session deciding to preserve free parking downtown—while declaring a climate emergency. Pure hypocrisy, he thought. "Don inspired followers before that word was used for Twitter," Holliday said. "He's an evangelical person. He probably *could* have started a cult if he wanted."

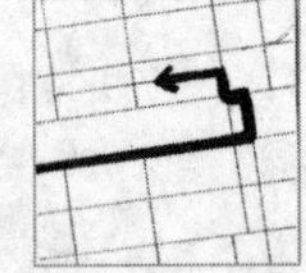

He did, in a way. There are more than five thousand Shoupistas on Facebook. They come to trade stories and ask for advice, share joy in food trucks and bus lanes, or gripe about yet another neighborhood ready to demolish itself to ease the parking shortage. Each of them had their Damascene moment when the world suddenly revealed its organization around the quest for parking. It was not just that Shoup had finally addressed a long-neglected aspect of urban planning. He did so with the elegance and simplicity of Pythagoras demonstrating the nature of a right triangle. Not only were Shoup's theories straightforward; the evidence was all around you, at every moment of every day. Parking could not be unseen. There was a bit of Solana Beach in every community, whether in the liberal, pedestrian-friendly confines of Manhattan, where residents rallied to preserve a parking lot from its destiny as housing for low-income seniors under the banner "Save Manhattan Valley," or in sunny San Diego, where a disgruntled business owner told the mayor "there's blood on your hands" after a reduction in curbside parking.

Don Shoup was raised a military brat. "My earliest memory was the attack on Pearl Harbor, so everything's been very calm since then," he said. The family followed his father's assignments, leaving Don with the rootless, transatlantic accent of an old-time movie star. He enrolled at Yale and met his wife, Pat, on a study-abroad program in England. They skipped the Harvard-Yale game to get married in the chapel under Harkness Tower. Pat, who is from Northern Ireland, went on to a career as an editor, which came in handy for her husband. The two of them would turn one of Don's economics conferences into a working vacation. Sitting on some hotel balcony, Pat would read his work out loud and make suggestions. The next day, she'd serve as Don's mole in the auditorium, soaking in the reactions as her husband, as often as not, told his audience they were full of it. She is in the elite tier of Shoupistas who have read *The High Cost of Free Parking* more than once.

Don had first taken an interest in parking's insatiable appetite for American land in the 1970s. For decades, he worked in obscurity, churning out papers on a subject that only mall developers and garage operators had critically considered since the early years of the auto age. Parking was absent from urban planning textbooks and from architecture curricula even as it became the single largest land use in many American downtowns. And then came *The High Cost of Free Parking*. His colleagues in the urban planning department may have pontificated on Serious Global Issues, but it was Don Shoup whose book got translated into Arabic, Russian, and Chinese. "I'm a bottom-feeder," Shoup often said about the field he pioneered. "But there's a lot of food down there."

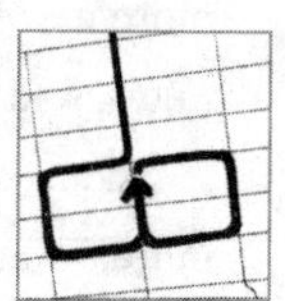

Parking was something to kvetch about, an animating subject lower than the weather and the traffic on the totem pole of small talk. But Shoup, who rode his bicycle to work each day through the streets of Los Angeles, had the cutting perspective of an anthropologist in a foreign land. He saw how parking hit a nerve. He collected newspaper clippings of parking space murders in a sheaf in his office, dozens of them each year. No clear-cut rain forest could upset an LA liberal more than an endangered bank of parking spaces.

A sense of humor helped sweeten Shoup's primary message, which was straight out of Econ 101. The reason the daily hunt for parking unleashed deep-seated territorial urges was not complicated: parking was too cheap. At least, for drivers: Shoup's calculations aligned with earlier estimates that the annual American subsidy to parking was in the hundreds of billions of dollars. You paid for it in the rent, in the check at the restaurant, in the collection box at church. It was hidden on your receipt from Foot Locker and buried in your local tax bill. You paid for parking with every breath of dirty air, in the flood damage from the rain that ran off the fields of asphalt, in the higher electricity bills from running an air conditioner through the urban heat-island effect, in the vanishing natural land on the outskirts of the city. But you almost never paid for it when you parked your car, which created a localized supply-and-demand crisis. You could read the whole postwar parking history of U.S. cities this way: it was *because* cities had been reluctant to free up curb space with market-clearing pricing that they had to resort to more extreme measures, such as demolitions, money-losing public garages, and parking requirements.

Shoup did a little back-of-the-napkin calculation. He took an estimate for how much a new parking space cost in 1998 ($4,000) and multiplied it by a conservative estimate of how many spaces existed per car (three) to conclude that there existed $12,000 in parking for every one of the country's 208 million cars. Because of depreciation, the average value of each of those vehicles was just $5,500 (all these figures in 1998 dollars). Therefore, Shoup concluded, the parking stock cost twice as much as the actual vehicles themselves. He threw in the capital cost of American roads, as well. In 1998, all of America's roads and vehicles *together* were about equal in value to its parking stock.

In 2005, to celebrate the book's release, Shoup was invited to speak at the APA conference in San Francisco, the annual gathering of the nation's city planners. He proposed two big ideas for San Francisco. The first was dynamic, demand-based pricing at downtown parking meters to free up spaces, charging for curb parking based on its availability. Shoup wanted San Francisco to create a parking market that would raise prices high enough to ensure free spaces on every block, as opposed to the familiar first-come-first-served system that leads to that lurching style of driving known as "cruising" for a spot—"parking foreplay," per Shoup—as well as countless altercations.

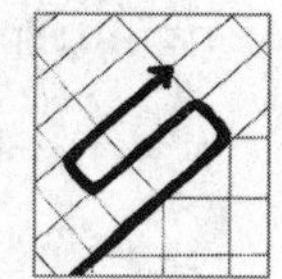

The second was an end to the parking-minimum laws that required new parking spots in every new or renovated building. "Half the profession thought I was crazy and the other thought I was dangerous," he told me, a little dramatically.

The idea of parking minimums, proposed in the twenties, rolled out in the thirties, and expanded nationwide in the forties and fifties, was obviously enticing: cities could force the private sector to fix the parking problem. No one would *pay* more for two parking spaces than for a studio apartment. Which is why city laws required developers build the spaces. Otherwise they would build apartments instead.

It was seemingly an elegant solution: governments would make builders increase the parking supply. Cities could require developers to build fire escapes, the Massachusetts Supreme Court reasoned in 1966 in a typical formulation—so why not parking spaces? Every city planner in America has a reference book of parking formulas that dictate, with the confidence, specificity, and evidence of a medieval alchemist, exactly how much parking must accompany a given land use. Their exactitude is mathematical.

But the parking minimums that govern development in every American city, Shoup discovered, were not very good. The idea was bad and the execution was worse. Instead, he wrote in *High Cost*, parking minimums displayed "a breathtaking combination of extreme precision and statistical insignificance." A typically prolix and arcane document governed construction in the city of Detroit, which requires one off-street parking space for every

> "tumbling apparatus" at a tumbling center;
> employee at a youth hostel;
> pool table in a pool hall;
> two employees in an emergency shelter;
> three beds in a fraternity;
> four beds in a nursing home;
> four seats in a theater;
> five beds in a boarding school; and
> six seats in a stadium, church, chapel, mosque, synagogue, or temple;

and one off-street parking space per:

> 100 square feet in an armory, substance abuse facility, assembly hall, beauty shop, or golf course clubhouse;
> 150 square feet in a courthouse or customs office;
> 160 square feet in a police station;
> 200 square feet in a food stamp distribution center, bank, laundromat, or medical marijuana caregiver center
> 200 square feet of water in a swimming pool (plus one per six seats of spectator seating)
> 400 square feet in a library, museum, ice-skating rink, or aquarium.

Industrial uses required two spaces for every three employees. An adult bookstore required three parking spaces, plus one for every one hundred square feet in excess of one thousand square feet. For retail uses, Detroit had a strange rule: if the store was small and free-standing (i.e., not in a mall), its parking requirements per square foot marginally decreased as the store got larger. But if the store was *very* large and part of a shopping center, the parking requirements marginally *increased* as the store got larger. Notice that the laws don't always use the same baseline: sometimes your parking is dictated by the objects inside the building (cribs, bowling alley lanes), sometimes by the size of the building, and sometimes by the number of employees.

Why does a nail salon require twice as much parking as a laundromat? Why does a police station require *slightly* less parking than a customs office? These were the questions Shoup sought to answer. The codes grew stranger still when you began to compare laws between cities that otherwise had similar designs and rates of car ownership. Parking requirements for funeral parlors were determined based on some combination of fourteen different characteristics, from the number of hearses to the number of families that lived on the premises. Mesa, Arizona, required more than five times as much parking for a high school as Kansas City, Missouri. Schools in Memphis and Fort Worth were ordered to provide three times as much parking as those in Tampa and El Paso. San Jose required twice as much office parking as Milwaukee; Omaha required twice as much as Denver. A restaurant that needed ten spaces in Memphis needed twenty-five in Nashville. A studio apartment that needed one space in Los Angeles needed two in Albuquerque. The rules weren't even internally consistent; Memphis and Miami had higher-than-average requirements for offices but lower-than-average requirements for restaurants. All this city-eating parking, empty most of the time anyway, was required by law!

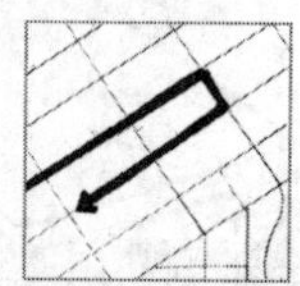

Thus far, I have mostly referred to parking requirements as a kind of asphalt *Odyssey*, a tradition passed down from generation to generation and copied from town to town. Which was true in the early days. But for contemporary planners, there was a specific villain here: the *Parking Generation Manual*, first published in 1985 by the Institute of Transportation Engineers, or ITE. This book is where America's bad parking ideas were codified and disseminated. The book of parking requirements is long and boring, but the premise is simple: every type of building creates car trips, and projects should be approved, streets

Louis Sullivan said form follows function; Donald Shoup said form follows parking requirements. Above, no parking required.

One space per 500 square feet of interior space.

One space per 250 square feet of interior space.

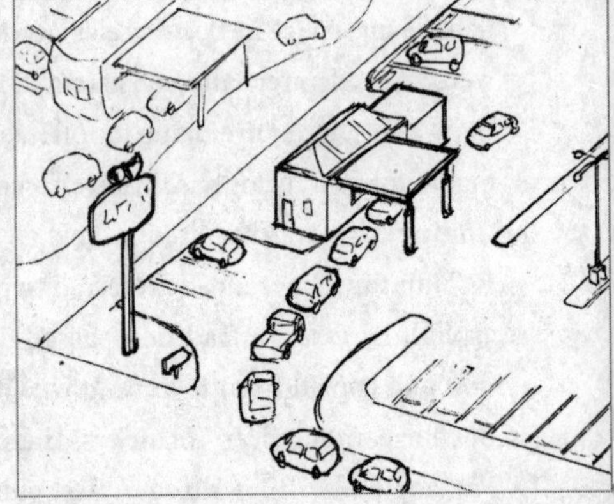

One space per 100 square feet of interior space.

designed, and parking constructed according to the science of trip generation. What became the blueprint for every new American building of the last sixty years began with a series of surveys, which the ITE recommended as early as 1950.

Daniel McKenna-Foster, who started work in 2019 as a planner in the college town of Corvallis, Oregon, hated enforcing the parking code. In 2020, he shared with me some examples of recently completed Corvallis projects: A building six hundred feet from the campus of Oregon State University with 228 apartments and 475 parking spaces. A 28-unit building between downtown and campus with 98 spaces. The Retreat at Oak Creek, a 330-unit building with 870 parking spaces required. The Domain Corvallis, with 292 apartments and 748 parking spaces. A duplex a few blocks away from the university and a grocery store: 9 parking spaces required. The town expanded the community center, which meant paving over a baseball field to build more parking.

Those were things you could count. His previous job, working in the isolated, spectacularly set Alaskan fishing village of Kodiak, may have been even more demoralizing. One guy wanted to build a little grocery store by the harbor to cater to cannery workers and fishermen coming off the water but gave up because he couldn't find enough parking. The brewery spent more than two years trying to get a parking variance to open an outdoor seating area. A guy building a house had to spend $20,000 and get a special permit from the Environmental Protection Agency to fill in a small section of the lake behind town to provide the required parking. All this gave the town the appearance, McKenna-Foster thought, of an unfinished development site.

In Corvallis, the clientele was different—this was a hippie-dippie college town—but the effect was the same. "People would come in all the time and say, 'I want to build this, I want to build that,' and I was the one who had to say, 'Oh, sorry, that doesn't meet the parking rules.' It doesn't align with what anyone wants to do here. The community says they want more economic development, more housing, and all these ideas were dying and no one even knew about it. No one tracks the ideas that don't happen. To watch as these dreams get pared down, hacked away. A beautiful ice sculpture and they end up with an ice cube. An ice cube in a tray of parking."

The result of all this, McKenna-Foster said, was not just more expensive housing, uglier architecture, less green space, and sprawl. As a college town with regular bus service to Portland and a nearby Amtrak station serving Seattle and San Francisco, Corvallis was one of a few places in America where a resident—say, one of twenty-six thousand undergraduates at Oregon State University—really could live without a car. Instead, ample parking drew people with cars and encouraged them to drive. Traffic got worse, not better.

The assumption behind parking requirements in Corvallis was that every new structure generated traffic, according to rules spelled out in a companion ITE manual, *Trip Generation*, first published in 1976. McKenna-Foster's view was that this theory was backward. An apartment building, he said, did not generate car trips any more than a banana generated fruit flies. An apartment building sitting atop eight stories of garage, on a street without sidewalks, linked by a six-lane, fifty-miles-per-hour arterial to a commercial area that is 70 percent parking by surface area would attract car trips. But the car trips were not an inherent feature of the building any more than the fruit flies were of a banana. It was the context that determined the way people would travel. This was obvious when you compared "trip generation" of identical apartment buildings in Houston and New York City. But it showed up in more subtle ways, too: a study of Philadelphia grocery stores showed that locations with visually obvious parking drew more drivers from the surrounding area than supermarkets that directly faced the sidewalk. Yet in Corvallis, as in most cities, parking was required by law and bundled into your rent. You'd have been a chump not to use it.

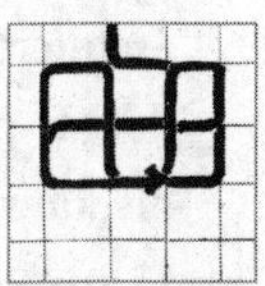

When McKenna-Foster learned about the ITE's books on parking, driving, and development in graduate school from his professor Michael Manville, who had trained under Shoup, it blew his mind. These texts were responsible for the look of everything around him. "I've always hated these big-box urban hellscapes, and you're gaining this secret knowledge that shows you, it's all based on *nothing*. The ITE is based on junk! This false precision reproduced over and over. You open the hood of the car and it's this junk engine made of Styrofoam cups and straws." It was not just that the parking minimums were bogus. The very *idea* of parking minimums was backward.

The ITE was not the only compendium of bad parking advice. A similar survey on commercial parking was published by the Urban Land Institute in 1982. The instructions:

1. Rank by busiest traffic all the thousands of hours the mall was open.
2. Design the parking lot for the twentieth-busiest hour of operation, a moment that would likely fall on a Saturday before Christmas.

For almost every one of a shopping center's 360 days of annual operation, there would be an all-day parking surplus. For nineteen hours every year, distributed over 10 busy Christmas shopping days, "some patrons will not be able to find vacant spaces *when they first enter*." Obviously, the spaces would also be empty all night, because the mall would not be allowed to share parking with a nearby apartment building.

This pattern was repeated across every land use. "Religious leaders advise 'Do not build the church for Easter Sunday,'" Shoup noted, "but planners ignore this advice for church parking requirements." Because churches require lots of parking on Sunday mornings but little at other times, they're awfully tough to park efficiently. (For developers and architects, to "park" a building is to provide the parking.) On Sundays, double-parking during services is the source of constant neighborhood disputes. The rest of the week, churches try to put that surplus parking to use. Some host homeless people who live in their vehicles. At Arizona State University, the local Mormon church offers discounted parking to students if they agree to take a religion class. Parking with the university can cost up to $800 a semester; parking with the Latter-Day Saints costs $15 (plus a bit of your soul).

Even putting aside the larger question of whether we could park our way out of traffic, there were problems with the ITE handbook. Buildings change, but parking could be built only once, so it was always built to the maximum *potential* occupancy of the building. And it was built to accommodate the peak *moment* of demand for that maximum occupancy. And both those figures were derived in places where people *already* drove everywhere. The ITE's 1997 data was based on nearly four thousand studies "primarily collected at suburban localities with little or no transit service, nearby pedestrian amenities, or travel demand management (TDM) programs." In other words, the ITE quantified the experience of sprawl and planners imposed it on small towns, urban neighborhoods, and commercial cores. A study of Portsmouth, New Hampshire, found that ITE data predicted twice as much traffic as actually existed. A 2013 study found the ITE overestimated peak traffic "generation" from mixed-used development sites by 35 percent, on average. Another study found the ITE overestimated vehicle trips in cities and underestimated trips on foot. The ITE didn't predict the relationship between new buildings and foot traffic until 2020!

All this explains why building to code produces a lot of empty parking spaces. Meanwhile, projects that don't fit in the ITE box incite widespread opposition before they can break ground. Because most parking lots are mostly empty most of the time, it's easy to overlook how this ubiquitous manual of overbuilding perpetuates its own advice, locking communities into what the parking scholar Todd Litman calls "the cycle of automobile dependency," in which car-centric transportation requires car-centric land use, which requires car-centric transportation, and so on.

It was nothing nefarious, said Randy McCourt, a traffic engineer in Portland and international vice president of the ITE who updated the parking manual for the first time in a couple decades in the early 2000s. "It's all volunteer!" he pleaded. "It's not like someone comes along with a million dollars and says, 'Let's go out and do some research!' I would cry if I heard that." He and his colleagues thought they were doing society a favor by collecting far-flung studies on parking lot usage. "We expected you to be smart! The thought was, we'd put it out there, you'd be smart and use it well. It was wrong to put it out there without the cancer warning in big, bold letters: 'If you want to be stupid, copy these numbers, you're a moron!'" But that is exactly what happened.

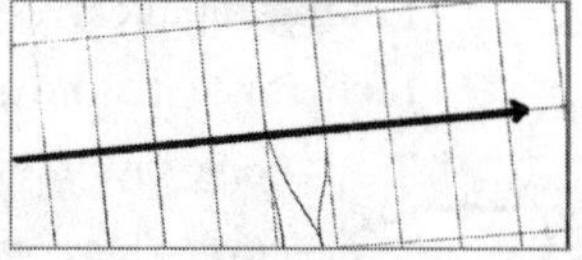

What Shoup showed in *The High Cost of Free Parking* was that all the requirements were pseudoscience. They were like astrology, he said. The planners who put them in place were nincompoops hiding, like the Wizard of Oz, behind a green curtain of outdated and misapplied research. Parking requirements had been copied from other cities, distorted by misleading evidence, and implemented without examination, where they had molded a half century of architecture literally built around (or, more often, surrounded by) parking minimums. The American modernist Louis Sullivan said form follows function; Don Shoup said form follows parking requirements. "Free parking has become the arbiter of urban form, and cars have replaced people as zoning's real density concern," he wrote.

In 2019, fourteen years after Shoup's book came out, ITE president Bruce Belmore renounced the idea of mandatory parking minimums in a preface to the organization's monthly journal. "Parking minimums make some broad assumptions, including the idea that all homeowners can afford a car, want to pay for a parking stall, and that the car is their preferred mode of transportation," the engineers' president wrote. "This works against many other policies a city creates to encourage sustainable development, promote active transportation, and serve low-income families. This discussion reminds me of the 1970s Joni Mitchell song Big Yellow Taxi in which she famously sings, 'They paved paradise and put up a parking lot.'" Regaining a piece of paradise, he wrote, demanded that cities and counties eliminate mandatory minimums, use data and pricing to manage supply, and create policies to reduce driving demand. The ITE's book ought to be guidance, not law.

But the engineers' concession meant little on the ground, said McKenna-Foster. "You go to your average yokel planning department, they're talking about cars. Nobody on the ground knows that ITE has changed their tune. Lisa in zoning doesn't care. She needs a number, and the

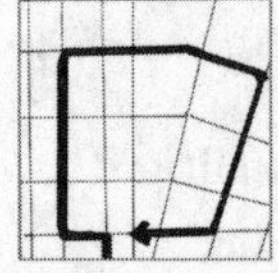

book says four hundred parking spaces." There were the neighbors. There were small businesses clinging to free parking and big ones afraid to charge. There were risk-averse politicians. There were developers who just wanted to go by the book and bankers who insisted they did. Americans knew something about parking, too. We had been looking for it all our lives.

❙ ❙ ❙ ❙ ❙

Don Shoup said asking if there's enough parking was the wrong question, since free parking invited driving. It was like asking if there's enough beer in the fridge at a high school party. The problem, Shoup argued, wasn't that there wasn't enough parking. It was that it wasn't priced properly. Curbside parking in the best locations tended to be free, while cavernous garages a few blocks away charged entry. Retail employees and office workers arrived early and took the best street spots, and when customers or clients arrived, they found no space at the curb. Studies estimated that approximately 30 percent of traffic in congested central business districts consisted of cars looking for parking. Commercial property owners heard these complaints and lobbied local governments to build more off-site garages—or demanded that rival merchants build their own private lots. These fiefdoms did comparatively little to assuage the overall supply crisis, though, since drivers often looked first to park at the curb. They also contributed to traffic, since even running nearby errands required moving the car from one private lot to the next.

This was the high cost of free parking. Charge higher rates for the best spots and lower rates for the worst spots, and everyone would fall into place according to the amount of time they needed to park and what the parking was worth to them.

Which brings me to the fourth thing that cities did to battle the midcentury parking shortage, one I haven't yet mentioned: they installed parking meters. Unlike urban renewal, public garages, and parking minimums, parking meters were not an attempt to compete with the suburbs on their own terms. They recognized that curb space was worth something, that cities were worth something. Before they were left to rust or, in Chicago's case, unwittingly sold off, the humble parking meter acquired a reputation as a kind of miracle pill for urban congestion. Shoup kept a parking meter in his office.

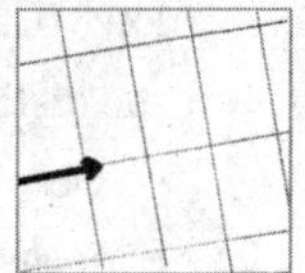

The story of the parking meter begins in the 1930s with a revelation on the part of an Oklahoma City newspaper editor named Carlton C. Magee: get the nine-to-five crowd to park ten, five, or even two minutes away, and you could save easy-access curb spaces for deliveries and customers. Eighty percent of the cars parked curbside in the state capital belonged to employees at downtown businesses. So Magee invented the Park-O-Meter, which replaced the inefficient and unreliable "chalk the tires" practice. Oklahoma City did a trial with one side of the street metered and the other unmetered. The city manager reported the results: "On the unmetered side is confusion, cars jammed together, fenders being bent, cars being pushed in front of fire hydrants, and traffic being impeded by those who are trying to back into cramped parking spaces, while shoppers can hardly find parking spaces open. On the metered side is order, sufficient room for every car to be parked and driven out quickly and easily, and there are usually parking spaces open so that shoppers can park within a block of any store or bank." By 1938, there were meters in eighty-five U.S. cities, and by 1955, all big U.S. cities had metered business districts and retail shopping streets.

Cops liked the meters, which saved time, raised money, cleared up traffic, and, most importantly, resolved arguments. Planners were dumbfounded by the results. "One had to see it to believe how completely the parking meters took command of the situation," wrote a Toledo traffic engineer. "One day it was bumper-to-bumper, and ill-tempered confusion; very soon it was timely movement in and out of the stalls all day long. The long-time parker removed his car to a lot or garage or out of the district."

Despite this positive reception, meters fell out of favor as urban decline accelerated in the 1960s. Panicked merchants sought to emulate the free parking provided in the suburbs. Developers were required to include free parking on new projects. Traffic engineers wanted moving lanes from sidewalk to sidewalk. And politicians were afraid of the backlash to raising rates while suburban malls trumpeted their free parking. Drivers had always hated meters. "This is just a combination of an alarm clock and a slot machine which is being used for further socking the motorist, who is already paying enough in taxes," wrote William Gottlieb of the Automobile Club of New York, opining on Oklahoma City's brand-new meters. There were meter vigilantes, like the cowboys in Paso Robles, California, roping meters and dragging them from the ground, and parking fairies, disobedient Good Samaritans who rescued absentminded motorists with rolls of quarters in a show of protest.

The result was that curb space itself fell out of favor. In downtowns and along busy streets, curb parking was banned. In small towns and on side streets, curb parking was made free. Either policy diminished the utility of the curb as a point of access to neighboring businesses. Good curb management had been a crucial part of well-functioning cities. In a 1970 survey, for example, curb parking spaces did not make up the majority of the stock in American cities of any size. But no matter how big the city was, the curb filled up first. In a small city where 40 percent of spaces were at the curb, 80 percent of observed parking took place at the curb. In a large downtown where just 15 percent of available parking was curbside, the share of parking that took place at the curb was 30 percent. Killing the curb's power as a reliable access point—through a ban on parking or through a ban on parking meters—reinforced the need for every building to provide its own personal parking, however destructive and redundant that practice might be. Instead of meters, cities did minimums.

Meanwhile, the initial function of meters—to impose order on the streets by pricing a scarce resource—was subsumed by a new focus: making money. Of course, this had always been part of the meter's utility for local governments. But since politicians were reluctant to raise meter rates, the primary way that meters put money in city coffers by the start of the twenty-first century wasn't from payments but from penalties. In fact, cities didn't even need meters at all to make a ton of money off parking—in a perverse way, the free-for-all engendered by removing the meters encouraged illegal parking, citations for which became a major component of revenue-driven policing. In a review of this practice in Ferguson, Missouri, published after the 2014 killing of Michael Brown, the Department of Justice told of a low-income woman who parked illegally one day in 2007. She received two citations and a $151 fine, plus fees. She attempted to make partial payments of $25 and $50, which the court refused. Then she missed her court date, resulting in an arrest warrant and an escalating series of fines. In the seven years that followed her parking ticket, the woman was arrested twice. She spent six days in jail. By the end of 2014, she had wound up paying the court $550 but still owed $541. All for a parking ticket. Counterintuitively, this state of affairs is exacerbated by cheap or free parking, which creates the supply constraints that make it necessary to break the rules, and haphazard enforcement, which requires cities to impose big fines to have any deterrent effect at all. When meter systems are working well, enforcement revenue goes *down*, because people can always find a place to park.

I I I I I

One of Don Shoup's first parking interests was cruising. A 1960s study of parking prices in London had shown the potential of high curb pricing to free up spots, reducing the amount of time drivers were parked—and the amount of time they spent looking for spots. In places where meter prices rose by a factor of four, every arriving driver saved more than *eight minutes* looking for parking. More modest price changes reduced parking searches by three minutes. In 1983, Don and Pat went to London and (in an experiment Pat would prefer to forget) re-created the study themselves. In places where street parking was cheap, it was really hard to find a spot. Don spent twenty-seven minutes trying to park at the National Gallery.

The next year, Shoup and his graduate students went to work trying to put numbers to *the parking problem* in Westwood Village, a mixed-use neighborhood of apartments, shops, and offices adjacent to the UCLA campus. To get a handle on the situation, Shoup and his students did something totally unreasonable: they went looking for parking spots themselves, over and over and over again. Parking prices in Westwood, as in most American neighborhoods, were backward: Garages, no one's first choice, were expensive. Street parking was cheap, if not free. A city study showed that at the peak hour of demand, 2:00 p.m., the curb was 96 percent occupied, while 1,200 off-street spaces remained vacant. Don and his students focused on the hunt for street parking in the evening, between 4:00 and 8:00 p.m., but made additional measurements during the lightly trafficked morning hours, too. By simultaneously searching for parking spots themselves *and* measuring turnover time at the metered curb spots, they could multiply search time by the number of new parkers to obtain an estimate of total time spent looking for parking in the neighborhood.

The figure was thirty-five hours every hour. The average cruising distance was a half mile. This single neighborhood, with its fifteen blocks of 470 underpriced meters, was generating 3,600 extra miles of extra driving *every single day*. A "reserve army of the unparked" in constant circulation. It added up to almost a million miles of driving a year, just looking for parking in one Los Angeles neighborhood. And Shoup and his team couldn't even count all the Angelenos who, heading for a doctor's appointment or a movie, drove around the block before settling for a garage. Putting various studies of road use together, Shoup concluded that nearly one third of all the cars in parking-scarce neighborhoods were looking for a place to park. If it takes three minutes to find a parking spot on a block, that block is generating sixty thousand extra driving miles each year. Shoup was like a Renaissance scientist, stumbling on the lost works of the twenties, thirties, and forties where parking was recognized as a complex and vital field of study and the parking meter venerated as a powerful tool. By the time he was teaching at UCLA, parking studies had entered a dark age. Parking meters were abhorred by everyone but municipal budget directors.

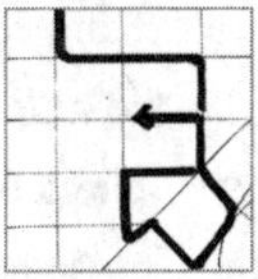

Among a new generation seeing the country's damaged urban landscape with fresh eyes, however, the professor's ideas found traction. You didn't need to tear down an entire city block to give drivers rock-star parking. All you needed were parking meters. Long before Shoup had earned the prestige to make parking a full course, one of his economics students was a young journalist named Bill Fulton. In those days, Fulton remembered, Shoup was considered something of an iconoclast by both students and faculty—the bearded, bicycling economist whose obsession with parking spaces (of all things!) did not strike everyone as very serious. Most of his colleagues were focused on regulation; Don was trying to deregulate. Plus, he was funny. Fulton was hooked. He spent an extra year in the program working on a thesis about planning and politics in Santa Monica; he even read one of the class textbooks to his girlfriend in bed. Fulton says it helped her get to sleep. Shoup says the proof is in the pudding: they got married, settling in Ventura, California, a beach city halfway between LA and Santa Barbara.

In 2009, after six years on the Ventura City Council, Bill Fulton was elected mayor. He found himself with a classic Shoupian problem: Main Street was a nonstop traffic jam as customers lurked for free parking. A hundred yards away, commercial lots and garages sat empty. Fulton reinstalled parking meters, which had been removed from Ventura four decades earlier. This was a pretty small intervention. Ventura's meters covered just three hundred spaces, and they cost just a dollar an hour. Pocket change if you were going to dinner, but enough to nudge Ventura's all-day parking hogs into walking a block or two from cheaper spots. (A two-hour limit that had been in place was hard to enforce, because parking officers found car owners would wipe the chalk off their tires. *Plus ça change*...)

The reception was contentious. Talk radio hosts in LA devoted a full afternoon to calling Fulton a dumbass. Tea Party activists collected ten thousand signatures to try to scrap the parking meters via ballot referendum. (That was blocked by a judge.) Some drivers just said it wasn't fair, because they could park for free at the mall. But, as Fulton pointed out, Main Street parking spaces were *better* than parking spaces at the mall. If you could drive inside the mall and park in front of the Sharper Image, Fulton reasoned, don't you think the mall would charge for that? And don't you think some people would be willing to pay for it? In

Ventura, it took all of thirty minutes for meters to solve the downtown traffic crunch, as employees and other long-term parkers retreated from prime real estate.

In city after city, the best street parking was cheap while garages were expensive. In 2012, Mike Manville compared street and garage pricing in the country's largest cities. Most parking in most U.S. cities was unmetered. In New York and Miami, 5 percent of spaces were metered—and the share fell to 3.4 percent in Boston and Chicago, 3 percent in Seattle, 2 percent in Portland, and 0.5 percent in Dallas and Houston. The most expensive meter in Boston was $1.25 an hour; the median off-street garage downtown was $12 an hour. With arbitrage like that, cruising for street parking was the rational choice for all but the shortest trips—where double-parking would suffice. The expected windfall from cruising in Boston was $10.75 for every hour you planned to park. The amount cruising saved you for every hour in the parking space was $11 in Philadelphia, $9 in Washington, DC, and $7 in Denver. No wonder everyone was driving around the block all day. Not surprisingly, in just a handful of Manville's surveyed cities did downtown garages hit 80 percent occupancy at peak hours.

There were people besides Bill Fulton who had figured out that parking pricing was backward. In the 1960s, merchants in Boulder, Colorado, objected to higher meter rates, fearing they would lose customers. Commuters grabbed the best spots early in the morning; shoppers got frustrated and shopped in the suburbs. In 1970, the city created a parking district to run both the meters and five public garages. The meters and the garages were the same rate, but a curbside time limit pushed commuters—as well as anyone who wanted to do dinner and a movie downtown—into garages. Parking revenue paid for bus passes for downtown employees and upgrades to public space, like benches and street trees. After eliminating parking requirements and charging for parking, this was the third leg of Shoup's parking stool: spend that money locally, through dedicated Parking Benefit Districts.

Pasadena and Santa Monica, two midsize cities on either side of Los Angeles, put in place similar initiatives in the 1980s and '90s. In those places, downtown businesses were given the option to build their own parking—but most chose to make payments toward the public garage system instead. Commuters and customers are accustomed to the arrangement; what they got in return were walkable, "park-once" downtowns where attractions were not interspersed with fields of asphalt.

In 2011, an experiment on a larger scale began in San Francisco, a city that had recently claimed to have the highest auto density of any major city in the world—more than ten thousand per square mile. "Parking," Mayor Dianne Feinstein said in 1988, "is our No. 1 problem." Two decades later, the San Francisco Municipal Transportation Agency (which runs transit and parking in the city) adopted one of the ideas Don outlined at the 2005 conference: setting the price of parking high enough that everyone could find a spot. In April 2011, in an initiative called SF*park*, SFMTA began to adjust the prices on seven thousand metered curb spaces around the city, which were monitored with occupancy sensors. The goal was to make sure that curbs were consistently 60 to 80 percent occupied, so that drivers would always be able to pull in. Every six weeks, the city would measure the average occupancy rate for curbs in specific blocks of time—a three-hour block on Saturday afternoon, say—and change the prices accordingly. If the block was more than 80 percent full, the price went up by 25 cents an hour. If the block was less than 60 percent full, the price got chopped. All this parking had once cost $3 an hour; now the city might have three different prices on each block each day. In the first year, the city made more than five thousand price changes.

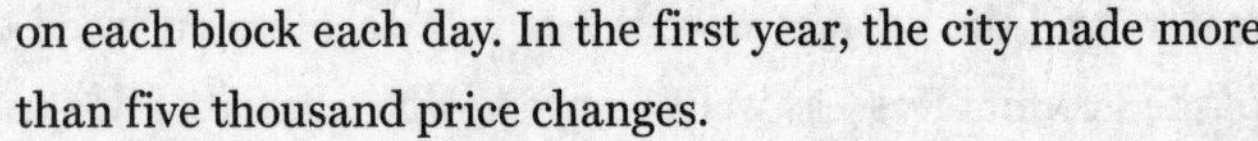

It worked. Drivers gradually responded. Consider the difference between Chestnut and Lombard Streets, which run parallel in the Marina District. Lombard Street is the main east-west thoroughfare connecting Interstate 80 to the Golden Gate Bridge. It's eight lanes wide, with a planted median, and traffic moves fast. Chestnut Street is half as wide and stacked with boutiques and independent restaurants. When SF*park* began, each street had meters priced at $2 an hour, with predictable results: it was almost impossible to find parking on charming Chestnut Street, while the curb on roaring Lombard Street was barely more than half full. Between July 2011 and January 2013, average prices for parking from 3:00 p.m. to 6:00 p.m on Lombard Street fell from $2 an hour to $1.70 to $1.25 to 95 cents, at which point occupancy jumped by ten points. Prices on Chestnut Street rose from $2 to $2.45 to $3.05 to $3.40, with curb occupancy slipping down. Finally, in April 2013, with Chestnut Street parking at $3.50 an hour and Lombard Street at $1 an hour, Lombard Street became the parking destination of choice for visitors to the Marina District. (The prices have continued to fluctuate since, in an effort to keep the neighborhood occupancy in equilibrium—if anything, the program has been criticized for taking too long to reach market-clearing prices.)

Curbs opened; garages filled. Citations in pilot areas fell by 23 percent—maybe people finally felt they were getting a service worth paying for. Price changes reduced the time San Franciscans spent looking for parking by 43 to 50 percent in pilot areas (and by 13 percent elsewhere). The results were so good the city expanded the program to cover twenty-eight thousand spaces, including lots and garages—and eliminated its parking requirements for new construction, the largest city to do so. In many places, parking got cheaper. The Performing Arts Garage, for example, went from being 25 percent full at $2.50 an hour to being 85 percent full at $1 an hour. Garage revenues rose by 10 percent. Double-parking dropped by 22 percent in pilot areas. Because drivers found parking faster, the total amount of driving in the pilot areas fell by 30 percent—2,500 miles *a day* of searching for spots and weaving around double-parked cars, vanquished by right-priced parking meters. Don thought it was the biggest change to parking policy since the introduction of the parking meter. Chicago had managed its meters to maximize revenue; San Francisco fine-tuned its system to maximize drivers' free time.

In 2019, fifteen years after his first appearance there, the APA returned to San Francisco and brought Shoup back, triumphant. The renegade from UCLA had realized his crazy ideas. In 2016, the Obama administration released a list of ideas to jump-start the country's creation of affordable housing in cities where new supply had all but dried up. Eliminating parking minimums was one of the suggestions.

CHAPTER 10

Parkitecture

Parking minimums had not just changed the feel of the street, the density of buildings, the cost of housing, and how much people drove. They had changed American design traditions, too. Consider the architecture of Los Angeles, which has been shaped and stifled by the need to provide parking. In the design of the city's buildings, you could trace the evolution of the city's parking laws, as required spaces wormed their way into first floors and front yards, cutting buildings off from each other and the sidewalk. Parking determined the concert schedule, the ticket policy at the museum, whether you could open a restaurant or renovate an abandoned building. Parking minimums were such a ubiquitous force in the city's recent development that it was hard to know with certainty their influence—perhaps people just wanted all this parking?—until, in a radical neighborhood experiment, they were eliminated.

The story of the liberation begins in the 1950s, with a girl named Carol Schatz. Carol had a narrow foot, and to buy shoes she went to Bullock's department store in downtown Los Angeles. She'd take the streetcar. She boarded in her neighborhood, Leimert Park, and rode the rickety yellow trolley northeast. Back then, the famous Los Angeles and Pacific Electric Railways, which had given Los Angeles the most extensive mass transit system of any city in the world, were clanging their way into obsolescence—as was the downtown where their routes converged. Out the window, Carol saw a changing commercial landscape drift by, one being rebuilt to accommodate and encourage Angelenos' unequaled love for the automobile. A new vernacular was taking flight. Billboards and brightly lit signs towered above the city's famous boulevards between the palm trees, with supersized writing to beckon speeding motorists. Rows of shops, restaurants, and theaters still pressed up eagerly against the sidewalks, but they were beginning to yield, one by one, to driveways and parking lots, slinking back from the street and leaving a gap-toothed line of storefronts behind them.

Not far from the Schatzes' house, one of America's first regional malls had opened in 1947. The Broadway-Crenshaw Center still had plate-glass windows along the sidewalk, but the grander (and better-used) entrance faced the parking lot. And what a lot it was. Ten acres, with space for two thousand cars—but advertised as accommodating seven thousand a day, thanks to turnover. It was front and center in the ubiquitous newspaper ads: "Plenty of free parking."

Carol and her family kept going downtown in the 1960s, because only at Bullock's could she find shoes that fit right. Bullock's wasn't just a shoe store; it was one of those retail palaces whose bounty at once announced the splendor of the world and seemed to contain it. The store had opened in 1907 and by 1960 stretched a full block down Seventh Street between Broadway and Hill, bridging a little alley where the Bullock's flower shop perfumed the air. Bullock's had a camera store, a luggage store, a bridal department; it sold televisions, Oriental rugs, china, glassware, and furniture. It had a beauty salon, a soup bar, and a carpeted, clubby restaurant called the Palmetto Room. Each corner of the building bore the store's name on a sign five stories high. From the roofs flew two enormous American flags; below, great green canvas awnings kept the sidewalks shady and cool. At Christmastime, crowds of children pressed against the window displays. A thousand Angelenos worked upstairs in the Bullock's corporate office, managing more than a dozen satellites across the state.

Malls like the Broadway-Crenshaw Center were a blow to the Downtown Business Men's Association, the group of tycoons that owned property, such as Bullock's, in the center of Los Angeles. There was no matter of higher concern to the beleaguered retail moguls than the parking problem. You could feel it from the trolley, which slowed in the gridlock of drivers cruising the streets for parking or, worse, stopped dead in its tracks behind a triple-parked car, fed-up straphangers streaming out the door to walk. In response, the Business Men's Association worked for decades to build support for a public downtown garage. The Pershing Square Garage, when completed in 1952, was their answer to the mall in the Schatzes' backyard. It too had room for almost two thousand cars, though driving the last car down, down, down into Pershing Square felt like going to the center of the Earth. In 1955, the DBMA put a Bullock's executive in charge of their Downtown Parking Plan.

They couldn't have known it then, but one measure of downtown's impending obsolescence was its increasing parking supply: The year the Pershing Square garage opened, downtown Los Angeles had twice as many spots as in 1930, in part because no one wanted to replace its demolished buildings. By 1957, downtown interests claimed the area had added another twelve thousand spots in the past five years, a matter of sufficient civic importance to warrant a downtown parking map on the cover of the *Los Angeles Times* at the start of the 1958 holiday shopping season. In the end, no number of parking spaces could save downtown LA from the many forces pushing Angelenos outward into the giant, unbroken suburb that would blanket every flat inch of the Southland.

By the middle of the 1960s, the vast, convergent rail network that reinforced downtown LA as the city center had been largely dismantled. The trolleys took one last trip down to the Port of Long Beach, where men with white-hot acetylene torches tore them apart for scrap. Bullock's finally bit the dust in 1983, not long after Carol Schatz graduated from law school and got her first job downtown: managing a detox center for public inebriates. Boosters like the Downtown Business Men's Association, even with Southern California booming and billions in urban-renewal money flooding in, had not succeeded at doing much beyond building an isolated, glass-and-steel office district up the hill from the historic downtown strip.

The most influential progress on parking was achieved by the parking requirements Los Angeles leaders had established in the 1930s (for residential construction) and 1940s (for commercial buildings). At the time, they were considered an incremental approach to an urgent problem. By the millennium, however, those laws had helped give the Los Angeles Central Business District an astounding 107,000 parking spots—the highest parking garage density in the world. One of the old Bullock's buildings has been converted to a parking garage. The gorilla had been appeased, but downtown Los Angeles had grown so peripheral on the Angeleno mental map that it was east of the city's "east side."

In 1990, Carol Schatz got a job at the inclusively named successor to the Downtown Business Men's Association, the Central City Association. In 1995, she rose to the post of executive director, the first woman in a good ol' boys club that had tried nothing and was all out of ideas. Little but the proximity to great Chinese food remained of the downtown of her youth. Schatz walked the streets and told herself: "This ain't coming back." It wasn't just that the office workers left on the stroke of five, zooming for the freeways like NASCAR drivers at the flag. Or the growing homeless population on the city's nearby Skid Row. Retailers also weren't interested. The midnineties recession sent the commercial vacancy rate up to 30 percent in the area's class A office buildings—meaning the glassy ones, with the helipads on the roof and the well-lit garages in the basement. As for the skyscrapers of an older era—sleek Art Deco towers with glazed tiles glinting in the sun; sturdy, Beaux Arts blocks caked in terra-cotta reliefs; solid, red-brick sentinels with handsome cornices and big square windows—they had become see-through. If you looked in the windows you could see right through to the blue California sky on the other side, because there was nothing in there—no dividing walls, no cubicles, no furniture. Owners took in rent from the check-cashing operations and swap meets and Chicano nightclubs downstairs, and that was enough.* Downtown Los Angeles had, after Chicago, the country's greatest concentration of early-twentieth-century architecture, but the sum of the buildings was little more than a set for movies like *Armageddon*. The model of the old Los Angeles downtown at the County Natural History Museum seemed so distant to local children it might as well have been Chicago.

Carol Schatz liked to say, "As long as LA is defined by two theme parks, a beach, and a sign, it can't be a great city." In the midnineties, she traveled to New York, where older commercial buildings—once condemned as firetraps to be demolished for highways—had become some of the coolest addresses in town. She dreamed of it happening in Los Angeles. And to make it so, to fix downtown, she concluded that the city had to get rid of a law that her own organization had once thought essential to the city's future: the minimum parking requirement. Thanks in part to the parking obsession of her midcentury predecessors, the whole neighborhood was frozen in the amber of parking law, a specimen from a time when you might have taken a streetcar downtown to buy shoes.

---

*It was enough, in part, because California had frozen residential and commercial property taxes in 1978, which has to this day left many downtown buildings with miniscule tax bills.

In 2017, a lawyer named Mark Vallianatos conceived a tour of Los Angeles he called "Forbidden City." It sounded mysterious, perhaps even indecent, but it was something like the opposite: an architecture tour with a heavy dose of regulatory history. The premise was simple. Los Angeles banned itself.

The Forbidden City was not a distant imperial fortress; it was all around. The familiar houses and apartment blocks of neighborhoods like Hollywood, Koreatown, and Mid-City; gated courts of stucco cottages grouped around grassy courtyards; handsome two-story houses in the style of old Spanish missions or Cape Cods, split into two (duplexes), three (triplexes), or four apartments (fourplexes). Hollywood apartment towers, with their schlocky appropriations of French châteaus or Chinese pagodas. Elegant, Bauhaus-inspired midrise apartment buildings. The Forbidden City is the everyday architecture of Los Angeles neighborhoods—the glamorous and the mundane, essential, quintessentially LA. All of it was illegal to build, because none of these buildings had enough parking spaces.

On a warm February day in 2020, I joined Vallianatos for a Forbidden City reprise. "We banned the parts of Los Angeles that people love the most," Vallianatos said, walking up the hill into Highland Park, an early streetcar suburb near Pasadena. Dressed in a natty green suit and thick architect glasses, the square-faced Vallianatos looked a little out of place in the California sunshine, and a lot out of place as he skulked around gates and peeked over box hedges. He was looking for electrical meters and mailboxes. That's how you figure out how many apartments sit behind a facade; it's how you know when what looks like a single-family home is in fact a fourplex. He approached a two-story house with a light-blue coat of paint behind neatly trimmed bushes. Five dials. Five apartments. Evidence that this particular building would be illegal to build in 2020. Circling around back, it was clear why: three measly parking spaces. And built for the small cars Angelenos drove in

1923, when the first tenants moved in. The tripartite garage looked like a toolshed.

If you wanted to build a five-unit building in Highland Park in 2020, you had to build at least five parking spaces (for five studio units), eight parking spaces (for five one-bedroom apartments), or ten parking spaces (for five two-bedroom apartments). Given those stipulations, on a lot this size, you wouldn't be able to build this building at all. It was an architectural fossil; the environment that gave it life was long gone.

"The overall theme is that most of these older neighborhoods in LA have a mix of smaller apartments and houses," Vallianatos went on. A dog barked, birds chirped, a drill whined in the warm air. Another rehab under way in the Forbidden City. One consequence of prohibiting such buildings from being built today is that the old ones are constant targets for luxury renovations. We passed an austere white-walled synagogue—no parking, forbidden—and paused below the scalloped red roof of a Mission Revival bungalow court with ten apartments around a manicured garden. Forbidden. In a new home in Los Angeles in 2020, as in virtually every other city and suburb in America, a parking space was as obligatory as a toilet. In fact more so. A two-bedroom apartment did not require two toilets. But it did require two parking spaces.

"We banned them through parking before we banned them through zoning," he said wistfully. "It's the city that could have been." Vallianatos's specialty was policy, not architecture. To him, the shape of buildings was a product of law first—and taste a distant second. (Shortly after we spoke, he read *The Great Gatsby*—is it just me, he thought, or is this book all about housing and cars?) Around the time Mark gave the first Forbidden City tour, he cofounded a group called Abundant Housing LA, which advocated for local housing growth—a contested subject, even as prices skyrocketed and homelessness increased. By day, he worked as an executive at the county transportation agency, LA Metro. It's no wonder he got interested in parking. Parking lies at the intersection of transportation and land use, a bastard field of study shunned by both architects and traffic engineers.

Most people in Los Angeles drive, of course. But by making parking spots as obligatory as bathrooms, the city—like virtually every jurisdiction in America—forced housing to bear the costs of driving. Most everything we have built in this country since the 1960s can be seen through Vallianatos's glasses: it is the architecture of parking requirements, and it is all around us.

In 1991, the journalist Joel Garreau wrote a book called *Edge City* about the suburban, highway-adjacent clusters of offices, retail, and hotels that make up the typical setting for white-collar labor in America today. He spoke to hundreds of developers about why these places looked the way they did, and what it meant. "The measure of time, individualism, and civilization, they repeat, is *parking*." Developers had two laws that explained "just about everything in the physical arrangement of Edge City":

> An American Will Not Walk More Than Six Hundred Feet Before Getting Into Her Car
>
> To Park an Automobile Takes Four Hundred Square Feet

Putting those two axioms together with the high cost of building parking structures, Garreau explained why all these Forbidden City buildings were missing from postwar American architecture: they had vanished into what the apartment builder Payton Chung called the Valley of High Parking Requirements. On one edge of the valley were single-family homes, fast-food restaurants, low-slung commercial box stores—all the familiar building types that could be comfortably "parked" at ground level, even if parking took up 60 or 70 percent of the property. On the other edge of the valley were high-density, high-value properties like offices, hotels, malls, and condos that could afford to build structured (or even subterranean) parking garages. Anything in between was impossible to build because it was impossible to park—surface parking would take up too much room; structured parking would cost too much to build. The Valley of High Parking Requirements was barren ground where nothing would grow. Ginger Hitzke's project in Solana Beach was in the valley. So was Pastor Nathan Carter's storefront church. And the fishermen's grocery store that Daniel McKenna-Foster had to shut down in Kodiak, Alaska.

Anybody who wanted to build a small apartment building in the United States in 2020 needed to confront a multivariate financial geometry problem that began with how many parking spaces you could fit on a lot. The size, quantity, and shape of the housing followed from there. Sometimes, with just one parcel, it was hard to make anything work at all. Buy the lot next door and you could unlock some economies of scale—like a driveway with stalls on each side. Buy four and—well, most small-time developers couldn't afford four, even if you could find four buildable, adjacent properties. In any case, parking was *the* immovable object at the heart of neighborhood architecture, not just socially, as in Solana Beach, but technically as well. "Parking is like

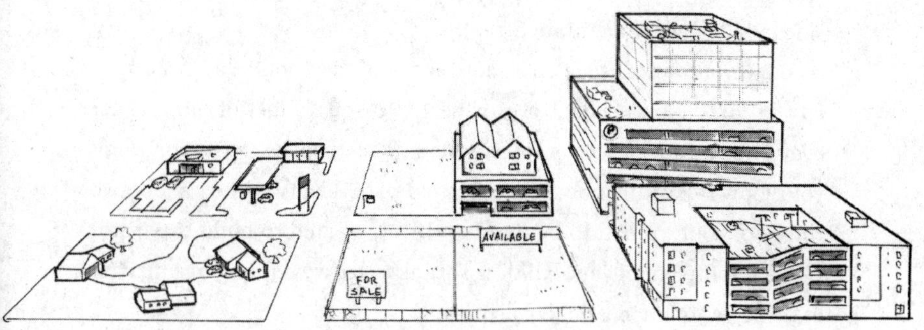

The Valley of High Parking Requirements. Anything between sprawl and high-density development was impossible to build because it was impossible to park—surface parking would take up too much room; structured parking would cost too much to build.

eggs," one builder said. "You can't buy just one, you have to buy a whole floor. . . . If you have to build one-and-a-half floors, you'll build two floors."

Mostly, America just stopped building small buildings. Parking requirements helped trigger an extinction-level event for bite-sized, infill apartment buildings like row houses, brownstones, and triple-deckers; the production of buildings with two to four units fell more than 90 percent between 1971 and 2021.

What apartments did get built were clustered in megastructures whose design was dictated by parking placement. One popular model is the "Texas donut," in which a ring of apartments encircles a five- or six-story parking garage (this is the type of building you see in the cool neighborhoods of growing cities). Another is the "parking podium tower," like Chicago's corncob Marina City, in which the housing sits atop the parking.

For mixed-used or commercial properties, the calculus is simpler, because so much more parking is required. There is less room to negotiate. Take the core of any small American town. Central parcels here were originally developed as commercial storefronts facing the sidewalk with offices or even housing above. Put twenty or thirty of them side by side and, voilà, Main Street.

But if you wanted to open a shop on one of those lots in an American city in 2020, you needed to provide 1,200 square feet of parking for every 1,000 square feet of interior commercial space. More than half your lot was parking now. If you wanted to build a two-story shop, two thirds of your lot had to be parking. If you wanted to build three stories, the footprint of your building shrank to barely more than a quarter of the lot, a totem in a field of asphalt.

For restaurants, the math was much worse. In most cities, ten parking spaces were required for every 1,000 square feet of restaurant, so your classic Main Street lot of 7,500 square feet could support a restaurant of only 1,500 square feet. Eighty percent of the lot was parking now. The developer Mott Smith, who works in Los Angeles, told me about his trips to present new projects at community meetings in the 2010s. "I had some architect friends, and we'd show the neighbors a picture from the community of some beautiful, zero-lot-line 1930s building with a café and a caption saying, 'What you want.' Then we'd spend the next hour explaining why the requirements make it so unless you're building a Taco Bell, you need not apply." Fast-food architecture—low-slung, compact structures on huge lots—is really the architecture of parking requirements. Buildings that repel each other like magnets of the same pole. Parking minimums were like "dark energy," Don Shoup wrote, that hidden force that powers the expansion of the universe. Parking minimums powered the expansion of the city.

In 1968, the architects Robert Venturi and Denise Scott Brown heralded this new phase of American architecture with a contrarian, pop appraisal of Las Vegas as a city worth studying, loving, even emulating. Their comparison of a supermarket parking lot to the Château de Versailles was a Slate pitch of its day:

> The A&P parking lot is a current phase in the evolution of vast space since Versailles. The space which divides high-speed highway and low, sparse buildings produces no enclosure and little direction. To move through a piazza is to move between high enclosing forms. To move through this landscape is to move over vast expansive texture: the megatexture of the commercial landscape. The parking lot is the parterre of the asphalt landscape. The patterns of parking lines give direction much as the paving patterns, curbs, borders, and tapis verts give direction in Versailles; grids of lamp posts substitute for obelisks and rows of urns and statues, as points of identity and continuity in the vast space.

And the Las Vegas they adored was downright urban by the standards of millennial exurban sprawl.

The other option, on the other side of the Valley of High Parking Requirements: twenty- or thirty-story buildings that are all garage from the waist down. In Austin, a 2020 office building called 405 Colorado placed a glass crystal of office (thirteen stories) atop a brick of parking (twelve stories). The architect, Turan Duda, likened it to a Brancusi sculpture. Austinites said it looked like a ring pop, or a glass molar on a stand. Forget the parking podium. This was a parking pedestal. Whatever you thought of 405 Colorado, it was honest about the fact that every modern American high-rise was half parking by volume.

Southern California's parking laws worked wonders. In 2015, Los Angeles County was estimated to have 18.6 million parking spaces, five for every home and more than two for every adult, including 5.5 million stalls in residential driveways and garages, 9.6 million spots in commercial and industrial lots and garages, and 3.6 million spaces at the curb. Laid flat it came to two hundred square miles of parking—14 percent of all the incorporated land in the county. Los Angeles had achieved something that was just about unparalleled in the entire world: it was a metropolis of more than ten million people where it was possible to park, mostly for free, at nearly every single residence, office, and business.

I I I I I

Vallianatos used to freelance at the cafés in Highland Park. He spent his days looking up the age of the structures around him, happily avoiding his assignments as he studied the progression of the city's zoning and building codes. Looking back at LA history, he saw the city's architecture moving in paired evolution with its parking laws. The clusters of cottages known as bungalow courts sprawled across Los Angeles in the 1920s, only in part because buyers found them charming, affordable simulacra of country home life. The model also permitted developers to put six, eight, or ten units on a single lot without making the expensive, unsightly jump to two stories. Critics thought them monotonous, dreary, and crowded. In 1934, Los Angeles decided to require one parking spot per unit in every multifamily residential project. The policy effectively killed the bungalow court; even if you could fit eight spaces at the back of the lot, the driveway to reach them would eat up half the living rooms.

When the building boom resumed after the Second World War, LA's developers pored over the parking code and developed a new specimen, the dingbat. The adaptation was simple: put the housing above the parking, perched on slender concrete poles. This was more expensive than simply sticking one garage in back, and it certainly made for a less attractive experience from the sidewalk, which was transformed into one big driveway serving the yawning maws of carport. But it allowed builders to put eight family-size apartments on a standard lot at low cost. The dingbat became a naturally occurring source of affordable housing in Los Angeles, like the triple-decker in Boston or the row house in Baltimore. Variations in the form—the dumbbat, the cheesebat, the halfbat—were classified by how they responded to local parking impediments, such as slopes or a lack of rear access. In 1958, Los Angeles banned the kind of street-facing, building-width garage that had defined fifties dingbats (in part because the huge driveways cannibalized street parking). Builders adapted with side and rear parking, though that often meant less space for apartments. In 1964, LA increased its parking minimums to require 1.5 spaces per two-bedroom apartment. Ding-dong, the dingbat was dead.*

When parking came calling, green space was often the first thing to go. Courtyards were turned into parking lots. In the 1960s, librarians at the beloved Los Angeles Central Library, a gilded ziggurat downtown, called a sick-out to protest their inadequate parking facilities.

---

*Those who did keep building in this style began to avoid two-bedroom apartments, an early example of how parking requirements discourage the construction of family-sized housing units.

The librarians wanted to pave the sculpture garden for parking; preservationists were aghast. Robert Alexander, partner of the SoCal modernist Richard Neutra, chained himself to a rock in the garden in protest. The librarians got their parking lot. The fountains and gardens were demolished, and the sculptures vanished.

Walking in Highland Park that day, we were watching this history unfold block by block—the building-by-building neighborhood equivalent of what Victor Gruen and urban renewal planners had tried to do downtown. Postwar structures began to cede the front yard to parking. Eventually, the whole ground floor became a parking garage. Planners thought that if you could get residents to stop parking their cars in the street, the nightmarish LA traffic would improve. Residents recognized that onerous parking rules would discourage the new construction crowding their neighborhoods. Apartments without parking, it was thought, would both lower neighborhood status and intensify the curbside melee.

This had consequences that went far beyond traffic. "I don't think they were thinking, 'This is going to extinguish all midrise masonry buildings in Los Angeles,'" Vallianatos observed on our tour. "It did, though." Occasionally, we passed a lot that just had nothing on it at all. "There's so many unbuildable lots in LA because of parking," he went on. A city stillborn.

There was something ironic in it all, Vallianatos thought after his first Forbidden City tour in 2017, when he led a group of fifty Angelenos around the prewar neighborhoods of Los Feliz and Koreatown. Zoning is often blamed for abolishing the kind of old-fashioned city streets Americans so love to stroll down when they visit places like Philadelphia or Savannah. On a purely visual level, however, Americans' distaste for new buildings today is often a reaction to the bigger, grayer structures developed in response to parking laws. Buildings got boxier. A 2005 LA initiative to spark infill building—in the interstitial urban spaces often used, for lack of anything better, as parking lots—produced a boom in townhouses that Angelenos seemed to mostly hate. Why were all these new buildings so tall? Why did they all look the same? The greatest determinant of their form, builders said, was the parking requirement.

A small version of that trade-off was at work in every residential project in Los Angeles. "You think architects design buildings, but actually we just arrange parking spaces," the Angeleno architect Daniel Dunham joked to me in 2019. Dunham, who designed midrise, affordable apartment buildings for a Santa Monica–based firm, was only kind of joking. "It's the first thing you think about. The spaces determine the column grid, and the columns determine the building." Putting structural support columns thirty feet apart is great for parking spaces, so that's what Dunham did, even though it created spacing on residential floors that's a little too wide for one-bedrooms and a little too narrow for two-bedrooms. "We end up planning housing modules around this unit that works for parking but not for housing."

In 2008, a wannabe restaurateur named Ben Lee had the idea to start a restaurant in Beverly Grove, a posh neighborhood in West LA. Lee had run a twenty-four-hour diner in Hollywood, and he had the perfect site for his new project: a building on Third Street where his father had, for a half century, run a carpet store. It was one of those older, workaday structures that had outlived its function as Floor Covering Unlimited Inc. but not its utility. The younger Lee convinced his father to let him turn the space into a West Coast rebirth of the New York staple Ratner's Deli.

There was one big problem: on this side of the Hudson River, the Jewish delicatessen would require forty-two parking spaces—about three times the square footage of the building itself. Lee would have to buy and demolish three neighboring buildings just to open his restaurant.

Fortunately, Los Angeles had come up with an alternative: rent some spots nearby and ask the city for a variance, an exception to the parking code. Across the street was a shopping mall with a five-story garage that was never full. So Lee rented a few dozen spaces from the mall for a valet operation.

Unfortunately, getting a parking variance in Los Angeles is, like trying to make it in Hollywood, a long and degrading process with little chance of success. Businesses that do get the variance often find themselves with severe restrictions attached. The Academy Museum of Motion Pictures, for example, recently constructed its building without parking, to take advantage of three adjacent, half-empty existing garages. The evident risks in this plan required a twenty-two-page variance, which suggested a "timed ticketing program" to help avoid a potential parking fiasco. No refunds, no early entry, and no guarantee you'll get in if you're more than thirty minutes late. Admission to this temple of Hollywood's cultural import has been conditioned on parking.

After Los Angeles finally sanctioned Ben Lee's plan to park cars across the street in 2010 (on appeal, and after many months of hearings), a nearby homeowner group filed a lawsuit against the City of Los Angeles, which Lee (as the beneficiary of the variance) had to defend. The suit alleged Lee didn't have exclusive title to the parking spaces he had rented. It took another two years for Lee to prove his legal right to those empty parking spaces in the mall garage, by which time he was down $100,000 and no longer on speaking terms with his father, who couldn't believe his son had gotten them into this mess. More than three years after he had begun work on the project, demoralized and out of money, Lee gave up the dream.

On a Forbidden City walk in 2019, Vallianatos brought his tour to the Buck House, a modernist duplex by R. M. Schindler, all clean white lines and cantilevers, a house made for the movies. When the Buck House was completed in 1934, Schindler's firm went beyond the code by providing a three-stall garage beneath one of the units. The home is a Los Angeles landmark, though now illegal in a handful of ways, in violation of the neighborhood's single-family zoning and the city's parking requirements. (It would now require four stalls.)

A home without a parking space may be illegal under current LA law, but that doesn't make it undesirable. On the contrary: given the choice between high rents and parking anxiety, plenty of Angelenos vote with their feet for neighborhoods like Hollywood or Koreatown, despite a curbside parking shortage so severe it has ended relationships. The comedian Jenny Yang called parking in K-Town "a blood sport." Despite its parking-challenged housing stock, Highland Park, where Vallianatos had spent so many days sipping coffee at his laptop, was hot. This longtime Latino enclave attracted newcomers with its walkable, prewar urbanism, quiet streets, and proximity to downtown. Figueroa Street was bustling; shops built before parking requirements crowded right up against the sidewalk, shading and beckoning passersby with sights and smells. A shrimp cocktail was painted on the window of a Mexican restaurant. A woman sold fresh fruit under a rainbow parasol near the curb. Nearby, East LA's creative workforce unfolded their MacBooks at the counter of a coffee shop. If apartments without parking spaces were hard to rent, Highland Park would have been a slum. Instead, it was one of the fastest-gentrifying neighborhoods in the country. A multigenerational Mexican American community lived in fear of the "renovictions" that brought granite countertops to the kitchens of the Forbidden City. For while it was illegal to build anything like Highland Park again, you could renovate these buildings for a sizable profit.

Vallianatos was searching for a particular building, and he found it: an unremarkable, four-story box perched on a quiet corner. The ground floor was painted olive green; the top three floors a blinding white in the morning sun. When it was built a hundred years ago, this was a hotel. "Little hotel rooms, some apartments, no parking. If this was torn down, you could build *nine apartments* with fifteen parking spaces. How many units are there here? Sixty. I don't know what the quality is, how the conditions are, whether the landlord's a good person, but it has been cheap housing for working-class Latinos for decades. And the fact that it's illegal is part of the problem we're facing."

The original *problem* was that there wasn't enough parking, and in that context, Los Angeles was a magnificent success. But the new problem, the one Vallianatos was talking about, was that Los Angeles was the least affordable city in the United States. Parking was one reason why.

| | | | |

To really grasp the impact of parking minimums, you had to see what happened when they disappeared. In 1999, Carol Schatz got Los Angeles to pass an Adaptive Reuse Ordinance (ARO) for downtown. This law was supposed to make it easier to renovate the area's aging, vacant buildings. It proposed an alternative seismic code. It granted a by-right exemption from the city's difficult permitting process. And it freed builders entirely from the obligation to provide parking when they turned commercial buildings into residential ones. Expectations were low. Just as early parking requirements had been viewed as an incremental solution to downtown's woes, so too relief from the requirements was seen as a half measure. "We had to make chicken salad out of you-know-what," Schatz said.

But just like that, the walls of the Forbidden City came crashing down.

The first builder to bite was an Israeli-born subdivision developer named Izek Shomof. Shomof came to California as a kid and worked for a spell flipping burgers downtown. It was a ghost town after dark. How dead was downtown LA? In 1991, Shomof was able to buy the former Los Angeles Stock Exchange, a twelve-story tower, for $2 million in 2020 dollars. It's probably worth twenty times that today. In 2001, Shomof's Spring Towers Lofts was the first building renovated under the ARO to open. Its three dozen apartments had fifteen-foot ceilings. Shomof carved a garage out of the first floor and the basement, though he was only able to get about twenty-five spaces—dozens short of what the code would have required. Some of the tenants parked downstairs; some parked a block away, and some didn't own cars at all. "Without the ordinance easing parking, downtown would be as dead as it was in the seventies, eighties, and nineties," Shomof said.

Then came Barry Shy, a secretive, quarrelsome builder who turned Shomof's model into a system. Using private equity, Shy was able to buy and renovate faded, vacant commercial buildings faster than anyone else. His apartments were relatively affordable, too—in part because the price of parking was never folded into the lease. Shy let tenants figure it out themselves. By 2010, a decade after the ARO, Shy was the second-largest residential landlord downtown and had created more than 1,500 new apartments.

But the guy who got the glory was Tom Gilmore. Shomof saw an opportunity; Shy was an operator. Gilmore was a true believer. There he was on the cover of the *Los Angeles Times Magazine* in October 1999, glowing in the setting sun, standing against the granite facade of the 1905 Farmers and Merchants National Bank. Gilmore bought it for $100,000, one one-hundredth of its original construction cost. Headline: RECLAIMING THE BADLANDS. In the spread, there was Gilmore again, looking like Bruce Wayne, tie dangling over the fire escape railing on the top floor of the Continental Building, with its Corinthian columns, cornucopias of terra-cotta fruits, and cornice of lions' heads. For many decades, this was the city's tallest office building. Now it was at the center of Gilmore's plans to revive downtown: the Old Bank District.

One colleague said Gilmore was like P. T. Barnum, meaning theatrical (and maybe full of it). The *LA Times* likened him to the renowned Protestant evangelist Aimee Semple McPherson, and to New York's master builder Robert Moses. A partner said he was like a "half-grown puppy with big paws," who'd come back from lunch with plans to buy five new buildings. "Not what you'd call employee material," said another. Overextended, undisciplined, always talking too much and running out of money. But also a charismatic, bootstrapping outsider, a "shanty Irish New York Goober" (his words) who saw no reason Los Angeles couldn't or shouldn't have a downtown. "LA's been a movie set for long enough," he said. "Now it's time for it to become a real city."

In the late 1980s, Gilmore got flushed out of New York, where he had run a middling architecture practice (though he was not, in fact, an architect) and hung out at Elaine's, the uptown clubhouse for the cool and the rich. As he later explained to a high school class, he asked his new friends in Los Angeles to show him the action. They tried Beverly Hills, Century City, Santa Monica—the centers of the West Side. No, no, no. "Good try. Show me the city, the place where it's really going on in the middle of your town," Gilmore said. "They went, 'Oh, oh, oh! You mean like downtown?' I said, 'Yeah, downtown,' and they looked at me like I was crazy. They were like, 'Well, nobody goes downtown. Nobody in LA even knows where downtown is.'" (No white people, at least—while the upper stories remained largely vacant, storefronts on Broadway did cater to the city's Latino population, and still do.)

Ten years later, Tom had become an Angeleno in every respect but that one: he loved downtown. Despite the fact that it rarely lived up to the inscription carved into the stone in Pershing Square, atop the mammoth underground garage, written in 1946 by Carey McWilliams about that very spot: "Here the American people were erupting, like lava from a volcano; here, indeed, was the place for me—a ringside seat at the circus." By 1999, downtown's asphalt cover was so extensive it looked like a nonmetaphorical volcano had erupted nearby. "We're ashamed of our downtown," Gilmore lamented. "We have dozens of beautiful old buildings, the kind that people die for in New York, and we treat them like eyesores, as if we're just waiting for them to fall down so we can sweep the bricks away and build another parking garage." For Carol Schatz, who had thought of New York as a model, this guy was a godsend. "We would do anything—and I repeat, anything—to make it succeed," she said of Gilmore's downtown vision.

Tom and Carol shared a theory about what had gone wrong in downtown Los Angeles: it had been subjected to the car-centric logic that governed the rest of the city. "Transportation was ultimately the primary mode of tearing apart downtown. Everything was done to facilitate the car," Tom observed. "A good 25 percent of downtown was demolished to create surface parking lots." Downtown had so much surface parking, Tom said, it looked like Dresden after the war. Throw a rock, you'd hit a parking lot. He did some friendly sparring with Harry Lumer, the local surface-parking magnate. "Surface parking is a pain in the ass," Tom would tell him. "The city looks like hell. Everything is a chain-link fence." And Harry, Tom remembers, would brag: "I've torn down more buildings in this city than any human being alive." The builder and the demo guy. Later, Tom would comb through historical photos of LA and match them up to Harry's lots (better known to Angelenos under the name of his cofounder brother as Joe's Auto Parks). In the basement of the Banco Popular building, Tom found a garage that had been set up on the grounds of an old ballroom. You could still see the ornate tiled floor beneath the oil stains.

Carol Schatz agreed with the diagnosis. (After all, her organization had done its share to help.) The whole building code was suburban. Downtown was like a captured village, prisoner to the laws of a conquering tribe of drivers.

People had tried to bring round-the-clock life to downtown Los Angeles before. A huge public investment in Frank Gehry's Walt Disney Concert Hall, which broke ground in 1992, was supposed to serve as a catalyst. But the county ran out of money after spending seven years building another huge underground garage. In the end, Gehry's wavy silver auditorium building wasn't opened until 2003. (Its lease demanded that the hall put on 128 shows a year—enough to generate the needed parking revenue. That first year, Disney Hall put on 128 shows.) In the late 1980s, a developer named Ira Yellin put 120 apartments in the Million Dollar Theater building on Broadway. But Yellin also had to build a 448-space garage next door, and ten years later, the project had proven so expensive he still hadn't turned a profit. No one had tried to convert a large office building to apartments since the 1970s.

But things were different now: operating under Carol's new ordinance, Tom Gilmore moved quickly to transform a full block of downtown. Under Gilmore's supervision, one vacant building after another was reborn as apartments. New residents supported little businesses downstairs, like video stores and restaurants, or the beloved Last Bookstore, which opened in 2005. Those businesses also got to play by the no-parking rules, and so they looked less like a strip mall and more like Main Street. Tom would offer free rent, sometimes for years, in order to jump-start the kind of street life he felt would attract residential tenants. That was another thing about parking: if you gutted the ground floor to park cars, you couldn't have any retail. And at that point, with everyone parking inside their own building, had you really improved on the suburbs? Tom thought not. Downtown living to him meant that you don't have to get behind the wheel to buy a toothbrush.

Skeptics thought he'd lose his shirt. Everybody in LA drove. And Tom would say, "I don't need everybody. I just need to fill this building." Ten million people lived in LA County; he needed a hundred of them. It wasn't just tenants who needed to be convinced. Banks refused to lend money to parking-free downtown buildings. Citigroup and Bank of America would not finance these conversions. For "comps"—comparable properties that demonstrate that a project is viable—Tom had to go all the way to Denver. There was just nothing in Los Angeles that fit the bill, parking-wise. For financing, he went to the Department of Housing and Urban Development, which had a flexible financing program available for creating housing in blighted areas. Downtown LA qualified. That was great for financing new apartments, not so great for marketing them.

In 2010, Michael Manville and Donald Shoup tried to isolate the effects of the new, laissez-faire parking regime downtown. Manville called up every downtown builder he could find and asked them how parking rules changed their approach to historic buildings. The new parking law wasn't the only factor: without the revised earthquake design rules, most agreed, nothing could have happened. High-end developers, whose buyers and renters wanted to park their cars on-site anyway, prized the expedited permitting process.

And yet: *every single project* that had been built under the ARO rules had constructed fewer parking spaces than would have been required by law. Developers built what buyers and renters wanted—and it was a lot less than what the law had demanded. Perhaps more important than the number of spaces was their location: instead of exclusive, on-site spots, developers chose to lease stalls from the downtown's many garages, most of which were empty at night and on weekends—exactly when residents needed them.

The former headquarters of Mobil Oil, for example, was reopened as the Pegasus Lofts in 2002. The developers provided less than 60 percent of the on-site parking that would previously have been required by law. The Gas Company Lofts, a thirteen-story limestone building fronted by a handsome trio of arches, provided just 20 percent of what would have been required—and offered tenants space in a garage across the street. Not exactly radical—but until 1999, totally illegal. Sixteen buildings renovated under the ARO offered no on-site parking spaces.

Manville tried to imagine the alternate universe in which the historic conversions were still limited by the on-site parking spaces builders had or were able to dig out—how would things be different? Downtown LA would have lost more than 2,500 of its new apartments, he concluded. Nearly half the new lofts would not have been built! And that figure surely underestimates the effect. With forty fewer units in each converted building, and accordingly lower profit margins, would the rehabs have attracted builders and lenders at all?

Liberated from parking requirements, downtown Los Angeles came roaring back. The population more than tripled in the first two decades of the millennium, to more than sixty thousand people. By 2020, there was an Ace Hotel, a Whole Foods, a Blue Bottle Coffee. Two of the new residents, as it turned out, were my friends Ian and Shea, who in 2019 rented an apartment in a turquoise palace of a building called the Eastern Columbia. At the millennium, this 1930 Art Deco landmark was largely vacant, the hands stopped and dials dark on its four-sided clock tower. In 2004, under the ARO, it was given new life as lofts. My friends' concrete-floored apartment looked out on the rubbery leaves of a bank of ficus trees. Ian could walk to the gym or the office, and Shea kept her car in the garage next door.

Developers thought a handful of buildings might be eligible under Carol Schatz's new ordinance. Instead, in the following decade, developers like Tom Gilmore used the ARO to turn more than sixty vacant old buildings into more than 6,500 apartments. That was more housing units than downtown Los Angeles had built in the previous three decades *combined*.

That wasn't the only thing going on downtown at the time; the Staples Center opened in 1999, a new rail line opened—along with the concert hall—in 2003, and about as many new apartments were built, hot on the heels of the historic conversions, in new buildings. But many observers believe the historic conversions lit the fuse for change. Dan Beckerman, the head of the company that developed the Staples Center, where the Lakers, Clippers, and Kings played, said at a 2018 event in her honor that Carol Schatz was "the most influential person in the renaissance of Downtown LA." Schatz said, "I was known as the queen of Downtown, and many people would say I still am." She was retired, but she still came to walk the square that was named for her in 2018—and, a half century after those trips to Bullock's, still came downtown to get her shoes fixed. "I remind the shoe repair guy that he's one of my subjects and he better do what I need," she joked.

Los Angeles did not suddenly become a place where people stopped owning cars. On the contrary: the car ownership rate has gone *up* in downtown Los Angeles as young professionals moved into a neighborhood once considered a last resort. What the transformation of downtown LA shows is how quickly a perceived parking shortage can turn into a surplus when the city doesn't force every building to have its *own* parking. And yet the absence of parking continues to be a barrier to the redevelopment of older buildings and neighborhoods across the city and the country, from Greenwich, Connecticut (where, as in nineties LA, upper floors are left vacant for want of required parking), to Rust Belt cities, where "unparkable" old buildings sit abandoned with a parking-sized padlock on their doors. Forbidden cities, everywhere. What makes this all the more strange is that for the most part, such parking-challenged structures—like Mark Vallianatos's beloved Highland Park ex-hotel—no longer provide the naturally occurring affordable housing they did when those buildings, and neighborhoods, were widely considered obsolete. Instead, precisely *because* they offer access to places where car ownership is optional, buildings without sufficient parking are among the most in-demand structures we have. In virtually every U.S. city, the most expensive neighborhood is a prewar, mixed-use streetcar suburb that would be illegal to build today. That scarcity ensures their high price point. No one would think, for a second, that we had built too many places like Highland Park, like Los Feliz, like downtown LA... to say nothing of parking-challenged places like Brooklyn's Fort Greene or Boston's Back Bay or Chicago's Lincoln Park. So why did we make it illegal to build more of them?

CHAPTER 11

The Shoupistas Take City Hall

The followers of Don Shoup started to pop up everywhere. The Shoupistas, the bottom-feeders, the people with shirts that read "Street parking is theft." Finally, there was someone to argue with parking-concerned neighbors at the city council meeting. The Shoupistas came armed with the promise of a better world through better parking: more affordable housing, more new businesses, more historic reuse, more walkable neighborhoods, less time behind the wheel. Downtown parking minimums were abolished in New Orleans, Pittsburgh, Austin, and Fargo. Parking near transit was made newly optional in New York City, Sacramento, Indianapolis, and San Diego. In Miami, a parking variance for small parcels produced a boom in small-lot houses, little teeth growing into a block's broken smile. Austin and Boston scrapped parking minimums for affordable housing. In city after city, reformers were getting their way.

The Shoupistas were designers, environmentalists, developers, planners, pedestrians, and small-business owners. Restaurateurs and food trucks. Start-up founders doing e-commerce and hippies riding bicycles.

People who didn't drive or didn't want to. They came from the Left, frustrated by a hidden nationwide subsidy for fossil fuels and enraged by the hurdles to building low-income housing, and the Right, thwarted by laws that told you what to do with your property with dubious justification. Preservationists who wished to see old buildings find second life and antipreservationists who wanted to see new buildings everywhere. Free marketeers who wanted dynamic parking pricing, and good-government advocates who wanted revenue for public improvements. The "yes in my backyard" (YIMBY) prohousing activists. The small-city restorationists of the Strong Towns movement. Architects who subscribed to the Congress for New Urbanism, the movement for traditional town building founded by Elizabeth Plater-Zyberk and Andres Duany, who with Jeff Speck called parking minimums the "single greatest killer of urbanism in the United States today."

Chrissy Mancini Nichols was working for the Chicago Metropolitan Planning Council, a regional think tank, when parking started getting in the way. "Everything we were trying to do on transportation or land use—parking just dominated every policy," she said. Not just bus lanes, which Chrissy knew were desperately needed to help the city's bus riders escape rush-hour traffic. City budgets: a tax on commercial parking accounted for 5 to 6 percent of Chicago's revenue; construction of a municipal parking deck might account for 10 to 20 percent of a suburb's budget. Midway Airport had long been a candidate for privatization, but after the parking meter deal, Mayor Emanuel thought it seemed too risky. "The CPM deal almost killed the entire P3 market in the country," Chrissy said. Consolation prize: the meter fiasco launched a handful of parking reformers into orbit.

When the city started to renegotiate the deal, Chicago CFO Lois Scott asked Chrissy to take a look. That, Chrissy joked, was when she started dedicating her life to the Chicago parking meter deal. Her blog remained the most detailed account of what happened when CPM and Chicago went to war over the bill for changes at the curb. By 2020, she had leveraged that mania into work as a professional parking consultant. "Everything revolves around parking," she said cheerfully, in one of a series of conversations we had that year. That sentiment might have been mistaken for a kind of professional boosterism—parking consulting was her job, after all. But as she launched into the story of the Chicago parking meters, I instead had the feeling of speaking to a self-assured healer who didn't shy from treating the sickest patients. "They all need help," she said. "And it's worth it, in all these places. Once they see the price of the garage, they think, 'Oh my God, we could build a school!'"

Even five years after the deal, Chicago parking still seemed totally backward. For example: Chrissy and her husband lived in an old pencil factory near the train tracks, not far from an L stop. Every day on her way to work, she passed the site of a tire shop that had gone out of business. The property, which belonged to the Chicago Transit Authority, was in the shadow of the L stop, a vacant lot behind a fence. The property sold. The grass grew, the grass was mowed. The snow fell.

The problem, one you'll surely have guessed by now, was that the lot was too small to provide the requisite number of parking spaces to make residential construction pencil out. Even in Chicago, even in the second decade of the twenty-first century, even next door to the L, this was the law. Chrissy fought it. At the Metropolitan Planning Council, she built a calculator to figure out how many new apartments Chicago's parking-heavy rules were suppressing. In 2015, citing an MPC study and quoting the organization's president, the Emanuel administration eliminated parking minimums on nine square miles of land on or near Chicago transit. The ordinance covered only a tiny fraction of Chicago's 218 square miles, but those nine square miles included eighty-two thousand parcels whose location on busy commercial strips and near L stations made them exceptionally well suited for Chicagoans without cars. That summer, 2015, the first new apartment building to take advantage of the parking-light ordinance opened on the vacant lot near the Paulina Brown Line stop. In the next three years, the city approved more than twenty-four thousand residential units in those areas. The share of large buildings including a parking spot for every unit fell by half. In 2019, the city expanded the law to cover bus routes. The movement to legalize old-style Chicago buildings, buildings without parking, the Forbidden City, finally swept up Nathan Carter's storefront church. He paid a penalty and quit his parking lot lease.

The lot by the Brown Line, however, had been set to become a one-story Walgreens, mostly parking spaces, had it not been for the intervention of Alderman Scott Waguespack's chief of staff, Paul Sajovec. Parking being the subject on everyone's lips in those years, Paul had picked up *The High Cost of Free Parking*, too. He pushed for something better than a chain pharmacy. "The joke is, whenever you go to a public meeting," Sajovec said, "you have to do everything in your power to steer them off the two subjects of parking and rats. People have this innate idea that no matter what you're talking about, the number-one thing you should be concerned about is finding free spaces on the street. If your number-one complaint is traffic, and your number-one request is parking, you have to understand how those things are at cross-purposes."

Even metered street parking in Chicago was still a mess, Chrissy thought—it was just a mess with very strict rules about how to clean it up. In 2013, she and a couple other budding parking fanatics, Lindsay Bayley and Jane Wilberding, cruised the streets of Wicker Park looking for parking spaces. In this they were not alone; Wicker Park was a neighborhood where residents often complained about parking. It was a neighborhood where almost 75 percent of the 11,650 street parking spaces were free. It was also a likely candidate for better parking policy: half the area was in Waguespack's district, and he and the neighboring alderman had both asked Rahm Emanuel to reinstate Sunday parking fees after the deal revision.

Chrissy, Lindsay, and Jane wanted for Wicker Park what anyone would want for a neighborhood business district: a park-once strategy. This was a kind of Victor Gruen philosophy adapted to the local level. Unlike auto-oriented strips with proprietary parking lots attached to each business (and sometimes patrolled by predatory tow trucks), neighborhoods with lots of curbside parking could (like malls) allow visiting drivers to park once and then forget their cars all day as they ran errands, roamed around, watched a football game at a friend's place, hit the gym, or attended a music lesson. But Wicker Park could not allow that, because its parking supply was balkanized between free and resident-only curb parking (jam-packed most of the time), private parking lots that belonged to specific businesses (always with space to spare, but only for customers, and empty all night), and metered streets whose high cost and tight two-hour turnover limits ensured that curbs were rarely more than 60 percent full.

Lindsay Bayley worked at the main regional planning organization, the Chicago Metropolitan Agency for Planning (CMAP), where she'd made the pitch that parking should be something regional planners paid attention to. Shoup's book, she said, "opened my eyes. No, the sky is not blue." CMAP couldn't tell the suburbs what to do any more than Chrissy's MPC could tell Chicago what to do, but Lindsay hoped that by taking an informed stance on parking, CMAP could throw its weight behind concerned citizens trying to avoid textbook parking errors—usually in the form of a $30 million brand-new garage, which would sit mostly empty except on special occasions and cost taxpayers for decades to come, when some well-placed parking meters would have sufficed. Old habits die hard. Lindsay could name, instantly and on one hand, the Chicago suburbs with paid parking. In her spare time, Lindsay would do things like ride her bike to the showroom of a new condo building, pretend to be a prospective buyer, and ask where the parking was. She had converted her daughter, who at the age of five would point out bollards and sidewalk bump-outs to her grandparents, and her husband, who worked on renovating an old candy store with no parking.

"This building is for the future," he told a doubting Thomas. "And in the future, everyone who drives will be dead."

Lindsay's intern from the Wicker Park study, Jane Wilberding, had gone on to be a full-time parking consultant like Chrissy. (Working, by the way, for Ana Russi's old boss "Gridlock" Sam Schwartz—parking reform may be a big tent, but it is also a small world.) Jane had grown up in Florida, a kid who hated cookie-cutter sprawl and relished trips to visit her grandmother in New York. Parking, she realized later, explained it all. "In Florida, parking will wipe out anything that's historic. Everything is so new, cheap, fast, and when everything is cut-copy, it creates this super-mundane environment people just want to move through." This was not snobbery, she insisted, but conscious design on the part of her clients, whose corporate strategy called for a frictionless shopping experience. Something so simple as putting the parking lot behind the store, so that the front door and windows abutted the sidewalk, represented an unappealing challenge to the status quo. Often, city parking requirements served as merely the baseline. Developers built extra parking in the hopes of pulling in a big-name retail client like Whole Foods. Whole Foods, for its part, had little interest in getting people to arrive by foot or preserving the urban landscape. On the contrary, drivers would go home with that many more groceries than pedestrians.*

Like many parking consultants, Jane tried to convince her clients that parking was a problem of pricing and management more than of supply. Transportation planning was really behavioral psychology. In July 2020, Jane took me on a bike tour of notable Chicago parking arrangements. Her favorite city view was from the top of a parking garage at a West Side hospital, a client she had helped convince to build more hospital buildings instead of parking garages. Looking out upon the

*Whether this is related to America's food-waste problem is a subject for further research.

long comb of skyline, she recalled conversations with clients. "The patient is like, 'We're sick. Our parking is messed up.' And we go in and we say, 'You're right, you are sick, but it's a matter of: Put signage here. Put the employees there, so that during the one-to-two-hour peak in the mornings, visitors can find spots. Get better technology to show where spots are open. Get some employees here on a shuttle from downtown, where X number of your staff lives within a half mile of these two intersections." And so on. The goal was always the same: save the client from spending millions on a new garage or tearing down an old building for a parking lot. "Parking would be the hip replacement," Jane said, "when you really just need to do a couple bridges every day."

Jane ranked some of the local attractions by their approach to parking. At the bottom was the White Sox ballpark on the South Side, with its ring of lots. "I've tailgated there," she said. "It's fine because you're drunk and you're with your friends, but you have to almost forget where you are to really enjoy yourself. That's what tailgating is. You have your beer, you have your friends, and you pretend you're not in a parking lot." Better sense could be found on the North Side retail corridor Division Street, where she, Lindsay, and Chrissy had succeeded in getting parking meters installed on a lively and busy stretch where drivers once left their cars for seven hours at a time. The new meters gave the city more flexibility with its Wall Street parking overlords, but more importantly, they made it possible to find a parking spot on Division Street by pushing long-term parkers onto the side streets.

Better still was Randolph Street in the West Loop, where the pandemic had prompted the sudden conversion of parking spaces into extravagant outdoor patios. Meters were coming to this part of town soon. "The curb is really the final frontier of parking management. There's going to be a lot of changes," Jane said. Lindsay had a story from this block that made her optimistic: "The perception that it should always be free is changing. I get my hair cut on Randolph, at Salon Lofts. We were talking about parking issues, as I always do. My hairdresser was the first to say, 'I think we need to have meters.' She needs to have a parking spot. And if she needs to get to a client, she's willing to pay for it. And her fellow hairstylists completely agreed! And I just sat there, like, 'This is amazing! Finally!'" It was nice to feel like the message was catching on. Lindsay and Jane were getting ready to launch, in the summer of 2020, the first national group dedicated to better parking policy.

I I I I I

It wasn't just Chicago where the tide was turning. In 2015, a Minneapolis doorman named Chris Meyer bought thirteen copies of *The High Cost of Free Parking*—one for every member of the city council. By 2021, the city had opted to eliminate parking requirements citywide. Meyer was appointed planning commissioner; Ilhan Omar, a staffer for one of the members who received the book, went on to win a seat in Congress, where she is one of at least three Shoupistas.

In Minneapolis, as in other cities, the impetus for reform was part and parcel of a broader reckoning over the racist history of land-use rules. The uprising Ginger Hitzke faced in Solana Beach, it turned out, put that city in impromptu alignment with many communities that had deliberately used parking minimums to banish affordable housing. Deliberately or not, reformers seized on this fact in Minneapolis and elsewhere: more parking meant less housing, and that was reason enough to do away with parking minimums.

When I starting writing this book in 2019, I lived in an area of Chicago called Edgewater. It was one of relatively few integrated areas in a city divided between rich and poor and black and white. In the late 1960s, shortly after the city established its first parking requirements, builders responded by erecting hundreds of short, squat apartment buildings in Edgewater called four-plus-ones. Four stories of apartments; one level of parking on the ground floor.

Community groups revolted. One leader called the four-plus-ones a "blighting time bomb." Mayor Richard J. Daley rushed to rezone the North Side lakefront, but the city council settled for a simpler tool: requiring one parking space for each unit. The four-plus-one boom ended immediately; you just couldn't fit enough spaces to make the projects turn a profit.

But the proliferation of the buildings, with their tiny apartments, left the neighborhood with a lasting stock of workforce housing. It's thanks to the four-plus-ones that Edgewater remains a bastion of diversity on the North Side; in 2020, you could rent an apartment two blocks from the L and four blocks from the lake for just $940—less than half the city average.

Many jurisdictions found their way to this sleight of hand, using parking requirements as a backdoor method of rejecting low-income housing. In 1973, the U.S. Department of Justice sued the city of Parma, Ohio, for racial discrimination, based in part on its very high parking requirement for new apartments. "Rigid enforcement of the 2½ parking space requirement [for each unit]," a U.S. District Court concluded in 1980, "is one of the ways in which Parma has been able to keep all low-income housing out of the community." What makes Parma unusual among American suburbs is only that such a suit was brought.

Consider some of the contemporary parking requirements in the suburbs of Boston. In 2020, Essex, Massachusetts, required 1.5 spaces for every bedroom in an apartment—so a four-bedroom apartment would require *six parking spots*! No one was building four-bedroom apartments in Essex, or any kind of apartments at all. Nearby Wrentham required three spaces for a two-bedroom apartment. Down the road, Danvers required two spaces for a studio.

This is effective because parking is just that expensive to build. In Austin, Texas, Habitat for Humanity has snuck out of sky-high parking requirements by adding an extra bedroom without a closet to a two-bedroom apartment and calling it a "two bedroom plus." No closet, no official bedroom, no parking space required. Not that the child who sleeps there will care.

Beginning in 2017, mandatory minimums were abolished entirely in Hartford, Buffalo, and San Francisco. Developers still built parking, of course. But in the first study of thirty-six projects undertaken since the Buffalo reform, half of new major developments came with fewer spaces than had been required. In Seattle, developers taking advantage of reduced parking minimums built 40 percent less parking than would have been required. Over five years, the reform lowered the cost to build new apartments by approximately half a billion dollars. In 2021, the California statehouse quietly abolished local parking requirements for low-income and senior housing near transit with its "Density Bonus Law." Oregon followed in 2022 with rules to scrap almost all parking requirements in the state's major cities.

You began to hear radical, Shoupian thinking from the strangest places—like from the Department of City Planning in sprawling Atlanta, where director Tim Keane did not mince words. "That has been proven time and again, in every single city in the world that the more parking you provide, the more people drive," he told WABE, the local NPR affiliate, in 2016. "We need to shift now, from a situation like this, where you have a heavy parking load associated with an apartment building in a very urban setting, to way less parking. I hear this all the time. 'Well, we don't want the density unless we get transit.' Well, I've news for you. You really have to start with the density and less parking. If you don't, then you've lost your opportunity, because once you've built that infrastructure, it's so difficult to undo that."

"There's a really direct connection between what we're trying to do on the transit front, and even the parking front, and the city's climate-change goals," Andrew Glass Hastings, the transit and mobility director for Seattle, told KUOW in 2018. "Instead of storing a private automobile in that public right of way all day, we're now able to use it in a way where potentially thousands of people are getting on and off a bus."

Generally, city planners were no match for angry citizens. But now, for the first time, some people were angry about there being *too much* parking. Reforms inspired by the top-down disasters of the urban-renewal era had given councils of concerned citizens ever-greater authority over matters of housing, schools, transportation, and other civic affairs. The power vested in these eager beavers was not necessarily good for democracy, since concerned citizens tended to be old, white, and wealthy. (And parking was often their number-one issue.) But the flip side of this was that any busybody with a copy of *The High Cost of Free Parking* could get up and make a pitch to help save an old mill from the wrecking ball or make the case for counting curb spaces toward the parking requirement for a new group of houses.

Tony Jordan was one such gadfly. He was the most single-minded parking reformer I ever saw, bursting with energy. He sent me messages about parking at all hours and channeled his enthusiasm into a TikTok account, @nofreeparking, where he used costumes, music, and special effects to spread the good word. And Tony wasn't a planner, an architect, or an engineer. He was just a guy who read a blog post about Shoup and asked his wife to order *The High Cost of Free Parking* on Interlibrary Loan to their apartment in Portland, Oregon. This was right after Tony had given up his car, in 2009. "A gateway drug to parking," he said. At home, he looked out at a surface parking lot for a bar. At the office, he looked out on a parking garage. Before long he was testifying at public hearings. He met people. Cyclists. Straphangers. YIMBYs. Tenants' groups. People whose kids had been hit by cars. In 2014, he started the Portland Shoupistas group, also known as Portlanders for Parking Reform. With a membership of more than four hundred, it was the first grassroots parking organization in the country, he boasted. "When you start tweeting about parking, people will find you." He went to a parking conference to debate John Van Horn, the cantankerous publisher of *Parking Today*. John's assessment: Tony was "articulate, thoughtful, and wrong."

Portland had been an early adopter in the trend of rolling back parking requirements: in 2002, the city had relieved builders of parking requirements within five hundred feet of transit. The result was 122 new apartment buildings, half of which had no parking at all. The others averaged less than one space per apartment. Controversy followed. Portland went back and forth on parking policy, reestablishing minimums and then later undoing most requirements. Parking remained a live issue. In 2021, the city's largest preschool, where Tony had sent his own kid, was evicted over a lack of parking.

In 2019, Tony joined the Chicago planners Lindsay Bayley and Jane Wilberding to start the Parking Reform Network. They recruited members from around the country and sent out stickers with Don Shoup dressed up as Uncle Sam: "I want you for the parking reform network." I joined. They sent us copies of *Spot's Parking Lot*, a children's Shoupista text by a member named Bridget Brown, who had started writing the book in her head as she walked past surface parking between the bus stop and her job in Minneapolis in 2002. *Spot* aside, this was supposed to be a grown-up version of the Shoupistas Facebook page—a more formal space for "practitioners," though many practitioners had, like Tony, little more professional planning training than reading Shoup. Then again, neither did their opponents who showed up at community meetings demanding more parking.

Through PRN, I met parking nuts of all stripes. The Honolulu-based activist Kathleen Rooney; Curtis Rogers and Evan Goldin, founders of the shared-parking start-up Parkade; Enrique MacGregor, advocating for parking reform in Dallas. Cary Westerbeck, a PRN member and architect in the Seattle suburb of Bothell who had seen his own projects thwarted by parking minimums, suggested that his local busybody group—Bothellites for People-Oriented Places—should just help people park their cars. He'd start a valet service to park cars around the corner from the restaurants drivers complained never had enough spaces. "We park your car. We'll do it for free! You sign a thing that says, 'I'll never complain about no parking again.'"

The Parking Reform Network Slack was a place to exchange tips and information: Can anyone point me to cities with Residential Parking Benefit Districts? Anyone have experience with hospital parking? How to best handle trash collection when street parking is tight? There were parking reformers from transit-rich cities like San Francisco and Chicago—but also from Austin and Dallas. "Framing the story of parking reform," read one PRN graphic. "Don't say: 'Parking requirements.' The word 'requirements' indicates something is required, implicitly that it is needed. It is also value-neutral. Instead use: 'Costly parking mandates.' Remind people that parking costs money and land to provide. And use the term 'mandates' which implies a heavier hand." This had the additional advantage of not looking like development deregulation to law-loving liberals—and might even tap into genuine, normie anger about beloved trees or buildings felled for huge parking lots.

In September 2020, the Parking Reform Network held its first forum—on Zoom, of course. Jane, Lindsay, and Tony had spent the year balancing the rollout with the twin convulsions of the pandemic in the spring and the antiracism protests of the summer. In August, Tony wrote a piece for *Parking Today*, "Systemic Racism Affects Everything, Parking Is No Exception."

"It's been a crazy year, and it's been difficult to feel like a time when we can expect people to think about things like parking reform," Tony told the assembly. But of course, they *were* thinking about parking reform. "It's great to see everyone who is into parking," Tony continued. "This is the first time I'm doing a parking presentation where I don't have a set of slides explaining Professor Shoup's three tenets. I'm hoping that if you're here you already know! How awesome is this? This is parking-related fun. We've been so excited planning this." They were working on assembling a digital research library and a parking reform "report card"—which was being helped along by an intern, a graduate student at the University of Illinois–Chicago named Andrew Kiefaber. The trio had assembled a group of parking-studies luminaries to make up the board, including Shoup himself, cheery as usual in a blue polo, calling in from Los Angeles. His advice? "Everyone should try and clone Tony Jordan for their city."

By the spring of 2022, their little club had grown to three hundred members. The Slack hummed with activity. They were mapping parking reform, grading cities, assembling a research library. They had partnered with the Singapore-based parking obsessive Paul Barter to make his podcast, *Reinventing Parking*, the official podcast of the PRN. "At times the pace of change, or success, moves like molasses," Lindsay Bayley admitted at one meeting. "I remind myself that Professor Shoup started working on this decades ago, and I feel as though his message is finally catching on." Members were doing things: Detroiters for Parking Reform. Fighting exclusionary parking policy in upstate New York. Parking permits in Denver. Racism and parking reform in LA. Trying to eliminate parking requirements in Edina, Minnesota, and Bend, Oregon.

Lori Droste, a council member in Berkeley, California, had succeeded in a five-year effort to eliminate parking minimums in her city. "Y'all are my kind of people, golly!" she told the assembly. "I can help you figure out how to talk about it to resistant constituents and how to bring people along. What I've tried to emphasize is that this is a very pragmatic, evidence-based approach to address the problems we hear about day in and day out—housing affordability, traffic fatalities." Droste had come to council with receipts: new developments of more than ten units in Berkeley used only 45 percent of all the parking they'd built. Another parking reformer, Patrick Siegman, supported her by making the case that parking reform did not harm people with disabilities, who are less likely to drive but more likely to have trouble finding housing. "Blind people shouldn't have to pay for parking spaces that they don't need and can't use," he wrote.

A reporter from Chicago, Courtney Cobbs, spoke for the group when she said, "I never thought that at the age of thirty one of my passions would be parking policy... but it is, and I'm okay with it."

In 2020, I went to visit the Shoupista factory on the west side of Los

Angeles. After four decades at UCLA, Don had retired in 2015 with a party on the top of the parking garage. Still, the bald, white-bearded economist came to campus most days, to his little office with the parking meter, with its stacks of printouts on the subjects that interested him right then: garage apartments, parking cash-out, the university's transportation-demand program. He still wore a bicycle pin on his lapel, but he didn't bike so much anymore, just occasionally to make sure he could. Instead he walked the two miles through sunny Los Angeles to the lush oasis of campus listening to parking podcasts.

Don taught the world's first university course on parking to a couple dozen undergrads and grad students, cupping a hand over his ear to hear his students' questions. When I visited, Shoup was delivering his introductory lecture on parking. In his tweed jacket and chunky leather shoes, he told the story of the parking meters in Ventura, where Bill Fulton had been roasted by shock jocks. He extolled a social media campaign for parking meters in Mexico City, whose flyers he had run through Google Translate. "Who ever *heard* of voting in favor of parking meters," he exclaimed. The bulk of the session was dedicated to understanding the evolution of parking arrangements around UCLA, of which Don surely has the world's largest collection of photographs. In the wealthy neighborhood across Hilgard Avenue, a parking permit system had left the curbs mostly vacant. "It's a full-time job just to *live* in those houses, but the staff needs someplace to park," he said. Whereas in neighborhoods with student housing, landlords auctioned off the public right-of-way as parking for their tenants. "Private affluence and public squalor, that's what we have in LA."

It was a spiel he must have delivered dozens of times, but zeal lifted his voice with each example, as he lauded the foresight of cities that had seen the light and decried the idiocy of those that had not. Musical, pouncing on the fools, bursting into laughter at one story or another as if, even after all these years, he *still* couldn't believe it had all gone down like this.

He was chuffed by the constant feedback. Thousands of parking apostles, from coast to coast, were trying to turn the page on a century of American city building. They were undoing parking minimums and fighting new public garages; they were drumming up support for parking meters, shared parking, parking benefit districts, bus lanes, bike lanes, and all the rest. Don Shoup's playbook was being put into action, and the results were starting to take shape. From downtown LA to rural New England, free parking was no longer a condition of building. "Cities and regional governments are looking to build more affordable housing, tame traffic, reduce greenhouse gas emissions, and reduce traffic injuries and deaths," Tony wrote in the introductory message to the Parking Reform Network. "As a result, parking policy reform is more vital than ever." In June 2021, Don invited a couple dozen parking reformers to join one of the final sessions of his course, as students presented their reports on a bill in the California legislature that would free all development near transit from parking minimums. The bill passed the State Assembly during the class to applause. A year later, Governor Gavin Newsom abolished parking requirements near transit in California and became the highest-profile politician to elucidate the simple logic behind parking reform. "Basically we're making it cheaper and easier to build new housing near daily destinations like jobs and grocery stores and schools," Newsom said in a video he released when he signed the bill. "This means more housing at lower prices closer to walkable neighborhoods and public transit. Again, reducing housing costs for everyday Californians and eliminating emissions from cars. That's what we call a win-win." Ever the scholar, Don was intrigued by the research opportunities. But he was proud, in his quiet way, to see a lifetime of research change policy in his home state. "It's only been fifty years," the eighty-four-year-old told a reporter. "It makes me feel grateful for longevity."

CHAPTER 12

The Market: Parking after Minimums

Starting around 2015, parking minimums began to fall in city after city. But for every downtown LA, where parking-free architecture burst forth, there was another place where changing the law hadn't changed much at all. Parking still got built. It still drove up the cost of housing and pushed everything apart, and it still sat mostly empty most of the time. Less parking might have saved everyone money, but no retailer or corporate office wanted to hear even a whisper of a parking shortage. More than saving money, what developers wanted was to avoid risk. New housing in urban neighborhoods was hitting the market at such a high price point that the relative cost of a garage looked small compared to its amenity value to millionaire buyers. And bucking the status quo on parking, even when it was allowed, invited conflict with neighbors, banks, government, and clients. The stories of the builders who did build less parking show just how difficult it remained, even when you didn't have to worry about city laws. Putting Shoup into practice wasn't always so simple.

In Austin, Texas, for example, a trio of reformers quietly banished parking minimums from downtown in 2013. But Austin did not have scores of old office buildings to convert, like Los Angeles, and it did not have a robust public transportation system, like Chicago. The wave of parking-free apartments didn't come. Builders kept building as they had before—a sign that the habits formed under seventy years of parking minimums would be hard to unlearn. The office-tower Brancusi was exhibit A. Local real estate people would say, "Even if you don't want parking, you want it for resale." You couldn't build it in later.

Architects had plans to reimpose street grids over the colossal footprints of abandoned malls. With the nation short millions of housing units, there were enough missing apartments to retrofit scores of car-dependent suburbs as walkable neighborhoods. But living without a car remained a sacrifice; even in cities like New York and Chicago you risked cutting yourself out of half the job market. There were only so many American neighborhoods that even had the bones to support a car-free life; those were exactly the neighborhoods where rents were highest, and many barely permitted new housing at all. Parking minimums were not the only thing standing between the status quo and the revival of vibrant, walkable cities.

For a builder, excising even surplus parking was tough. Parking may have been expensive and underused, and the curb right there for the taking, but arguing about it—paying months of interest on a construction loan to fight with the neighbors—was also expensive. Parking cost money, but it bought the acquiescence of politicians, lenders, and neighbors. Builders often concluded that deviation from surplus parking was a risk they were not interested in taking.

The first developer to build without parking in Portland, Oregon, in 2007, had to fly up a credit officer from Wells Fargo in San Francisco so he could see for himself the number of people riding their bikes or taking the bus. When Minneapolis removed parking requirements near transit in 2015, developers were so reluctant to buck convention that the city council president said she couldn't even get their support for repeal.

This happened even in the nation's most densely populated areas. In New York's East Harlem, a mall of 485,000 square feet insisted on building a 688,000-square-foot garage. On a Saturday before Christmas, it was only 38 percent full. In the Bronx, the Yankees threatened to move the team out of New York if the city didn't provide two thousand extra parking spots along with the team's new, smaller stadium, which sits at the intersection of three busy train lines. The city acquiesced, issuing $237 million in tax-exempt bonds to expand the parking system, paving over the neighborhood's last regulation baseball diamonds to do so. By 2020, the garage was so underused that the concessionaire was bankrupt and owed the city more than $133 million.

Sometimes getting the parking right took some trial and error. Target told Washington, DC, it wanted to open its first inner-city store in 2008, but only if the District built the company a 1,000-car garage. (Zoning required 1,700 spaces.) In its first decade of existence, the $47 million structure was never half full. The city rented out spaces to commuters; Target went on to open more urban stores—some, as in the DC suburb of Rosslyn, with zero parking.

Walmart was downsizing its famous parking lots, so expansive the company welcomed RV drivers to pull in and get a little sleep. "Every time we re-evaluate, we pull [the parking requirement] down a little bit," said John Clarke, Walmart's head of real estate. "That means on a big store, we went from 1,200 to 800 spaces. It has a big impact: on the size of land needed for store, the cost of striping and cleaning the parking lots, just to light it at night. It's a significant factor for the facility to have one less stall." Rumor has it that the beloved, secretive grocery chain Trader Joe's also secures leases with less parking—which would constitute both a direct savings and a competitive advantage over peers who require larger and more remote sites. The store's cramped lots have become a comedic touchstone: "May your dreams always be bigger than a Trader Joe's parking lot." "My car insurance doesn't cover the Trader Joe's parking lot." "Oh so you're into BDSM?? Have you ever tried to find parking at Trader Joe's on a Saturday afternoon??" Trader Joe's was the future parking reformers wanted.

To understand the slow pace of change, in the summer of 2020 I went to visit Clay Grubb, a developer who built and operated offices and housing across the Sunbelt. Grubb had given up his Lexus and rode an electric bike, or the bus. For a distant meeting, the millionaire took a cab. That got a look from his associates. "Clay, did you just... get out of an Uber?"

This might have passed for eccentric rich-guy behavior in Chicago or Seattle, but Grubb lived in Charlotte—a sprawling Sunbelt city where not owning a car meant either you were down on your luck or you hadn't turned sixteen. Grubb was fifty-three, and he was not down on his luck.

He was the CEO of Grubb Properties, a 250-person firm that built thousands of apartments in the southeastern United States. The company had pulled in more than a billion dollars for its investors since 2002, for a return of more than 40 percent. Grubb could take his thoughts about the bus fare directly to the head of the transit agency; they met regularly.

Grubb concluded that parking is anathema to housing affordability. That was both because of the cost of building, he told me, and because of the cost of driving: in 2021, Americans spent more than $800 a month or nearly $10,000 a year on new-vehicle ownership, according to AAA. (Median per-capita pre-tax income in Charlotte, for comparison, is $40,000.) The high cost of getting a car for each adult has created a cottage industry of subprime auto loans—high-interest, long-term debt. America's outstanding car balance almost doubled in the ten years between 2010 and 2020, from $740 billion to $1.3 trillion, eclipsing credit card debt, and dealers now make more money on loan interest and insurance than they do selling cars.

In 2020, Grubb won approval to build the first parking-free apartment building in Charlotte in nearly a century. "This is a vote between cars and housing," he told a wary city council. The council chose housing.

For the most part, however, Grubb was not an affordable housing developer in the strict sense, using tax credits to build apartments that get distributed by lottery. He could talk a big game about parking, but his apartments rented on the open market. His tenants had a lot of other choices, in a city that was, by one measure, the sprawl capital of the United States. Of the twenty-five largest metro areas in the country, none had a lower population density than Charlotte.

In 2001, Grubb tried his hand at a mixed-use building—that is, a building with both apartments and stores in the same place. Common in prewar America, such structures had been largely zoned out of existence—while those that endured deteriorated under federal "redlining" rules that made renovation, refinancing, and sale difficult and expensive. His first effort to revive the form in Charlotte was the Latta Pavilion, a pair of sturdy brick buildings of five stories. One was a closed box around a large interior courtyard; the other had an E shape, like the old offices, hotels, and apartments built before air-conditioning that tried to provide as many windows as possible. It was a "new move" for Charlotte, the local paper wrote.

When I visited in 2020, the ground floor of the Latta had a tattoo-removal shop, a barber, a lighting store, a waxing parlor, a nail salon, a restaurant, and a café. In the middle, a driveway opened into the dark mouth of a garage that changed Clay Grubb's life. Here he was trying to build Charlotte into a city, and he was required to spend $13 million on an underground parking garage. What he got for his trouble—a building that looked like it might be in Brooklyn—was a very Brooklyn response: a bunch of retail tenants angry that their customers couldn't find the parking. Cost-wise, his next project was even worse: parking wound up costing $50,000 a stall. And this was in 2002. After those early parking bills came due, Grubb built a model to track how much parking was being used at his projects.

And then he made a breakthrough: he could have his projects share parking spaces between them. Take his office in Charlotte: It was in a boxy concrete office building that shared a garage with his new rental property across the street. Office workers filled up the garage during the day; right as they started to head home, residents arrived.

Why wasn't this model more common? Because if the buildings had different owners, this would have been illegal. But since Grubb dabbled in office and residential, he could double up on the garage. And increasingly, he did. One project from the 2010s in suburban Charlotte was a good example. The office was 110,000 square feet; it required (by law) about 350 parking spaces. The apartment building contained 288 units; it required (by law) about 350 spaces. But by sharing the garage, Grubb knocked 700 spaces down to 480 and saved more than $5 million in capital costs on parking construction. At 480, he's got an extra 130 spots for folks who sleep late or work from home. There was another element working in Grubb's favor here. Instead of paying to operate two separate garages, he just paid for one. He said it cut his annual operating costs by 40 percent.

What Grubb was doing with parking, by mixing offices and residences, was unlocking the same twenty-four-hour efficiencies in one project that are typically associated with big-city neighborhoods. Sidewalks, sewers, streets, and even electrical grids are used more evenly, over the course of a day and a week, in neighborhoods that share homes and offices, schools and restaurants. But shared parking is extremely unusual in the broader world of U.S. development, despite the many complementary uses that don't require parking at the same time (schools and apartments, offices and apartments, banks and bars, and so on).

Charlotte was one of America's fastest-growing cities, a bit of promotion that came echoing through the PA system at the airport every five minutes. Along with "a big city with a small-town feel." For many years, that could have been interpreted to mean: a huge suburb. Which is what Charlotte was. The city was so suburban that a geographer who calculated the orientations of its streets—cul-de-sacs hung from the spokes of farm roads that connected long-gone villages to the county courthouse—found that Charlotte more closely resembled Paris or London (tangled, without rhyme or reason) than any of its orthogonal American peers. With its tiny, gridded downtown and vast hinterland, Charlotte had the urban form of a Triscuit atop a plate of spaghetti.

But the city was changing: Charlotte got a basketball team in 1988, a football team in 1995. The city grew by 35 percent between 1990 and 2000 and *again* by 35 percent between 2000 and 2010. Which means that Charlotte in 2020 was already twice as big as it was when Clay Grubb was a young law-school grad at his parents' company trying to make his mark. No large city in the country grew faster.

From the top of one of his office buildings, Grubb could look down on his own project, Link Charlotte, and the one next door. His was a Texas donut: a six-story apartment building wrapped around a garage.

Across the street from Grubb's property was Novel Montford Park, a rental complex by a rival developer called Crescent Communities. Novel Montford Park looked like Link Charlotte. It too had a seven-story parking garage, but without office workers nearby, this one sat empty all day. "They don't share their parking. They didn't get a subsidy. They have to try to get about $400 a month more in rent than we have to get over here," Grubb said proudly.

Situations like this draw builders into a vicious cycle: Parking garages cost so much money that developers must raise rents. To justify high rents, developers get into an arms race to provide amenities—roof gardens, cycling studios—which add costs. And then before you know it, everything is a "luxury" development. In 2018, Grubb wrote an op-ed for *The Charlotte Observer* where he made the case outright: "If my firm, Grubb Properties, were to build a 300-unit apartment community with moderate rents in downtown Charlotte today it would cost in excess of $75 million. If we could build that same apartment community without having to provide parking, the cost would be closer to $60 million. This $15 million reduction in total cost would allow for an average monthly rent reduction of over $250, making the apartments affordable for a far greater percentage of Charlotteans." Saving $3,000 a year in rent is not an insignificant figure in Charlotte; it would account for about 10 percent of the income of a poorer family.

Grubb had a strategy: he wanted to build affordable housing—not the kind that you need to win a lottery to get, but the kind that can be rented cheap because it was cheap to build. This was a controversial point. Some left-wingers didn't believe that housing was a market good; that rents would fall if development was cheaper; that more housing might mean cheaper housing. In many markets, supply had gotten so tight that new housing was de facto luxury housing because that's what people would pay for it.

Housing scholars countered that people like Clay Grubb occupied a crucial niche in the housing ecosystem. If we consigned the production of affordable housing to subsidized builders whose regulated apartments were rented via lottery, as happens in high-cost cities like New York and San Francisco, we would never come close to achieving the scale of production to fix what was, in reality, an across-the-board housing shortage. Despite the cranes outside your window, the country produced fewer new homes in the 2010s than in any decade since the Second World War. We needed, in other words, more people like Grubb—developers who could provide a nonluxury product, and make money doing it.

Why weren't there more builders like Clay Grubb? There were the neighbors, who labeled his affordable, parking-free project a "monstrosity" and gathered four hundred signatures for a petition about a parking shortage. There were the politicians, who didn't always like their parking codes but certainly relished the power to issue dispensations on a case-by-case basis. Even jurisdictions without parking requirements often required some form of political review, at which the lack of parking became a subject for horse-trading. Grubb had a strategy for them. When he went to purple districts, like the Denver suburb of Aurora, where he planned to build four hundred apartments across from a cluster of hospitals, he played to the "market forces" crowd: "It's a free country. Let me build my apartment building the way I want to, and if people don't want to live here because there's no parking, well, that's my problem." In deep-blue districts, like Charlotte, he played the affordability card: "This project will get more expensive if I have to build parking up to code. Or it won't get built at all."

Most important were the lenders, scrupulously conservative when it came to something so fundamental as parking. That included banks, which viewed deviation from the parking norm with great suspicion. Grubb's faith in a car-free or car-light clientele was not enough to make them believe. If he went under, they'd be left holding the bag.

And it included the Department of Housing and Urban Development, which Grubb considered enemy number one in his quest for leaner projects. Those bureaucratic box checkers, he fumed, had made him add *hundreds* of unnecessary spots to an apartment project near the University of North Carolina in Chapel Hill—a project for which Grubb had enlisted the celebrated Danish firm Copenhagenize to design bike paths and install bus stops. HUD was not on board. And so the parking got built, and the project costs went up by $2 million, and the rents rose by $1,400 a year.

On a subsequent project in Atlanta where Grubb's apartments abutted an office and shared a garage, Grubb simply lied to HUD and told them he would not share parking. "A year or two from now, I may be in jail," he told me in 2020. "They can foreclose on our project, but I was able to get our office lender comfortable."

❙ ❙ ❙ ❙ ❙

Building parking-light offices also required some ingenuity. David Cunningham was the senior director of Dallas-based Granite Properties, which owned about forty commercial office buildings around the country. Cunningham had never heard of Don Shoup; his epiphany came from tensions with his tenants, who started to demand greater and greater amounts of parking with their leases. Many of Granite's older buildings had been built to postwar parking codes in Sunbelt cities like Dallas, Houston, and Atlanta, which meant three spaces per one thousand square feet of office space—a recipe that was already half parking by square foot. Cunningham was concerned. Were buildings built to the code already out of favor with parking-hungry office tenants?

In 2015, Cunningham started counting cars. Every spring, he'd count across the firm's twelve-million-square-foot portfolio for two straight weeks between 10:00 a.m. and 2:30 p.m. No holidays. For every property, he took the busiest garage hour of the two-week stretch. Then, measuring each property's vacancy rate, he scaled up that peak-hour count as if the building were 100 percent leased. The average occupancy across the entire portfolio was 1.9 cars per one thousand square feet of office space. The busiest location, in the suburbs of Atlanta, had 2.6 cars per thousand square feet.

"To further put that into perspective," Cunningham told me in 2020, "we determined that we owned a portfolio of twenty thousand parking spaces. On any given day, approximately half sat vacant. To put it in even greater perspective, when we calculated how much it cost us to build that, it cost us one hundred million dollars *just* to build the vacant ones. One hundred million dollars in investment sitting fallow, nobody using it. And that's just in our portfolio! It's forever wasted. Millions and millions and millions of dollars in concrete and steel waste. It is just obscene.

"Urban Atlanta, that's thirty-eight a space," he said, meaning: $38,000 for every stall in the garage. "Cut five hundred spaces? You do the math. It's twenty million bucks!" This was typical. In Las Vegas, an aboveground parking garage built to code added 50 percent to the cost of the building. In Los Angeles, 32 percent. If the garage was underground, those figures rose by double digits. And as David Cunningham pointed out, tenants often demanded parking allotments that went well beyond the code.

What explained this huge mismatch? These offices were not in Midtown Manhattan; walking there was all but impossible. David determined there were lots of reasons the number of cars in the garage rarely met expectations: sick days, business travel, vacant positions, vacations, working from home (keep in mind, this was before the pandemic). Still, the facilities guy who told firms how to pick parking knew which side his bread was buttered on: he would get fired if there wasn't enough parking, but he'd never have to answer for a lease that was in line with the office market at large. At a highway interchange in North Plano, Texas—an affluent edge city north of Dallas—Granite built a 330,000-square-foot office for mortgage lender Fannie Mae. Fannie Mae insisted on 5.5 spaces per one thousand square feet, nearly twice the Plano code. It would add up to 1,815 spaces for just 1,550 desks. "At the same time," David said, "they were starting to whine about the cost of the project." The exchange went:

> FANNIE MAE: "How can we reduce our costs?"
> DAVID CUNNINGHAM: "Well, how about building 1,550 spots?"
> FM: "How much will that save us?"
> DC: "$4.4 million."
> FM: "Okay."

"We built to four point seven per thousand," David went on. "Still sixty percent more than code. They occupied the entire building, got all their people there, and guess what the maximum number of spaces they ever used? Eleven hundred. It's code. If we'd built just a little north of code, they'd still be fine. But now they've got an additional five hundred stalls there that they spent six million dollars in their lease for fifteen years, car parking they'll never use. And this is far North Plano, *suburbia* suburbia; the only way you can get here is to drive. I guess you could ride a bicycle, but you'd have to cross a few freeways." The Fannie Mae project was hard to forget, because David worked next door, and

Fannie Mae's was one of six garages he surveyed from his office window that never had a single car on the roof. (The view from there did not have the romance of rooftop parking in downtown Chicago.)

Cunningham said his data made a convincing presentation to city planners, who in their hearts often knew that parking minimums were not good policy. Unlike with residential projects, there were no neighbors to placate when you built offices, and he was routinely getting variances to build smaller garages than his rivals. "Architects, across the board, will tell you we've been overparking for years. But they draw what they've been told to draw." Unable to convince corporate tenants to right-size their requests, Cunningham subjected them to a sleight of hand. If a tenant told him they wanted five spaces per thousand square feet, he guaranteed it. And then—the secret to his success—he double-booked their spots, leasing the same spaces to two tenants at once. "Not *once* have we had a tenant unable to park." With a fraction of the money saved on surplus garage construction, Cunningham installed sophisticated parking-management systems to collect data and help commuters find spots.

❙ ❙ ❙ ❙ ❙

Even if you could double-book your office tenants, cajole your lenders, and get a variance from the city code, you might not be done jumping through hoops. That was the experience of Culdesac, a huge, mixed-use development that got underway in 2020 in Tempe, Arizona, a midsize city that borders Phoenix. Culdesac's founders, Ryan Johnson and Jeff Berens, were college roommates at the University of Arizona in Tucson. A decade later, they called their company "the world's first post-car real estate developer."

Armed with a heavily annotated copy of *The High Cost of Free Parking*, the two men secured a sixteen-acre plot near the campus of Arizona State University that they advertised as the first car-free neighborhood built from scratch in the U.S. (In a while, anyway.) The site sat along a light-rail line connecting Tempe to Phoenix, and would include more the six hundred residential units in 167 row house–sized buildings, twenty-four thousand square feet of retail, including a grocery store, and thirty-five thousand square feet of amenities. Those included features like dog parks and shared courtyards that, the pair said, were possible only because the project had been liberated from parking requirements.

This was not a one-off. "Our concept could be ten times bigger," Berens told me in 2019, when the site was just a dirt lot. "Transportation is innovating; real estate hasn't caught up." The offer on the table for Culdesac's future residents: lose your car, gain a neighborhood. Johnson did not own a car himself. Tempe, he liked to say, has a higher population density than Austin or Boulder, Colorado. But the idea was supposed to be applicable in other cities, too. Tempe was just the beginning.

Still, to get the project past the local government, Culdesac had to do something unprecedented: make residents affirm in the lease that they would never park a car here or in the adjacent neighborhood. Culdesac residents cannot make use of the public right of way as their neighbors do, or they risk eviction. It's an extraordinary concession, but that's what it took to get apartments without parking spaces approved in the Valley of the Sun.

These three endeavors—Clay Grubb's apartment buildings, David Cunningham's offices, and Culdesac's master-planned neighborhood—showed the challenges of moving forward without parking, even if you could get around municipal laws. But they also showed that parking-free or parking-light development had a shot in the car-dependent Sunbelt, which was anything but incidental. Streetcar urbanism in Minneapolis and San Francisco might have been an easier target for reformers, but the real work of giving Americans the right to walk would have to come in the sprawl. That's mostly what we had. And sprawling cities like Phoenix and Charlotte were the places that were growing the fastest, thanks to their sunshine and low housing costs.

Retrofitting suburbia was going to be hard, but there was reason for optimism about a future in which families might move from three to two cars, or two to one: Journeys to work accounted for just 15 to 20 percent of trips, even before the pandemic. More than half of all trips in the U.S. were under three miles. In other words, half of all trips could be accomplished on foot, on a bike, or on a small electric vehicle, if roads were designed for that kind of travel. A surprising number of Americans already lived within half a mile of a retail cluster of more than twenty-five establishments, even in drive-alone cities. The share was 31 percent in Las Vegas, 40 percent in Atlanta, 55 percent in Los Angeles, and 67 percent in Miami. That number would grow if parking could be decoupled from housing and retail. Meanwhile, the rise of remote work, e-commerce, and small electric vehicles like e-bikes and scooters made car-light living easier than ever.

There was another thing: the root cause of 2021's hockey-stick home price appreciation, escalating rents, overcrowding, and homelessness was that the country was millions of homes short. Where and how we built them wouldn't just change the way their future occupants lived. They could also change the way whole neighborhoods functioned, by creating the tax revenue, consumer power, and critical mass to support transit service, a grocery store, a café, or a day care. There were ideas about how to retrofit suburbia in big ways: megadevelopments like Culdesac, housing built over dead malls, street grids traced across acres of parking. The biggest idea of all might have been one that was all but invisible from the street: taking over the garage.

CHAPTER 13

How Americans Wound Up Living in the Garage

At the start of 2020, José Trinidad Castañeda was living with his mom. Reluctant to drain his savings in a rental market where a one-bedroom apartment went for north of $1,500 a month, Trinidad Castañeda shared a small house with his mother and two sisters. This made him typical of his generation: Even before COVID-19, 46 percent of eighteen-to-twenty-nine-year-olds lived with their parents. After COVID-19, that figure rose to 52 percent—the highest mark since the Great Depression.

What made José atypical was that the hypothetical apartment that was out of his reach was not one in Boulder, Colorado, or Washington, DC, or Cambridge, Massachusetts, to name just a few cities where high rent has forced young people into cramped, shared quarters. He was living in Orange County, California—land of the ranch house and the three-car garage, the crucible of modern American conservative politics, and not a well-known destination for the young and hungry. This was a place where generations of exiles from the country's eastern half had arrived, eager to abandon the problems of the older cities—racial conflict, the counterculture, high taxes, Democratic politicians. Trinidad Castañeda's hometown, Fullerton, is where Richard Nixon went to high school. Liberals used to complain that Orange County, the place "all good Republicans go to die," in Ronald Reagan's words, had exported its pious, antigovernment politics of white grievance to the country at large. But in recent years, Orange County had become more like the places its residents once sought to escape. In 2016, Orange County voted for the Democratic nominee for president, for the first time since 1936. In 2018, Democrats swept the county's seven congressional seats. The county had become majority minority, and 30 percent of its residents were foreign born. The orange curtain separating these suburban idylls from Los Angeles to the north had come tumbling down, and with it, one cycle of big-city problems in particular had arrived: high housing costs, overcrowding, and homelessness.

When I visited Trinidad Castañeda in February 2020, the California presidential primary was just a couple weeks away, and he had his hands full. In a café in downtown Fullerton, he ordered an iced dirty chai with oat milk and searched for an outlet to charge his dead HP laptop. No sooner had he found a seat against the wall than he was rushing up again—out the door, across the street, into the trunk of his car. "Don't even look at that mess," he said, grabbing a black shoulder bag full of campaign materials and heading back inside. This was how it went: one minute someone was asking him about the beaded starburst pouch of white sage around his neck—"It's a good conversation piece," he said later—and the next he was stumping, talking up his two simultaneous political campaigns, for the Orange County Democratic Central Committee and for Fullerton City Council. Like presidential candidates, he referred to his election in the definite future: "When I win my city council race..."

In a way, with his leather shoes, black slacks, and crisp white button-down, he was out of place here, in this café near the campus of Cal State Fullerton. No one else was wearing a button-down shirt; the other patrons were dressed in Kobe Bryant jerseys and tank tops, grinding away on term papers or chatting with friends. On the other hand, this crowd represents his Orange County. No one here was white. Like Trinidad Castañeda, they were the children and grandchildren of the immigrants who settled Orange County in the seventies, eighties, and nineties—Mexican, Korean, Indian, and Vietnamese Americans. They were coming of age in a suburban city that had gone from being two thirds Anglo in 1990 to one third Anglo in 2020, mirroring countywide trends. Trinidad's whole extended family lived in Fullerton. His relatives were in the Lemon Street Murals, a local Chicano artwork. In 2008, a white city council member tried to get the murals erased, arguing that the imagery would make people associate Fullerton with gang activity. Today they're being restored by local artists and city grants.

Like Los Angeles to the north and San Diego to the south, Orange County was experiencing a severe housing affordability crisis in 2020, one that got worse and worse every year. The median house sold for $730,000 in 2019, making homeownership affordable to just 15 percent of the population. This was a policy issue for Trinidad Castañeda. He advocated for a Safe Parking Program, which made Fullerton the first city in Orange County to open a commuter lot to homeless Californians sleeping in their cars. He helped convince the city to abolish its fees on accessory dwelling units (ADUs), also known as backyard cottages, granny flats, or garage apartments, which led to local ADU permits jumping from three in 2018 to forty-four in 2019.

It was also a personal issue. It would take the thirty-year-old almost fifteen years of his nonprofit salary to afford the median house in Orange County and take his place among his aunts and uncles and cousins in the neighborhood. Trinidad Castañeda was not the first person to have this problem. Housing has been expensive in coastal California for a long time. Because the predominant California neighborhood is composed of single-family homes, it's tough for anyone who's not in a traditional, nuclear family to find a place that's even the right size, let alone the right price. There were two areas in Fullerton with apartment buildings, where Orange County's young teachers and firefighters doubled and tripled up in apartments, as if this were the tightly packed Mission District of San Francisco and not the unending sprawl of the Southland. Fortunately, almost every single one of those sprawling homes—and certainly most of the one-story ranch homes in Fullerton—had a large, separate space that had never really been used as intended: the garage. Which was where Trinidad Castañeda was planning to live.

Trinidad Castañeda has a wide face, a politician's bright smile, and jet-black hair that's long on top and buzzed on the sides. He drove his Hyundai in the erratic fashion of a man whose city is rolling by the windows a little too fast for his own tour. Here a friend who asked José to build her a backyard rental unit. There a neighbor with an illegal ADU. Here José's uncle, who would like to move his grandmother into an ADU; José said he'll build it for them when he's done with his own. "All of them want to do this." His mom's place, where he was living at the time: that garage could be a two-bedroom. One more illegal ADU—a Filipino family was living there. How does he know this? "They love me; they want me to marry their daughter. That's not going to happen." But he might help them get their illegal ADU on the books. "I don't like to say illegal," he corrected himself. "Unpermitted."

José's father, a Mexican immigrant who worked as a cardiac technician at a hospital, owned a place on a quiet street here that he was renting to a family of Mexican immigrants. This was where Trinidad Castañeda was raised before his parents split up. It was a modest house, beige with a brown roof, palm tree in the front yard. Trinidad Castañeda was not a fan of palm trees. "Ecologically useless," he scoffed. He was working on an urban forest management plan for Fullerton and rattled off a list of native, drought-ready plants. In addition to running for city council and the county Democratic committee, he drew his salary as an organizer at an environmental nonprofit and was also helping his dad restart his side hustle, a restaurant that burned down after an illegal marijuana greenhouse next door caught fire on New Year's Eve. In short, José Trinidad Castañeda was possibly the busiest man in Orange County. He was up with the sun and still up long after it set. A good number of the issues that motivated him, though—transportation, housing policy, immigration, energy—were entangled in this seemingly obscure issue of legalizing garage apartments. "I don't see the need to use garages to store cars," José told me. "The street is fine. I don't understand why we need the car inside. The weather is always good, and it's not going to rain."

The garage at his childhood home was easily the size of a small studio apartment: five hundred square feet. Trinidad Castañeda got a home equity line of credit for $50,000 and drew up his own plans. He downloaded and taught himself AutoCAD, the architectural drafting software, and fiddled with his designs until his computer got so hot he had to put it in the refrigerator. The tenants in the house, whom he'd known for years, were happy to park their two cars in the driveway in exchange for low rent. "I've always had dreams of building the ADU," Trinidad Castañeda said, as we perspired in the stuffy air of the garage, which smelled of laundry detergent and motor oil. "I want a Murphy bed. I want to have meetings, do organizing."

He drove to a contractor nearby, wind chimes rattling below his rearview mirror as he swung the car across traffic, jumping from one idea to the next. "I watch a lot of the Netflix shows—*Tiny House Nation*, the interior design competition. But when you can see it up close it's different." He had come to Horizon Remodeling once before, looking for inspiration. No one had time to talk. This time, he wanted to know if his advocacy at the city council—getting the city's ADU fees eliminated—had helped their business. It had.

He ran a hand over a splash guard of dark glass tiles in an offset pattern. He liked that. "One of the ideas from the shows is for tiling to break up the wall paint. They capture some of the sunset light. The windows will hit the kitchenette from the southwest side; it'll be really nice to capture some of the sunset colors." He had wood-panel flooring stored from his parents' renovation, but if there wasn't enough, he would go for linoleum tiling (easier to clean) with some rugs. He looked over a shower the size of a small car. "That's pretty big." A marble countertop, he thought, was too much. "Yeah... we're probably not going to do this." He wanted to spend $25,000 to $30,000, which would be on the very low end for an ADU conversion. The line of credit went to $50,000. But when you did things yourself, you could cut some corners.

"Moving there will give me a chance to, not so much start over, but really come into my own as a community leader," he explained later. "Without the baggage of 'Oh, you're a millennial, you live with your parents, whatever.' It wipes that away." José was a levelheaded guy, but it drove him crazy the way the older homeowners would write him off as some kind of illegitimate candidate: He was a native son. He'd played youth soccer with the Fullerton Rangers and Little League baseball with the West Fullerton Terminators. He'd been a parks and rec commissioner and served on the community emergency response team. He'd helped get a park built. So what if he was going to live in a garage?

❚ ❚ ❚ ❚ ❚

There are more than eight million single-family homes in California. They are the state's architectural DNA, not just a building style but a foundation of California culture, a determinant of how the government functions, the way people get around, the neighbors you have, and the neighbors you don't. Thomas Pynchon wrote of the mystical experience of seeing them from above: "She looked down a slope, needing to squint for the sunlight, onto a vast sprawl of houses which had grown up all together, like a well-tended crop, from the dull brown earth; and she thought of the time she'd opened a transistor radio to replace a battery and seen her first printed circuit. The ordered swirl of houses and streets, from this high angle, sprang at her now with the same unexpected, astonishing clarity as the circuit card had. Though she knew even less about radios than about Southern Californians, there were to both outward patterns a hieroglyphic sense of concealed meaning, of an intent to communicate."

Dana Cuff, the director of the cityLAB research center at UCLA, had gotten a message. "When you think about the housing and environmental crises, the two biggest dilemmas out there in my mind," she told me on the phone in 2020, "the suburbs are where they can be solved." She began with a radical idea: Los Angeles ought to be twice as dense as it is now. For four decades the city had been doing its best to move in the opposite direction, paring the legally buildable skyline of neighborhood after neighborhood back to chimney height. And while legalizing three- and four-unit houses had become a popular target for activists in Minneapolis and Portland, it was hard to imagine homeowners in Los Angeles letting that happen here.

Inspired by the wave of historic conversions that had taken place in downtown LA, Cuff proposed bringing that laissez-faire attitude toward parking to an underused, historic structure far more common than the downtown office building: the home garage. California had passed a law permitting accessory dwelling units in 2003, but various local rules, and in particular the associated parking requirements—you had to add parking for the new unit *and* replace the parking lost from the converted garage—rendered the law all but unused. It was easy enough to renovate an old garage but impossible to find three additional parking spaces on your property. This state-local tension was a persistent feature of California housing politics. The state had first required cities to adopt ordinances permitting so-called second units back in 1981. In Los Angeles, however, to get approval for an accessory dwelling unit required a public hearing and a nonrefundable $1,900 application fee (more than $4,000 in 2020 dollars). The country's second-largest city issued only two dozen such permits a year.

In 2016, Cuff and California State Assembly member Richard Bloom cowrote a bill that would *really* legalize ADUs throughout the state, with or without parking if within a half mile of a bus stop or train station. The rule covered most of Los Angeles and much of its suburbs. It passed easily the following year. Cuff was not modest about what they had quietly accomplished: "It's not only that we've doubled the density of the state of California, we've eradicated single-family home zoning." Eighty percent of residential land in Los Angeles had been zoned exclusively for single-family homes. You could double the families now. Cuff thought it represented the biggest new market for residential real estate since the postwar suburban boom.

Single-family zoning was supposed to be the great, untouchable foundation of American local politics. The 2016 ADU law had undone it across California with the promise of infill growth that would be all but invisible—what advocates would come to call "stealth density." Still, for its proponents, the reform offered many of the same benefits associated with more dramatic efforts to liberalize land use in and around U.S. cities. Cheaper housing units in high-opportunity neighborhoods. Higher densities that would enable more local commerce, better public transit service, and more walkable areas. Rental income to help aging homeowners stay in empty-nest houses. Smaller units for older residents looking to downsize in their own neighborhoods, or for on-site caregivers. Privacy and affordability for young adults.

Abolishing local parking codes turned out to be the key that distinguished the law Cuff wrote from the failed effort fourteen years prior. In California, big-city ADU permits rose from 654 in 2016 to 8,785 in 2018. In Los Angeles, in particular, homeowners jumped at the opportunity. Citywide ADU permits rose from 254 in 2016 to 5,429 in 2018. The units were concentrated in the Valley—the suburban expanse north of the Santa Monica Mountains. More than 2,400 ADUs were classified as "conversions," usually from existing garages. Another big chunk of the permits simply replaced an obsolete garage with a small house.

This meant that *one in five* new permitted housing units in the entire city of Los Angeles in 2018 was built in someone's literal backyard. At least one in ten was crafted out of a garage or replaced one. Both categories, evidently, were dependent on the 2017 state preemption law, liberated from the poison pill that was the parking requirement.

Cities fought back with fees, permit delays, and other cumbersome procedures. But in 2019, the California state legislature went further. New, comprehensive laws allowed additional "junior ADUs" on some lots. They mandated a sixty-day approval. They quashed fees for ADUs of less than 750 square feet. They preempted homeowners' associations and deed restrictions. They made sure cities would not impose owner-occupancy requirements. And they forced cities to allow garage conversions near mass transit without new parking spaces.

I I I I I

From an aesthetic standpoint, the golden age of the American residential garage coincided with the development of the first automobiles. Early cars may have been rich men's toys, but they were also fickle and dangerous machines requiring daily professional upkeep, and their storage reflected this marriage of status and risk. In 1906, *House Beautiful* showcased some of the more handsome designs: Colonial, Tudor, and Craftsman-style garages, often accessed through a fanciful arch modeled after the porte cochere of Parisian hotels. "Few subsequent designs surpassed them in size and dignity," wrote the architectural historian J. B. Jackson in 1976. "A second story accommodated the chauffeur; the storage space itself was large, well-lighted, and efficiently planned, often with a turntable (to eliminate having to back out), an overhead hoist, and a pit. This last feature disappeared when cars were designed to give access to the motor from under the hood instead of underneath.... Only after the chauffeur had cranked the motor into action, tested the sparkplugs and the tension of the leather fan belt, checked the oil and poured in a gallon or two of gasoline did the car, figuratively speaking, join the family."

We can watch the home garage racing toward its modern form in the buildings of Frank Lloyd Wright, whose evolving accommodations for cars anticipated and influenced national building trends. In 1910, Wright completed a tank of a house on Chicago's South Side for local businessman Frederick C. Robie. Wright's three-bay garage, accessed through a courtyard, may have been the first attached garage in an American house. (He had tried to put a garage in the basement of an earlier project, the Cheney House, only to see his plans repeatedly rejected by the city council.) At the Robie House, Wright's garage was distinguished from the rest of the Prairie-style house only by its wide, out-swinging doors. Inside he dug out a mechanic's pit and installed a station for washing the car and cleaning its components. The ceiling was concrete, in case of accidents. The attached garage was a status symbol that implied the owner could afford elevated fire insurance rates. Even in 1919, it was rare enough that a writer could note, "Putting a garage in a house may sound like a joke, but it is not."

It would have sounded like a joke to many urban Americans. As late as 1936, only one in four *new* houses had attached garages, according to a survey in *American Architect*, to say nothing of those built in the previous decades. Even the few American city dwellers who owned their own houses lived on narrow, deep lots offering just twenty-five feet of street frontage and stretching back one hundred feet. The garage was therefore located in an independent structure at the back of the lot, abutting the service alley in cities like Chicago or joined to the street by a pair of concrete tire paths in cities like Los Angeles. This, J. B. Jackson wrote, was "an unsightly arrangement, and it had the effect of completing the ruin of the backyard."

And the backyard *was* a ruin. Covered in asphalt or gravel, the area behind the house was "a utilitarian space where trash was burned, clothes were washed and hung up to dry, and unneeded household items were left to rust." It was in front of the house that children played, in the yard or in the street, in view of the neighbors. The border between private and public space was the porous alcove of the front porch, a place for supervising those kids, flirting with a classmate in the respectability of the public view, snooping on neighbors doing the same, or adroitly greeting relatives or salesmen who weren't quite welcome inside the domestic sanctum. This was the function of George Washington's long front porch at Mount Vernon—to greet, in a shady chair that supplied a veneer of hospitality, an endless stream of callers who weren't welcome inside.

In the 1920s, the backyard began to supersede the front porch as the primary domestic outdoor social space. This switch would be accelerated by the arrival of indoor enjoyments like television and air-conditioning, as well as appliances like washers and dryers, which freed the backyard from its workaday purpose, but it began with the automobile. Prior to widespread car ownership, streets were multifunctional public places suitable for hawkers and markets, stickball games and snowball fights, the storage of construction materials, and waste disposal. The roaring car traffic associated with Henry Ford's Model T cemented the street's sole purpose as a thoroughfare. The children's book *The Wind in the Willows* offers an early glimpse of the way drivers navigated the terrain. Behind the wheel emerges "Toad at his best and highest, Toad the terror, Toad the traffic queller, the lord of the lone trail, before whom all must give way or be smitten into nothingness and everlasting night." The suburban cul-de-sac was the fruit of newly widespread car ownership—and a refuge from it. In 1922, *House Beautiful* noted strains of front porch fatigue: "the increase in motor-traffic, the dust and proximity of other houses tend to make the front porch less desirable each year . . . One prefers [porches] turned away from the trivial drama of the street with its hucksters and milk wagons and gossip." At the Tenth National Conference on Housing in 1929, one speaker declared that the dirty old backyard, of all places, could be repurposed to offer "charm and sanctuary from a too noisy world"—away from "front porch promiscuity."

But it was less the question of how cars moved than of where to keep them that changed the shape of the American house. This shift from front porch to backyard coincided with the forward march of the garage, out of the backyard and into the house itself, as the car (later, cars) assumed its prime place in family life. Wright led the way. With his Usonian houses, a series of middle-class dwellings he designed beginning in the 1930s, America's foremost architect invented a new word, *carport*, to describe an attached, sheltered overhang for car storage. This innovation is traditionally credited to Wright's employee and contemporary Walter Burley Griffin, who included a breezeway for car storage in a 1910 house in the Chicago suburbs, but it took another two decades for Wright to begin preaching the gospel of carports to the nation. In Wright's hands, carports made a seamless addition, nestled in the shadows beneath his great, horizontal cantilevers. He preferred the carport to the attached garage for the same reason he disliked basements: closed garages were likely to become just another place to gather household clutter.

Nevertheless, the implements of the closed, attached garage were all in place and awaiting the postwar housing boom. Overhead garage doors were commonplace by the 1910s, electric garage door openers by the 1930s. Early subdivisions may not have had interior spaces for cars—at the most famous of them, Levittown, east of New York City, the entire house was barely the size of a modern three-car garage—but the attached garage became de rigueur in the 1950s as mass-transit ridership plummeted and the car reinforced its dominance. The result was the most fundamental change to the structure of the American house in centuries. In addition to its superlative size, the garage became the preferred entry point to the house, relegating the front door to ornamental obsolescence. The effect of this huge, liftable white wall, when joined with a pair of windows above, was almost human. James Howard Kunstler wrote that the garage door gave new houses a "slack-jawed" mien. In later tract-home models, the garage was the lone street-facing element of the house. Now it was the human door accessed via side path—a perfect role reversal from the early-twentieth-century bungalow.

With the wicker chairs and painted spandrels of the porch relegated to photo ops in older houses and replaced by the blank door of the garage in newer ones, the gateway had become a barrier. Flirtation and courtship, in Beth Bailey's memorable phrase, moved "from front porch to back seat." As much as half of what had once been the front lawn was now occupied by a wide, concrete apron of driveway, a place for Dad to wash the car, teenagers to play H-O-R-S-E, or Mom to catch the last minutes of what NPR editors call a "driveway story"—a segment too good to turn off. "What the stork's nest on the chimney of the northern European home traditionally signified," wrote Jackson, "the basketball backstop over the garage door signified for the American home: a child-oriented domesticity." Together with the eternally unoccupied curb and the garage interior, this driveway could take the home's parking capacity up to six or seven spots in a pinch. Here, parked at home, the American car would spend more than half its life.

Americans and their architects have always been miles apart on the question of whether such garage-forward houses are practical or irredeemably gauche. Even those architects who otherwise celebrate single-family-home neighborhoods, however, generally want to make the garage a less prominent feature of the landscape. (In urban settings, home garages do not even add to the parking supply so much as privatize it, removing street spaces in favor of garage access.) Architects worried about the look and about the types of streets they were creating. In 1999, planners in Portland, Oregon, developed zoning laws to require the car house be subordinate to the human house, dubbing the garage-thrusting style the "snout house" because the garage stuck out toward the road like the nose of a pig. "Basically, we want a house to pass the 'trick or treat test,'" City Commissioner (later mayor) Charlie Hales said at the time. "So when kids come around to trick or treat, they actually get a sense that somebody lives in the house, and they can find the door. Imagine that." Halloween offers perhaps the best opportunity to imagine how lively those early suburban streets would have been on a hot summer night. But kids are clever, and in some suburbs, the little ghouls beg for candy at the garage door instead.

Another bit of wisdom from Wright, who would go on to pass off a glorified garage ramp as the world's most iconic art museum: the garage *would* fill up with stuff. On a trip to Los Angeles in the winter of 2020, I stayed in the garage of a 1917 Craftsman bungalow in Hollywood. As with many early-twentieth-century houses, the little one-car garage was set at the back of the lot, accessed by a long, narrow alley along the lot line. Inside were a bed and a washer and dryer, adding a private fourth bedroom to the house. One parcel south, the garage was a home office. One north, I heard the muffled sounds of band practice.

I had forgotten, until that moment, that America developed a whole genre of music named for the fact that we don't actually need to park our cars in our garages. Buddy Holly had supposedly given birth to garage rock in Lubbock, Texas, but Southern California's ubiquitous car holes would go on to nourish bands like Weezer, Incubus, Blink-182, and Linkin Park. California had the additional lore of the garage as a place where dreamers could retreat with their big ideas; Disney, Mattel, Hewlett-Packard, and Apple are some of the companies that claim to have been founded in a California garage.

This role of the garage as a workshop, closet, and rumpus room is foreshadowed in the word itself, a French coinage that initially referred to a storage space, with the French root *gar-* a cousin of the English *war-* as in *warehouse*. One reason Dana Cuff thought garages could be the place to double California's population density was that no one seemed to actually park their cars inside them. In a 2012 study of thirty-two California families, researchers found that just eight of them stored the car in the garage—for the rest of them, the garage was too full of *stuff.* The instant familiarity of the "garage sale" is a reminder of the room's primary household function, an eddy in the stream of domestic life.

As tempting as it was to crank up the amps or start the Uber of pet food, the most important innovation in garage use was far and away people *living* in them. This trend found cultural expression in the TV show *Happy Days*, in which Fonzie lived over the garage, but has become more widespread in the twenty-first century as housing costs outpace incomes. By data-mining real estate listings for words like *casita*, *guest suite*, and *in-law quarters*, researchers at Freddie Mac determined that in 2020 the United States had 1.4 million ADUs. First-time listings of properties with ADUs were growing by more than 8 percent each year. In 2000, fewer than nine thousand U.S. homes sold included an ADU. By 2019, that was up to seventy thousand. Not surprisingly, the ADU inventory was highest in California, Florida, Texas, and Georgia—states where the housing stock is heaviest on single-family homes. ADUs offer a much-needed alternative, especially in minority neighborhoods.

Still, most of them are probably illegal. And because of that, estimates remain woefully imprecise. In some of Cuff's fieldwork, she found neighborhoods of Los Angeles where three in every four houses had illegal ADUs. One project looking at home sales estimated twenty-five thousand unpermitted units in Los Angeles County. After fifty years of prioritizing parking over housing, people were righting the imbalance themselves. They would live in the garage. Or even in the parking lot.

In Southern California, the phenomenon had taken off in earnest in the 1980s, when the *Los Angeles Times* estimated that approximately forty-two thousand garages were sheltering two hundred thousand people

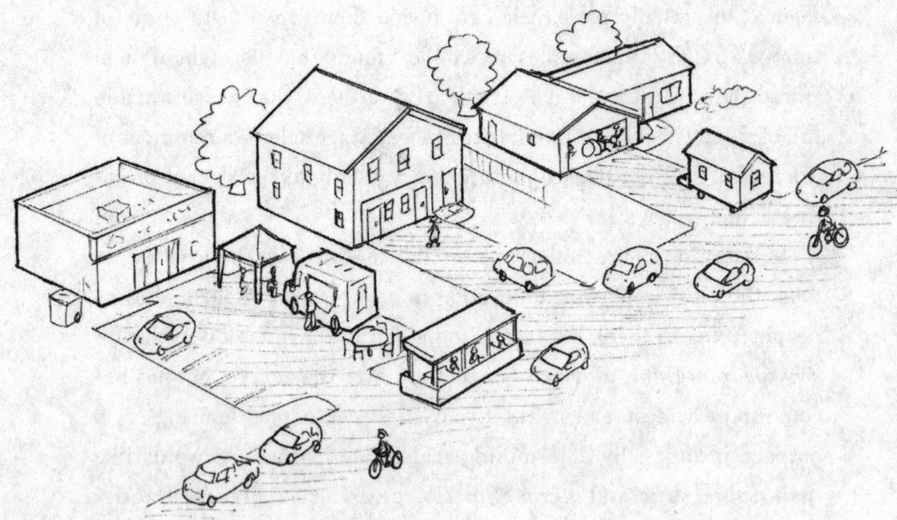

That garage units had become so common was evidence of the astonishing arbitrage between parking (required at every house, unused by most, with little market value) and housing (forbidden in most neighborhoods, desperately needed, and worth much more).

countywide. In South Gate, a small city east of Compton, city surveys suggested that one in five residents was living illegally in a garage. The city evicted hundreds of families every year. "Displacing people is wrong," Reverend Ben Vinluan, a Methodist minister who headed the South Gate Ministers Association, told the paper. But the greater wrong, he said, was to have "illegal aliens living in your garage to collect money."

That garage units had become so common was evidence of the astonishing arbitrage between parking (required at every house, unused by most, with little market value) and housing (forbidden in most neighborhoods, desperately needed, and worth much more). People complained about parking, of course, but no one would ever pay very much for it. But housing was a different story. New arrivals to the Southland,

Mexican and Central American immigrants in particular, desperately needed cheap accommodations. The amplest resource available to them was the Southern California garage. Because these dwellings were unpermitted, tenants often put up with substandard conditions and lived at the mercy of their landlords.

After the Great Recession, a starker arbitrage emerged between the West Coast's supply of parking and its supply of housing: homeless people sleeping in their cars. In 2019, more than sixteen thousand people were living in their cars in Los Angeles County. The City of Los Angeles developed an alternative to homeless shelters called "safe parking," supervised parking lots where homeless people could park and sleep without fear of being arrested, robbed, or assaulted. Long Beach City College created a program for students to sleep in its parking lot. Cities like San Diego, Seattle, and Phoenix (as well as smaller municipalities like Palo Alto and Encinitas, California) developed similar programs to meet the need. José Trinidad Castañeda helped create the one in Fullerton. In Las Vegas, during the early days of the COVID-19 pandemic, the city turned over a parking lot to homeless people in tents, giving everyone a parking space to live in.

At the same time, cities tuned up parking regulations to criminalize vehicular homelessness—or at least push people sleeping in their cars into out-of-the-way areas like industrial zones. In 2019, Los Angeles banned sleeping in vehicles on residential streets or within a block of a park or school (an earlier, blanket prohibition had been struck down in federal court). Fremont, California, placed boulders along a frontage road near the Tesla factory to discourage people from sleeping in cars or trailers. Missoula, Montana, banned overnight parking near the airport. Across the western United States, a housing shortage and a parking surplus had produced a tragic but unsurprising compromise.

One reason that garage conversions made for successful policy in places like California and Oregon was that they sounded like DIY projects, merely a step up from a backyard toolshed, embedded in the notion that a man's home is his castle and the yard his domain. Once the barriers were lifted, however, ADU construction in Los Angeles became the Wild West. Contractors staple-gunned advertisements onto telephone poles. Architects changed their practices to respond to the new market. Start-ups backed by Silicon Valley claimed they could convert a garage to a home in just twenty-eight days and aimed to make that work at scale—adding thousands of backyard homes every year.

For José Trinidad Castañeda, the project in Fullerton was not taking twenty-eight days. He'd been to Home Depot practically twenty-eight times. He came to the house almost every day of 2020 but struggled to balance all that he'd taken on. He'd dropped out of his city council race, focused on a special election slated for the following year. And the ADU was behind schedule. He had wanted to finish it in June, with a hard deadline on the Fourth of July, but he had completed only an outdoor shed for the washer and dryer. His father's tenant, Marvin, was a contractor, and José had hired him to work on the house.

Compromises were made. The garage opened on the side, and José had hoped to pull the street-facing wall out by several feel, expanding the footprint inside. "That was not the way I wanted it to go," he said that summer. But not doing that structural work, he said, also lowered the total project cost by a factor of five. The kitchen had been flipped to the other side of the unit; there would be no sunset glow on the backsplash. They would still be adding a larger window. "I value maintenance more than aesthetics," he said. What he saved on interior fixtures he would make up for with plants to enliven his new home.

But his sense of purpose was still strong. One day he had arrived early to a meeting with Marvin, who was himself trying to rent out one of the rooms inside the house. An elderly couple, mistaking him for Marvin, thought that he was putting the garage up for rent. Valerie was from Puerto Rico; Agosto from the Dominican Republic. They had lived in the neighborhood for three decades, working for the past five years as caretakers for an elderly woman nearby. When she passed away, her daughter evicted them. "Oh, we could get a dog!" Valerie told her husband, imagining their life in the new garage apartment and tearing up in front of José, who then had to explain the mistake. This was going to be his house, not theirs. "I wanted their dream to come true too," he said later. They wound up paying $1,000 a month for a single bedroom.

CHAPTER 14

Planting Gardens in the Gutter

Right as the need for housing began to muscle out parking space in California's home garages, another bastion of car storage was coming under attack. This was the curb. There was hardly a more obvious place to look if you wanted to find room for the functions of a modern city. Relative to the history of the street, the omnipresent banks of parked cars on each side were a relatively recent phenomenon. The land was worth a lot, to lots of different people, and at the beginning of the twenty-first century a wave of prospectors came upon the curb with new visions of what could or should happen there. This chapter chronicles their rise to power. The curb had long been treated the way cities saw their waterfronts: a free-for-all, a dumping ground, and little more. But waterfronts had been reassessed. Many people saw gold in the curb, too.

Few places have a greater gap between the sticker price and hidden value of a parking space than California, but one of them is New York City. The city's curbside parking wasn't just the cheapest in the nation compared with nearby garage prices. It also offered some of the best rent bargains in the world, if you wanted to do anything but store a car there. The price gap between a Manhattan storefront rent and the public asphalt plot that lay across the sidewalk had fascinated observers going back to William Phelps Eno, the inventor of the traffic light. (Prior to Eno and the automobile revolution, this opportunity was less obvious, since streets were used for a variety of commercial and leisure purposes—the city had, since 1761, required vendors to move every half hour.) Based on the rate a wig seller paid a store owner to operate on the sidewalk in front of his shop in 1977, at the city's economic nadir, William H. Whyte concluded that a Midtown parking space ought to go for as much as $20,000 a month. Instead they went for nickels on the hour.

One of the first entrepreneurs to seize the opportunity was the ice cream man. In part, the ice cream truck's raison d'être was derived from restrictive zoning: neighborhoods of homes, parks, and playgrounds were often not that close to a place you could buy ice cream. Whether the truck showed up to a suburban jungle gym or a cluster of housing projects, it was always a welcome sight. But with New York City's high commercial rents, ice cream truck drivers were also taking advantage of mobile food vendor permits that went for just $100 a year.*

Ice cream truck appearances are circumscribed by unwritten curb-control maps established by custom, negotiated by handshake, and enforced with violence. The history of ice cream truck rivalries is bloody. In 1969, armed rivals held up two Mister Softee garages in Brooklyn and the Bronx, taking nothing but the vital blender blades from thirty-nine trucks—rendering them useless before the blockbuster Fourth of July weekend. (In East New York, an accomplice also kidnapped a Mister Softee driver and blew up his truck.) In 2004, a pair of Bronx seniors selling ice cream with their fifteen-year-old granddaughter were

---

*Strict permit caps have produced a lively black market. On the resale market, the city's limited permits are leased for $20,000 and more.

left in critical condition after a former apprentice beat them with a wrench over a route dispute. "A route is money," the couple's fourteen-year-old grandson coolly observed.

In the spring of 2021, I dialed up Maria Campanella, who inherited her dad's ice cream truck in Bay Ridge, Brooklyn, and called herself the Ice Cream Girl. The routes in her neck of the woods used to get hammered out at the truck depot. She had heard stories of a wayward driver getting acid thrown in his face, even a man who'd been killed. "You used to get a wanderer, and you'd have to beat him up. I was a girl in a guy's world. They had no respect for me at all. If I let them stay there one day, that's it, it's their route. I remember fist-fighting, grabbing them out of their truck, throwing them down their steps. These guys would fight back. 'I fuck your mother. Get the fuck out of here!' Close their window? I knock it right out. I don't want to talk to your boss. You give me the phone, I throw it. All I want to hear is: you're starting your truck." The man who spit on Maria Campanella got his windshield bashed in with a gardening hoe. She got booked for that one. "I've had confrontations where you had to get rid of him no matter what it takes. I'm a respectable girl."

That has long been how it goes in the ice cream truck business, where the baseball bat is as important as the blender blade. In 2013, fed up with franchise fees, a Mister Softee entrepreneur named Dimitrios Tsirkos changed the names of his trucks to *Master* Softee. Mister sued, and won. But drivers with Tsirkos, now under the name New York Ice Cream, successfully fought their way into Midtown Manhattan, the city's most profitable turf. "You will never see a Mister Softee truck in Midtown," a driver told a reporter. "If you do, there will be problems, and you won't see him there very long." Mister Softee vice president Jim Conway said he would love to get his drivers into the heart of Manhattan, but they were too afraid for their own safety. In 2016, a New York Ice Cream driver hit a pretzel vendor in the head with a baseball bat near the Museum of Modern Art.

This situation persisted until 2019, when the city unleashed a sting it called Operation Meltdown against seventy-six ice cream trucks, including many of New York Ice Cream's purple-and-white vehicles. Between 2009 and 2017, the city alleged, these six dozen soft-serve vehicles had amassed 22,495 unpaid parking tickets—most on just forty-six trucks—for a debt of $4.47 million, or nearly $100,000 per truck. These tickets included 846 instances of blocking crosswalks, 1,192 fire hydrant infractions, and sixty-three times blocking curb cuts. All the photos in the complaint were of New York Ice Cream trucks; 99 percent of the tickets were concentrated in the zone New York Ice Cream had claimed as its turf. Tsirkos, the New York Ice Cream kingpin, was named as one of six officers who "dominate and misuse the corporations they own, operate or control"—as were forty-two alleged shell companies registered at the Queens garage he co-owned, the one whose address was printed on the New York Ice Cream trucks. Those companies had names like Ice Mania Inc., Twirly Twirl Ice Inc., Softee Taste Corp., and Super Softee Express Corp. Other defendants registered in Queens or the Bronx included Meathead Inc., Privilege Inc., Ice Boyz Inc., and Boyz of Midtown Inc.

Why hadn't these trucks been booted long ago? Because, the city alleged, their owners traded them for token prices, as little as $200, between scores of shell companies. One ice cream truck, which racked up $219,000 in unpaid fines between 2010 and 2017, was traded twelve times between thirteen different shell companies, adopting thirteen different license plates in the process. Each time, the truck would be transferred before the city could collect.

A new breed of entrepreneurs was taking advantage of the same core arbitrage between high commercial rents and low parking fees: food trucks. In Texas and Southern California, Mexican immigrants had long operated taco trucks out of commercial parking lots and on downtown curbs. The first taco truck of the modern era, which opened in LA in 1974, was remodeled from an old ice cream truck. Residents of cities like Austin and Portland had eaten from food trucks for decades, but the trend went mainstream in the early 2000s as culinary entrepreneurs embraced the low overhead and flexibility that came with a mobile kitchen. Many restaurateurs thought of food trucks as a way to gain a following, an income stream, and a proof of concept that could pave the way for a brick-and-mortar joint. But restaurants soon saw the attraction in mobile outposts, and many opened their own; reported sales from U.S. food trucks doubled between 2012 and 2017.

And that was despite laws pushed by restaurants to restrict their rent-free competitors. New York permits were cheap but limited, ensuring a lively resale market. At the behest of the Illinois Restaurant Association, Chicago forbade food trucks from serving within two hundred feet of any food service establishment—seriously limiting their territory downtown—and required they carry GPS transmitters to relay their movements to regulators. A cupcake truck sued; the restriction was upheld in the Illinois Supreme Court. Cities like Minneapolis and San Antonio have similar rules.

▮ ▮ ▮ ▮ ▮

In the summer of 2005, a San Francisco landscape architect named John Bela was thinking about the work of Gordon Matta-Clark, the artist whose project "Fake Estates" incorporated and auctioned deeds to microplots of leftover, "useless" urban space. Bela's firm, Rebar, found "unscripted fragments" of land in San Francisco in the form of curbside parking spaces. One day that September, Rebar paid the meter, rolled out some artificial grass, and set down a wooden bench and a potted tree on Market Street. Within minutes, two strangers were sitting and chatting. The project caught the attention of the Trust for Public Land, and a tradition was born: Parking Day. Rebar wrote an eight-step manual to guide participants, who emerged all over the world. A jumbo mancala board along a curb in Singapore. Mind-bending art installations in Montreal. Cafés and coworking spaces on the curbs of cities from Madrid to Santa Monica.

The event also inspired the City of San Francisco, which engaged Rebar to begin a program to build "parklets"—plots of curb that could be rented out long-term by businesses as spillover seating and green space. Parklets spread from San Francisco to places like Berlin and São Paulo, not just in curbside parking but in all manner of leftover urban space that had, in a previous era, been considered de facto parking lots. In Marseille, it is said, you do not find a parking space—you create one. Every city had ambiguous surplus territory like this. In Mexico City they were called relingos: "Asphalt and paving-stone trapezoids and triangles remained like odd pieces of a jigsaw, the origin and purpose of which no one remembers any longer, but which, equally, no one dares to either destroy or use in any permanent way."

New York City had one of those in a gentrifying waterfront neighborhood that real estate developers had branded Dumbo ("down under the Manhattan Bridge overpass"). In 2007, the city's new transportation commissioner, Janette Sadik-Khan, decided to turn the asphalt triangle in the shadow of the bridge into a little plaza—a prototype for what she called the Public Plaza Initiative. "A short time ago, this was a barren parking lot," she said at the ribbon cutting. "But people immediately filled up this space as the green came in." The green, in this case, was mostly paint—though the triangle was also ringed with plants spilling out from heavy concrete planters to keep the cars from reclaiming the space. "It is a New York City traffic principle that any street space not occupied by a car will become occupied by a car unless protected by a physical barrier or law enforcement agent," she wrote.

Sadik-Khan had grown up in Greenwich Village, the primal site of Jane Jacobs's "sidewalk ballet." More of a contact sport like rugby, she thought. When Sadik-Khan started working for the city in the late

1980s, she asked her mother, who had covered city hall for the *New York Post*, what department to aim for. "If you want to touch people's lives every day, you have two choices," her mother said. "Sanitation or transportation." She rode on the seat of her husband's bike, a one-speed fit for rough-and-tumble eighties New York they called the Tank, as he stood and pedaled them downtown.

By the time she passed the audition to become Michael Bloomberg's transportation commissioner, halfway through his twelve-year reign, New York was a different place—richer, taller, cleaner, more diverse. Mainly, it was more crowded. Nearly a million new New Yorkers had packed in, with the population surpassing the city's midcentury apex. And that didn't count the daily inflows of tourists and commuters; each group came in ever greater numbers. Since the 1950s, the number of vehicular registrations had risen by more than four hundred thousand. The number of cars entering Manhattan each day had more than doubled, to 1.85 million. The streets were jammed—not just with personal cars but with all the gas-powered instruments of a modern city: garbage trucks, fire trucks, ambulances, and police cars; delivery vans and box trucks; limousines and dollar vans and yellow cabs, soon to be replaced by sleek black Ubers; ice cream trucks and food trucks; school buses and city buses and tour buses; vans belonging to exterminators and electricians and plumbers and locksmiths.

Weaving between them all, in the greatest number of all, were the city's browbeaten pedestrians.

Carving out more space for cars was impossible; they had taken virtually everything available—the park from Park Avenue; the stoops from Lexington Avenue; the trolley lines from the Brooklyn Bridge; the carriage paths from Central and Prospect Parks; the curbs from vendors of ice, watches, knives, and fruits. But making space for people was easier; you could do so much with so little. Bloomberg's team was convinced you *had* to. The mayor thought a million more New Yorkers were on the way. If they wanted to drive too, the traffic would simply never move again.

Pedestrians got short shrift in New York: the city plowed the snowy roads clear for drivers but left women with strollers and men in wheelchairs to try their luck on slushy crosswalks. Streets designed to speed the passage of cars left pedestrians at risk; hundreds died each year and thousands more were injured. Buses crawled around double-parked cars and cyclists gamely navigated a deadly obstacle course. Everyone silently endured the honks and breathed in the air shimmering with exhaust. Unpaid parking tickets of many hundreds of dollars could get you the boot; jumping the $2.75 turnstile could land you in jail.

Sadik-Khan hired a Danish architect, Jan Gehl, to survey the streets. Children and the elderly made up 30 percent of the city's population but just 10 percent of its pedestrians—a sign, she felt, that they didn't feel comfortable out and about. On many busy streets, pedestrians outnumbered people in vehicles but received far less space. Little had changed since William Whyte's 1974 survey of the east side of Lexington Avenue between Fifty-Seventh and Fifty-Eighth Streets, which showed thirty-eight thousand pedestrians walking the twelve-foot sidewalk between 8:00 a.m. and 8:00 p.m. Over the same twelve hours, the nine-and-a-half-foot-wide curb lane was used by twelve cars carrying all of fifteen people!

Some of that imbalance could literally be fixed overnight, with a coat of paint.

That was what the team had done with the parking lot in Dumbo. Paint and planters. Basically, a Home Depot job. And once you started thinking of it that way, the possibilities were limitless. New York City had 6,300 miles of streets. They made up 25 percent of the city by area. The transportation commissioner, Sadik-Khan realized, was New York City's largest real estate developer. At the three-way intersection of Broadway, Fifth Avenue, and Twenty-Third Street, the Department of Transportation claimed another big quadrilateral of asphalt to be repurposed as pedestrian space in the shadow of the Flatiron Building. No sooner had construction workers deployed their orange barrels to divert traffic than a group of art students sat on the roadway and started to sketch. The implication was clear: those busy Manhattan sidewalks harbored unmeasurable demand for more public space. This Flatiron triangle was particularly notable because the plaza lay just across the street from a lovely park. One of the planners explained: "Why would so many people choose the plaza over the park? For the same reason that people at a dinner party gather in the kitchen instead of the living room or dining room."

After this busy merge had been carved into islands of café tables, awnings, and flowering vines, Sadik-Khan turned her eyes up Broadway. The iconic street, slicing diagonally across the grid, had created some very distinctive triangular plots, which in turn gave rise to the recognizable forms of the Flatiron and Times Square. But those same intersections had created a traffic-planning nightmare and a surge of crashes that injured drivers and pedestrians. Getting rid of lanes on Broadway, the DOT believed, would actually speed traffic in Midtown and clear out space for people in the city's congested heart. When Sadik-Khan told Bloomberg she wanted to pedestrianize Times Square, he told her it was the stupidest idea he'd ever heard. Ten minutes later, he was convinced. The temporary plaza was established in the summer of 2009 and populated, at the last minute, with 350 beach chairs from a Brooklyn hardware store. The experience was uncanny: you could put your feet up right at the center of the world. Pedestrian injuries fell by 40 percent; car crashes by 15 percent. In 2014, the plaza was made permanent with the installation of car-proof bollards and raised concrete paving stones speckled with steel discs that reflected the lights. The beach chairs were replaced by long granite benches that gave New Yorkers and tourists a place to sit. Three in four New Yorkers said the plaza had improved "dramatically," and commercial rents tripled.

New York activists had been trying to take back street space from cars since the 1960s, when Jane Jacobs and Shirley Hayes campaigned to eject vehicle traffic from Washington Square Park. Many of them had focused on securing space for bicycle riders. In 1973, hundreds of bikers calling themselves Transportation Alternatives rode from Central Park to Washington Square, where speakers demanded the city include bike lanes in its attempts to comply with the newly established Clean Air Act. Pete Seeger played the banjo. But progress came slowly: Bike lanes were installed, then ripped out. Cars were banned from Central Park on Sundays in 1966 and on Saturdays in 1967—but the city did not kick cars off of the park paths on weekdays until fifty years later.

To Sadik-Khan, making it easier to ride a bike in New York was a no-brainer. One in four adult New Yorkers rode a bike. More bike riders meant less traffic and fewer travelers on the stressed subway system. Biking was free exercise, produced no emissions, and required little parking beyond the city's ubiquitous, naturally occurring bike-lock infrastructure: parking signs. Biking was just a pleasant—and fast!—way to get from place to place. But it was also dangerous, and frightening, not least because drivers seemed to view bikers as fair game.

One of Sadik-Khan's first steps as transportation commissioner was taking a trip to Copenhagen, where she borrowed an idea for New York: use the parked cars to protect the bike riders. By putting the bike lanes between the sidewalk and the parking lane, you had an instant wall between cyclists and speeding traffic. Cycling boomed; injuries fell; drivers went nuts. In Brooklyn, neighborhood groups spent six years suing over the installation of a bike lane that ran adjacent to Prospect Park, though traffic moved at the same speed as before. "I'm going to have a bunch of ribbon cuttings tearing out your fucking bike lanes," mayoral candidate Anthony Weiner said in 2013. The front-runner, Christine Quinn, quipped: "Bike lanes, I put that now in the category of things you shouldn't discuss at dinner parties, right?" The Brooklyn borough president, Marty Markowitz, rewrote the lyrics to "My Favorite Things" and sang "My Favorite Lanes" at a council hearing in protest. (His favorite lanes were not bike lanes.)

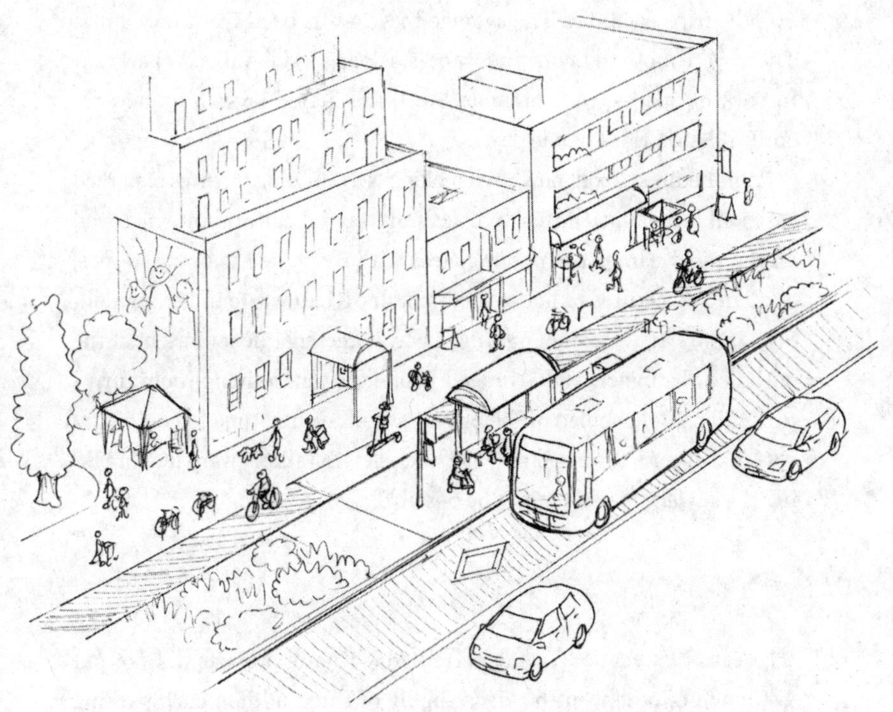

A wave of prospectors came upon the curb with new visions of what should happen there: bus lanes, bike-share stations, food trucks, car-share parking, parklets, loading zones for freight, pickup and drop-off areas.

Then there was Citi Bike, the bike-share system whose stations required swapping hundreds of car parking spots for thousands of bike parking spots. Dorothy Rabinowitz, a member of *The Wall Street Journal* editorial board, argued the failed community revolt to halt the Citi Bike stations showed that "the bike lobby is an all-powerful enterprise." But after the kvetching about lost parking spaces had subsided, the shared blue bicycles proved to be a huge hit. In September 2020, the system had almost 180,000 annual members, who made more than

80,000 trips each day. The average bicycle was used five times a day. There were more than one thousand stations on sidewalks, in parks, or in parking spaces. In September 2021, the shared bikes hit a new record: 135,005 rides in one day.

"A millennium from now, archaeologists examining pictures of parked cars will be convinced that vehicles were sacred cultural totems based on the way we lined our public spaces with them, like so many statues, and built structures to house them," Sadik-Khan wrote in her memoir, *Streetfight.* "If, instead of parking a car, I erected a Bedouin tent at the curb, fed the meter, and arranged inside the tent a living-room furniture suite, I'd be hauled off before my sweet tea had time to cool." That was in 2018. As it turned out, the bike-share stations were just breaking the surface of what might be possible.

▮ ▮ ▮ ▮ ▮

Despite the controversy, Janette Sadik-Khan's projects did not put much of a dent in the city's supply of three million curb parking spaces. But the bike-share stations did exemplify, on an enormous scale, a new way of thinking about the curb that went beyond the old parking meter. Not surprisingly, one company interested in thinking about curb uses besides parking was Uber—the ride-hail giant whose cars now made up a significant share of traffic in central business districts, often stopping for minutes at a time to pick up or drop off passengers, but rarely parking. In 2018, Uber commissioned a study with the San Francisco consultancy Fehr & Peers that coined a new concept: the Curb Productivity Index, which attempted to think about curbs not by Morgan Stanley's crude measures of profit but in terms of total utility. If a couple parked their car for four hours, those twenty feet served just 0.5 people per hour. If an eighty-foot bus stop served 100 straphangers in four hours, 6.25 people were served per hour per twenty feet of curb. In reality, bus stops serve far more people than that—in San

Francisco, a bus stop served about 160 times more people per foot of curb per hour than on-street parking. Between bus stops and car storage on the productivity index were a variety of other uses: bike-share stations, food trucks, car-share parking, parklets, loading zones for freight, pickup and drop-off zones (hence Uber's interest in the question).

Human utility was a squishy metric, but you could weigh curb access in cold, hard cash, too. What made New York's ice cream truck sting Operation Meltdown anomalous was the method of ticket avoidance—but not the number of tickets the drivers received. Underpriced curbs forced virtually anyone who wanted to do business at the curb to collect hefty fines, revealing, in a roundabout way, just how valuable that point of access was. A commercial truck in New York City easily racked up $10,000 or more in parking violations each year. One box truck logged nearly $30,000 in fines every year between 2016 and 2019, which suggests the value buried in the parking privileges of policemen, teachers, and other city workers. Defending the practice of parking in bike lanes, a spokesperson for the U.S. Postal Service explained on Twitter that if postal workers had to park legally, they could never deliver the mail in a timely or efficient manner. This was indisputably true.

Down at the New York City Department of Finance, it was not unusual to see lawyers representing delivery companies fight over technicalities on parking tickets. (Half the disputed tickets are dismissed, often on misspellings—which is why it pays to have someone like Ana Russi working the curb.) Just four companies—FedEx, UPS, and the grocery delivery companies FreshDirect and Peapod—accounted for more than five hundred thousand parking summonses in New York City in 2018. And that was just the times they got caught! Many of those companies had deals to pay a discounted rate on their tickets and avoid the boot, in exchange for not taking up the city's time disputing violations. (UPS paid $14.4 million to do business on New York streets, after the "scofflaw we can trust" discount of $6.6 million.) It was an example of the way cities profited from unmetered streets and parking chaos. In New York, every one of those twelve million tickets was a reason not to change the status quo.

And yet: each of those double-parked delivery vans was effectively removing a lane of traffic from circulation, which meant that New York's rapidly growing delivery economy had the power to strangle the street grid. One study, of Athens, Greece, suggested that eliminating double-parking could reduce traffic congestion by 30 percent. On Santa Monica Boulevard in Los Angeles, 44 percent of vehicles stopped at the curb were double-parked—and 80 percent of those were ride-hail pickups and drop-offs. A study of 2,900 trips in downtown Seattle found that commercial drivers at one parcel delivery company spent 28 percent of their drive time looking for parking, creating traffic and driving up the cost of doing business.

One problem standing between cities and better curb management was that, when it came to getting data, most cities were where Chicago was in 2008: focused on revenue from meters and tickets, and not thinking a step beyond. Officials did not even have maps of how curb space was allocated—let alone know whether a given space was full, and how often.

By 2020, however, several companies had emerged to try to quantify the curb. Passport, CurbIQ, and Coord were just three start-ups that were chasing after this uncharted territory. If Morgan Stanley had been able to wring billions from Chicago's curbs with the simplest technology—parking meters, jacked up to maximum prices—what might a well-meaning city planner be able to achieve in a congested metropolis like New York? How much revenue, and public welfare, could be unearthed at the curb? Stephen Smyth, the founder of Coord, had much the same pitch as Donald Shoup: the land was valuable, and it was being sold for far below market price (or worse, given away).

Coord, which was backed by Google's city-focused Sidewalk Labs venture, went way beyond parking meters. Doing business from a grubby coworking space in Midtown, Smyth's company had digitized the curb rules of dozens of cities, often by sending employees out to pound the pavement and chart, block by block, the Borgesian map of parking rules—a hydrant here, a driveway there, two-hour parking here, residential parking permits there, yellow paint, red paint, lawn chairs—that made up the bulk of public signage in the American city. The value proposition was simple: Coord was gathering information that cities themselves did not have, and that could not be easily mined from Google's Street View data. (Too many parked cars to clearly see.)

Curb parking rules were quite possibly the most complicated rules of the road there were, challenging for locals and unintelligible to visitors. In Los Angeles, where totemic parking signs sometimes carried five vertical feet of information, Coord digitized more than thirty-five thousand signs and thirty thousand stretches of curb on seven thousand blocks. It took twelve weeks and more than twenty surveyors. (Which seems bad until you remember how many days and nights it took Chrissy, Lindsay, and Jane to survey Chicago's Wicker Park. In Los Angeles, it took two Coord workers two hours to get information on how a mile of curb was being used.) The resulting digital map offered vivid proof of the mess, not just in cities but between them: where Romaine Street crossed from Los Angeles to the city of West Hollywood midblock, two-hour free parking during the day and permit parking from 10:00 p.m. to 8:00 a.m. changed to unlimited free parking during the day and permit parking from 7:00 p.m. to 7:00 a.m. Not exactly user-friendly stuff. In San Francisco, some parking signs were updated each year with the San Francisco Giants' entire summer schedule, with three sets of instructions for day games, night games, and away games.

In Aspen, Colorado, Coord collaborated with the city in 2020 to transform commercial loading zones into "Smart Zones" that delivery trucks could reserve. What SpotHero had done for garage use in Chicago by making thousands of spots reservable online Coord was trying to do for commercial curb use. The company figured it could offer companies an irresistible two-for-one: quit wasting time looking for parking, and pay tiny user fees instead of budgeting for reams of parking tickets. In Aspen, more than one hundred drivers signed up—about half from national fleets like Sysco, FedEx, and Coca-Cola—and made more than one thousand reservations during the program's hundred-day trial.

I I I I I

In 2020, I got an email from a man named Howard Yaruss, who was the chair of the Transportation Committee of Community Board 7, one of fifty-one local associations that govern neighborhood politics in New York. "I have been in the middle of parking wars," Yaruss began, before adding: "Full disclosure: I started many of them."

The most dramatic curb changes in New York City had come in the Manhattan core: the pedestrian plazas, the parking-protected bike lanes, the biggest stations of the Citi Bike network. But most of the city was residential neighborhoods, threaded with commercial thoroughfares following bus or subway lines. Perversely, it was in the neighborhoods that New York's nastiest parking disputes occurred. It was in the neighborhoods that the city had, since the 1950s, imposed its dreaded "alternate side" regulations, which required drivers to move their cars for ninety minutes once or twice a week. Merchants routinely overestimated the share of their clientele that arrived by car, and resisted bus lanes and bike parking accordingly. Resistance to the idea of dedicated loading zones was so strong, even as daily deliveries from Amazon and company became routine on every block, that fire hydrants became de facto loading zones. DOT officials joked they should just solve the double-parking problem by installing more fire hydrants. (Neighborhood Facebook groups, meanwhile, asked if they could do away with fire hydrants to create more parking. Starving for parking? Why not die in a house fire too?) Because the streets were so narrow, it took only a few double-parked cars to create a roadway obstacle course or an impassable logjam, or simply pen one's car in for who knew how long. Howard Yaruss lived in an apartment building on Central Park West, where he reckoned nearly every occupied apartment got a delivery every day. "Guess how many loading zones we have? Zero," Howard told me in 2021. "The DOT keeps telling me they have to keep studying what the optimal number is. And I say, scientists have been studying the optimal number of hours a person should sleep for centuries, but we know it's not zero."

The reason parking was such a challenging topic in New York neighborhoods, ironically, was the same reason activists saw limitless potential to remake the streets: people just didn't drive all that much. Not only did most New York households not own cars; many who did own cars did not use them to commute. Curb parking in New York was, in reality, long-term car storage—as the city began to refer to it in presentations, to the fury of its audience. Activists saw that as reason to be optimistic about new ideas for street space: You're not even using this thing! Car owners saw it as an exoneration: We aren't causing all this traffic! We're just driving Sammy to his cello lesson on Thursday afternoon.

Yaruss was an economist, so the idea of free parking in a neighborhood of million-dollar apartments naturally had caught his eye. "The most common use for public space on the Upper West Side is long-term car storage, and when you start to think of it that way, it becomes an outrage. Any time you have a system where you give away billions of dollars of stuff for free, you're going to have abuse," he said. "Once you start seeing it for what it is, you start to look at it differently. There has to be a more inspired use of this space than long-term car storage." Howard had grown up near Coney Island, a born-and-raised second-generation New Yorker. Howard was such a local that when he drove up to Vermont for a bike tour on the country roads, his parents fretted: Where would he find a parking spot? On the Upper West Side, he got a "How ah yah?" every other block.

He had been radicalized by a series of traffic deaths in the neighborhood: Cooper Stock, nine years old, killed by a turning taxi in 2014. Madison Lyden, an Australian tourist on a rented bicycle killed by a garbage truck in 2018. Many, many more pedestrians and cyclists had died in that time, inside and outside his district. Sometimes, a fix seemed so simple: for kids like Cooper, Yaruss wanted to "daylight" busy intersections, removing the parking space nearest to the crosswalk so that turning drivers and crossing pedestrians could see each other earlier and more easily. For cyclists like Madison, the solution was even more obvious: a curb-protected bike lane on Central Park West. Each of these designs, unfortunately, would require removing parking spaces. Yaruss failed to convince the city to daylight intersections on the Upper West Side. But he did push for a bike lane, which overcame a lawsuit by a neighboring condo building—with help from a scathing letter from the dead girl's mother—and was constructed in 2019. It took two hundred parking spaces away, a point that neighbors will not soon forget.

That was an appetizer for the idea that Yaruss floated to the Community Board in 2019: charging for street parking. Just as license plate readers and cameras had eliminated the hassle of tollbooths, new technology was emerging that could make paying for parking just as seamless. Don Shoup had proposed the idea in a *Times* op-ed in 2018, noting that the city's three million on-street spaces were 97 percent free and covered 6 percent of New York's land mass. Seventeen square miles of land. Thirteen Central Parks. Pricing just half those spaces at $5.50 a day, Shoup calculated, would raise an astounding $3 billion a year, enough to bond a new subway line. The $5.50 number was not incidental—that was the cost of a round-trip subway fare.

Yaruss took up the idea in 2019 with an op-ed in the *New York Daily News* that made a radical proposal: trade free parking for free transit. By metering *all* the city's parking spots at $6 a day, he reasoned, the city would raise as much as the nation's busiest mass transit system collected in fares each year. The estimate was conservative, since a free transit system could also abandon all the expensive machinery of fare collection (or continue to charge for commuter railroads)—and the costs of prosecuting fare beaters. It was progressive, since New York drivers were wealthier and whiter than their counterparts on the subways and buses. It was even, Yaruss dared to suggest, an idea that regular drivers (the gigging bass player, the locksmith, the UPS guy) might grow to like, since it would clear the curbs of all those cars that were used only a few times a month. No one alive could even remember a New York before free street parking, Yaruss noted. "It's like gravity."

At the public meetings after Yaruss proposed studying the issue, his neighbors did not buy it. "This issue upsets me so much, to stand here and not cry about it . . ." Jeannie George trailed off. "You say you have left-wing principles, but you're looking at us as some revenue source, some cash cow. Do you look at your family members and how much revenue you can squeeze from them? This is our community and it's being destroyed." Another speaker said Yaruss would take away her ability earn a living. "It's the government interfering with our rights," said Stilmore Gabriel. "I'm going to lose my way of life," said Abraham Poliente, an artist. "I carry paintings all day long. If I lose my parking spot, I have to leave the city." That last refrain was a real concern: New Yorkers with car-dependent jobs who had moved to a depopulated city decades earlier were finding it hard to maintain their way of life.

Leonard Daniels, very first speaker at the December community board meeting, called Yaruss out by name. "We need to get our parking spaces back. Not lose spaces. Put the bike racks on the sidewalk, Howard, or give up your garage space—because you are conflicted." It was true that Howard parked his car in the garage of his building. At $725 a month, it was not an affordable option.

But there were also many people who sounded sympathetic to Howard's idea. Sam Zimak said cars had changed since the fifties, and maybe car storage should change, too. Barbara Rice made the analogy to smoking inside, once a right, now unthinkable. Lisa Orman said, "Our current curbside benefits the minority at a huge cost to everyone else. . . . We need a rational system that emphasizes the public benefit for our limited public space." Another speaker, Beth Orlan, claimed to represent the silent majority of New Yorkers who did not own cars. "I represent the majority of the people in this neighborhood and on this island. This guy," she gestured to the previous speaker, "says we can't privatize public space. Well, a long time ago, we gave public space away to private cars."

Complaining about how hard it was to find parking was old news. Complaining about parking itself? That was very new. Yaruss knew his idea was fanciful, almost a taunt. Just a proposal to study something. But he started a conversation, one picked up in the newspapers and by candidates for mayor and council. Why *was* it free to store your car in the public right-of-way? And what else could we do with the space?

CHAPTER 15

The New World

In some ways, it felt like I had wished on the monkey's paw. Do you know that story, where a man is granted three wishes that come true in the worst possible way? I started writing this book in part because I had experienced a sudden revelation. All along the streets of our cities, and in a good many public plazas and parks as well, we had consigned a vast amount of public space to the long-term storage of cars. Some time ago in the murky past, we had collectively decided that the best use of this space was for cars to rest and recuperate before their next journey. In big cities like New York and Los Angeles, where real estate was expensive, the twin ribbons of asphalt on every curb held immense value. This was some of the most expensive land in the world. And you could have it for free, provided you used it for just one thing: parking.

I wished that others might see it that way. See all this public parking like it had never *been* parking, and it was up to us to decide what to use it for. A well-kept parking lot has an air of permanence, like Zeus had stamped the blacktop down with a thunderbolt, but have you ever seen one decay? It happens fast. Water pools and the surface begins to crack. The ground freezes and thaws and heaves, and the tarmac buckles. Seeds settle into these fissures and sprout, and the imperceptible, daily growth of their roots and trunks split man's best pavement in two. Before you know it, the parking lot belongs to the birds and the bugs. It was a Pizza Hut; now it's all covered in daisies.

I wished for others to share my epiphany, to recognize the tremendous potential of all the land that lay hidden beneath the chassis of a thousand parked cars. And then the monkey's paw part: As I began to write this book, the coronavirus pandemic shut down half the world. But for the ambulances, traffic vanished, and the air cleared. Some lucky few had fled to the country, but most urbanites were left with the unsettling experience of an empty city. The cramped feeling of an apartment without public life; the silence of streets without cars. As if someone had pulled the plug from a tub, traffic drained out of cities overnight. Streets were deserted. Lots, garages, and curbs were empty.

Suddenly, the fact that virtually every commercial and civic space in the country had an asphalt shadow next door looked like a stroke of genius. Church was one of the first institutions to relocate into parked cars. In Virginia Beach, megachurch parishioners honked once for *amen* and twice for *glory hallelujah*, while a local FM station broadcast the service and the band. In West Virginia, a pastor reported that parishioners were less inhibited. "There's always a lot of people sitting there, with their arms crossed, and a frown on their face, but they were singing along. . . . I definitely saw more people getting to cut loose and open up and really worship." And at an Easter service in Omaha, Reverend Greg Griffith exulted in the honking. "I love that we just broke Satan's eardrums."

Overbooked hospitals received patients in the parking lot. Marriage bureaus held ceremonies in the parking lot. The Philadelphia school district suggested students without high-speed internet at home attend class in school parking lots. Teachers also sought speedy parking-lot wi-fi. So did a Pennsylvania mother of four named Kate Baer, who, from her minivan in the Panera Bread parking lot, wrote a collection of poetry that wound up on top of the *New York Times* bestseller list.

In October 2020, I attended a town meeting in Massachusetts—Alexis de Tocqueville's great subject in *Democracy in America*—that had been moved in its entirety to a parking lot. Elected officials sat in an open-air tent, speaking into microphones. Hundreds of citizens sat in their cars, voting with clickers and following the action on a hyper-local car radio broadcast.

The awareness that the COVID-19 virus did not spread outdoors came painfully slowly. At the beginning of April, Oakland announced it would close seventy-four miles of streets to cars, to give people space to get outside. Cities like San Francisco and Chicago soon followed suit. At the end of April, the Lithuanian city of Vilnius decided to speed the reopening of its cafés, bars, and restaurants by offering public space for socially distanced tables. By midsummer, almost every American city and suburb had done the same.

Within weeks, in cities from coast to coast, the atmosphere changed from plague-induced lockdown to outdoor carnival. From suburbs like San Carlos, California, to old urban neighborhoods like Boston's North End, restaurants moved table service into the parking spots they once thought they couldn't live without. In San Diego and Austin, sacrosanct parking requirements were tossed aside without a second thought. Parking lots filled with tables, and all America ate outside. *The Onion* joked that LA had opened dining areas on the median of the 101 freeway, which wasn't *that* far off—at the Glendale Galleria in Los Angeles, diners ate inside the parking garage. Yelp reported a boost in consumer interest in restaurant strips that had blocked cars entirely, relative to their peers: diner traffic to Chicago's Fulton Market, where the Parking Reform Network's Jane Wilberding had showed me the future of parking, was up 25 percent compared with the city at large. San Francisco's Valencia Street was up 18 percent. Eighth Street in Boise, Idaho, was up 29 percent. And Boston's Little Italy, in the city's crowded North End, was up 61 percent.

Nowhere did the coronavirus challenge the culture of parking like New York City. Hammered by the virus and wary of eating indoors, New Yorkers turned the whole city inside out. It was like a tale from Italo Calvino's *Invisible Cities*: the whole existing metropolis had become suddenly obsolete, and a replacement had to be built alongside it. The replacement city was simple at first: Tables and chairs hauled out into the curb lane, shielded by a bank of propped-up shipping pallets. Picnic tables. Service through a window. But by the end of the summer, with restaurants assured indefinite access to the curb space corresponding to their storefront, the curbside structures had grown into full-fledged buildings. Janette Sadik-Khan had joked about a Bedouin tent in the parking lane, but reality had leaped far ahead. By the end of 2021, almost seven thousand New York City restaurants were doing table service in the parking lane. Their outbuildings had blossomed into fantastic curbside gazebos. Some were hung with potted flowers and paper lanterns. Others offered rows of velvet-curtained booth compartments, like you were traveling on the Trans-Siberian Express. Raw plywood was so 2020.

Mayor Bill de Blasio touted the program as a lifeline for the city's endangered hospitality sector, which it was. But the change was much more fundamental: space that had for decades been reserved for free car storage was now being used by dozens of people every hour, with some parking spots generating hundreds of dollars in sales tax every day. Some restaurants made more money in the pandemic summer of 2020 than they had in 2019—despite the absence of tourists and commuters. Hundreds of thousands of New Yorkers sat and ate in the street, turning thoroughfares into plazas from South Brooklyn to the Bronx, multiplying encounters with friends and neighbors. Streets with high concentrations of restaurants, like Koreatown and Little Italy, became semipermanent street festivals, spectacles of faces and voices. On some blocks, the streeteries had taken over almost every single parking space. When indoor capacity restrictions were lifted after mass vaccinations in the spring of 2021, nobody moved. Everyone wanted to be where the action was: outside.

Drivers challenged Mayor Bill de Blasio on the taking of the parking spots, on an urban landscape that had been wholly transformed in a matter of months without any community input. "Of course, that's more important than parking spaces for cars, to save 100,000 jobs. It's not even close!" the mayor retorted. For all the talk of metamorphosis, by critics and fans alike, of the city's three million curbside parking spaces, the restaurants had taken just 8,550.

The paradigm shift was under way beyond outdoor dining. The elimination of personal cars from Fourteenth Street in 2020 paved the way for a bus lane that boosted travel speeds by 30 to 40 percent, raising ridership 25 percent on weekdays and 30 percent on weekends. It also created a rapid crosstown thoroughfare for ambulances, fire trucks, delivery trucks, and other essential services. The Brooklyn-born entrepreneur Shabazz Stuart developed a bicycle-parking module, Ooneepod, to help New Yorkers with small apartments and no elevators safely park their bikes outside. In the space of one car, Stuart could shelter and secure ten bikes. The idea was "amazing," said the future mayor Eric Adams in 2021, and should be expanded "throughout the city." Sanitation Commissioner Kathryn Garcia inaugurated in 2020 a program called Clean Curbs, which allowed the city's Business Improvement Districts to relocate trash from sidewalks to sealed containers in parking spots. New Yorkers had become so accustomed to trash embankments along the sidewalk, gorging grounds for rats the length of your forearm, that it seemed almost inconceivable the solution could be so easy. Comptroller and mayoral candidate Scott Stringer said, "Priority No. 1 is repurposing curb and street space for pedestrians, bikes, buses, strollers, wheelchairs, restaurants, retail, and various public uses. . . . Parking space is valuable and we shouldn't be giving it away to private automobiles for free." The future Manhattan borough president Mark Levine wanted to change the city's zoning, allowing garages to rent street-level space to delivery companies for staging so they could transfer boxes to carts and bikes for local delivery in reserved "green loading zones." Whole Foods had already come to the realization on its own that trucks were a waste of time, space, and money; its Manhattan stores loaded cargo bikes for delivery at the curb outside.

If this was what a city could do with 8,500 spots, what could it do with 50,000? With 500,000? In a 2021 report, Transportation Alternatives made a pitch for reclaiming 25 percent of the street space New York had allocated to cars. What could we have? Thirteen new Central Parks. Five hundred miles of bus lanes; forty miles of busways; 38 million square feet of community space; better visibility at every intersection; a thousand miles of open streets; 5.4 million additional square feet for restaurants, businesses, and cultural institutions. Three million square feet for pedestrian space, wheelchair access, benches, bus shelters. Eighty feet on every block for loading zones and trash collection. And a block of space for play and outdoor learning outside every single one of the city's 1,700 public schools.

❙ ❙ ❙ ❙ ❙

For much of the twentieth century, America exported its car culture. Suburban, car-centric retail had sprouted in cities around the world, borrowing American standards for parking minimums. (In Germany, the Nazis seem to have developed the idea independently.) Just as Victor Gruen had unhappily confronted his own creation in the suburbs of Vienna, countless city centers watched suburban developments sprout on the periphery. More cars meant a better life, and city dwellers from London to Beijing slouched outward to emulate the progress of places like Los Angeles.

But the tide has been turning for decades now. Japan was one of the first countries to counter mass motorization with parking policy, starting with an overnight parking ban and culminating in a "proof of parking" law: you must have a registered parking space before you can register a vehicle. What gives a Japanese street its particular, alluring affect is simple: there is no on-street parking.

Latin American cities led the way handing streets back to people. Bogotá had pioneered Ciclovía in the 1970s, opening miles of streets every Sunday for families, joggers, cyclists, and vendors. More than two million people participated. Dozens of cities followed suit. In Brazil, cities like Rio de Janeiro, São Paulo, and Brasilia routinely closed highways to cars. Curitiba, Brazil, is renowned as the birthplace of bus rapid transit—a low-cost way to move large numbers of people down what had once been congested avenues. Mexico City adopted a Ciclovía-type

All along the streets of our cities, and in a good many public plazas and parks as well, we had consigned a vast amount of public space to the long-term storage of cars.

event every Sunday on its grand Paseo de la Reforma and eliminated parking minimums.

In Europe, where car ownership rates were higher, reform had also taken off. In Amsterdam, overrun with traffic in the 1970s, a group of mothers said "Stop de Kindermoord" ("Stop Killing Children") and started a movement. In 1975, the Netherlands experienced 20 percent more car deaths per capita than the United States; by the twenty-first century, the Dutch had 60 percent fewer car deaths per capita. Amsterdam had been transformed from gridlock into a city so oriented toward people (and people on bicycles) that it no longer served as a useful point of comparison—too unrealistic.

In 2004, the Greater London Authority replaced the UK capital's parking minimums with maximums. Nearly every London borough followed suit. The amount of parking that had once been mandated was now a hard limit. In the seven years that followed that decision, London constructed 144,000 fewer parking spaces than it would have built under the old law. The city has quietly become the standard-bearer for reversing a policy that America exported to the world: "No other major city has reformed its parking requirements on such a radical, comprehensive scale," wrote the researcher Zhan Guo.

Progressive politicians in Oslo, Norway, took power in 2015 with a plan to prohibit cars in the city center, where most residents did not own cars. Shop owners revolted; the city recalculated: it banned parking instead, removing all 650 on-street spaces in the central zone. In their place rose playgrounds, cultural spaces, benches, or bike parking.

In Paris, Mayor Anne Hidalgo eliminated thousands of curbside parking spaces to create room for bus lanes, bike lanes, and loading zones, and planned to get rid of half the capital's curb parking—seventy thousand spaces—by 2025. One winter day in 2020, her deputy mayor for transportation, Christophe Najdovski, welcomed me into his office of the Gothic city hall, overlooking one of the administration's signature projects: a two-way bike path running down the rue de Rivoli, the city's great east-west thoroughfare. Like his outspoken boss, Najdovski gave me a speech I was unlikely to hear from a local politician back home. Cars represented just 11 percent of trips in Paris but took up 50 percent of public space. He estimated that Hidalgo and the previous mayor, Bertrand Delanoë, had already gotten rid of twenty thousand or so street parking spaces. Hidalgo enlarged sidewalks and planted trees. She also pedestrianized the highways that ran on either side of the Seine River, creating two popular linear parks for strolling and socializing.

Coupled with the capital's investment in buses and trams, it was working to get people out of their cars: transit use rose by double digits between 2010 and 2020. Paris's vast portfolio of garage spaces (about six off-street spaces for every one at the curb) was emptying out. Some were yielding to underground mushroom farms. In another, I heard a man practicing the saxophone. Najdovski wanted to get rid of the public garages, too: "They're like vacuum cleaners for cars," he said, pulling in drivers from the city's suburbs. For Parisians, this fight gained new urgency every spring when weather patterns trapped smog in the bowl-shaped valley. There were days when the air in Paris was worse than Beijing or New Delhi. "Let's replace these tens of thousands of cars with tens of thousands of trees," Najdovski suggested. When I returned a year later, Hidalgo had used the pandemic as an excuse to plow huge bicycle highways through the city, tracing the routes of the most popular metro lines. They still occupied a fraction of the street compared with cars but moved more people every minute. Hundreds of Parisian schools now had car-free streets outside their doors, where the noise of tires and engines had been replaced with the sounds of chattering children. Like Amsterdam, Paris suddenly moved beyond a point of comparison. You didn't need to take very many parking spaces to transform a city.

Conclusion

In the United States, the pandemic changed the dynamics of parking. No longer would peak-hour traffic and high parking rates send commuters to mass transit. Downtown parking garages recovered faster than trains and buses as wary workers returned to the office in cars. On the one hand, the future of mass transit looked hazy. On the other, some Americans were freed from their lengthy commutes and newly invested in their neighborhoods, where trips were shorter and street space was being seized for people. A surge in online shopping left brick-and-mortar parking more oversupplied than ever—and double-parked delivery vans all over the place.

Everywhere, signs pointed to big changes in the place of parking in American life.

The biggest commercial parking operators consolidated under one company, REEF, an enterprise backed by more than a billion dollars in venture capital banking on the end of parking as we know it. REEF's goal: providing "thriving hubs for the on-demand economy" by "reimagining the common parking lot." In plain English, that meant "ghost kitchen" restaurants focused on delivery; last-mile sorting hubs for FedEx, UPS, and Amazon; or simply adaptive reuse in all the country's excess garage space. "We have these pods, which arguably are not pretty, but they're functional. They can support any kind of application," Ari Ojalvo, the CEO of REEF, said in 2020. "If you want to put a grocery store in there, put a grocery store in there. Laundry, put laundry." Parking operators were dinosaurs, and REEF was going to make it easy for entrepreneurs to access the undervalued space in its 4,500 lots and garages, which contained more than a million parking spaces. "I have received a number of calls from operators across the fruited plain asking about ParkJockey," wrote *Parking Today*'s John Van Horn, referring to REEF's prior name. "Who are they? What does their software do? Yikes, are we prey?" Yes.

The transition to electric vehicles also posed a threat to the old ways. Suddenly, the free-for-all hunt for parking spots made even less sense than usual. Electric vehicles promised the most fundamental change to curb space since the parking meter—or else imperiled the curb's viability for long-term car storage. For residents who park on the streets of cities like Philadelphia, Boston, and Chicago, electric car adoption is a challenge. At the start of 2020, New York City counted just 5,800 electric cars among its 2.4 million registered vehicles. The situation is only slightly simpler in multifamily housing with off-street parking, where condo boards and landlords must devise their own solutions to charging infrastructure. Where can it safely be installed? At what charging speed? Who should pay for it—all drivers? Just the electric car drivers? All residents? That process will have to be replicated on a municipal scale for electric cars to become the standard in the country's largest cities. To avoid the prohibitive cost and waste of a car charger in every parking spot, cities will need to come up with more sophisticated ways to dictate how curbs are used to make sure every driver gets the power they need, and to ensure older neighborhoods where people park on the street don't get left behind. Extension cords hanging out the window are not going to cut it.

But that is nothing compared to the shake-up in store if autonomous vehicles one day master the roadway. Already new cars can park themselves; if that technology can be applied at the scale of a parking lot, the amount of space needed to store cars will shrink dramatically as stalls get narrower and access lanes vanish. Imagine your morning commute in a future of autonomy: You live in a big house, far from the city, because what's an extra few miles driving to work when you don't have to steer? Instead of hunching over the wheel in stop-and-go traffic, you're typing away on a laptop or taking a nap. The traffic moves faster because robot cars can drive close together, communicating about conditions ahead. There is never an accident closing the left two lanes. But the traffic also moves more slowly because there are *so many people driving*. Children get on the road the moment they're too big for a car seat. Old people never need to stop. Many people with disabilities, like blindness, are on the road now, too. Because driving is better when you don't have to drive, many of yesterday's drivers are spending more time on the road now, too.

But the real change happens when you get to your destination. Your car drops you off in front of work and goes to look for parking. Since driving is cheap and parking is expensive, your car leaves downtown entirely—perhaps it settles in on a cheap lot by the highway or along the curb in a nearby residential neighborhood. If you're just running a quick errand or having a coffee, maybe your car doesn't park at all. Maybe it just circles the block for an hour until you're ready to get back inside. If you're short on cash, maybe your car enters a taxi fleet for the day, ferrying around strangers for a couple hours. In any event, the value proposition of a big downtown garage, a fat block of high-priced parking like John Hammerschlag's Poetry Garage, disappears. Parking as we knew it is dead, and something else can take its place.

At times, as I reported and wrote this book, the path forward from a policy perspective seemed clear. Abolish parking minimums and let developers build the amount of parking their clients want. Break garage rents apart from apartment rents so carless tenants don't have to subsidize their neighbors' driving. Recognize that more parking means less housing, especially affordable housing. Let different uses—an office and an apartment building, a school and a movie theater—share parking. Charge for the best street parking, and use parking prices and enforcement not to generate cash and cycles of punishment but to manage city streets. Invest the proceeds in the neighborhood. Let architects design environments where people can walk. Ask drivers to bear some of the externalities of automobile use. And turn some of that extra parking into something new.

You might go further. One of the ironies that has emerged in recent years is that central, walkable neighborhoods have become in vogue among rich people who own more cars. In some such places, like Manhattan or central London, developers are building more parking than they need to—because luxury buyers are willing to pay a premium to park in them. Getting rid of parking requirements may not be enough for such places to reduce air pollution, vehicle deaths, and traffic congestion; parking maximums might be necessary.

For drivers, which is to say, for most of us, most of the time we go anywhere, a parking-reformed world would be more convenient. Easier to park, even. Professional drivers at delivery companies, for example, would benefit from a more professional parking system. But parking reform does ultimately mean undoing some of the advantages drivers have amassed since they conquered the landscape a hundred years ago. From behind the wheel, some of those changes—parking spaces vanishing for a bus lane, a row of saplings, a restaurant patio—will be frustrating. But my hope is that drivers will not see those changes only through their windshields, and that making it harder to park might also make it easier not to drive.

A world with better parking would allow us to find our feet. Without parking baked into the streets and the architecture, and without fixing the density of residents and the style of commercial activity, how many more people could live in walkable places? How many car-dependent places, freed from parking law, could grow into neighborhoods where people could ride a bike? Where a family with three cars could get by with two and a family with two cars might manage with just one? Where kids could walk to school again?

Initially, I had worried that the parking reformers were after something nobody wanted. Sure, parking had eaten up cities and pushed them apart. But hadn't most Americans happily accepted the trade-off, decamping for suburbia—with its obligatory driving and ample parking, day or night—at the very first opportunity? Americans wanted to drive. They wanted bigger homes with yards. The city created by parking requirements was not pretty, and maybe the parking was poorly managed, but it was the result of a real preference. Not only did Americans continue to move to the suburbs, but they moved en masse to the least walkable regions in the country—to places like Austin, Texas. If there was one thing that united parking reformers, above all, it was that they didn't drive. Maybe they were just bunch of weirdos, tilting at mechanical arms.

But as I worked on the book, I became convinced it was the opposite: a substantial share of Americans did want to live in places they could walk around, and some were even willing to give up their cars to do so. The vast subsidy for car parking was just part of the way the deck was stacked in favor of suburban life, from the mortgage interest deduction to biased lending practices to gerrymandered school districts to cheap gas and other unpriced externalities of driving. But in spite of all that, the most expensive places to live in the country were, by and large, densely populated and walkable city neighborhoods. If the market was sending a signal for more of anything, it was that.

No sooner had I been convinced of this than the balance of city parking changed. On a deep level, the parking obsession kept people out: Parking laws made infill development impossible. Parking concerns torpedoed affordable housing. The financial and political obligation to provide parking served as a limit on urban density and ensured that high-opportunity neighborhoods would remain the province of the few. But on a superficial level, of course, parking was access. The environments the parking reformers idolized had gone in the span of a few generations from slums facing the bulldozer to unaffordable and exclusive. Parking-light neighborhoods were the hottest neighborhoods in town. As the focus of city planning shifted from quality of life to equity, I could see how free parking could serve as a consolation prize for residents who had been pushed into the car-dependent periphery. Not to lure them, as in Victor Gruen's day, but to offer them a small recompense for our inability to give them a home here.

When I met Greg Anderson in Austin, Texas, in the fall of 2020, he was on a haircut strike to protest the city's "pile of shit" land use code. "We care deeply about auto storage but we don't give two hoots about housing," he told me that fall on the terrace at Austin's LINE Hotel. "It's just devastating." Anderson worked at the Austin chapter of Habitat for Humanity, where he was trying to develop the organization's first parking-free housing on a lot downtown. His boss at Habitat was worried that no one would want to live there and that no banks would finance the project. She asked *me* if I had any comps. In the end, they sold the land.

Greg made the argument that living close to the center of Austin, in the city's walkable quadrants, was many people's first choice—a preference borne out in real estate prices, which descended from the city center to car-dependent periphery like rings on a target. Even in the heart of Texas, you'd pay a premium to live in parking-challenged neighborhoods. But most people did not recognize the trade-off between affordable housing and accessible parking. On the contrary: the more expensive neighborhoods became, the more vital *everyone* considered their free parking, whether they lived there or not. The very people making it impossible to build new housing—to build that inclusive twenty-first-century city—could put forth free parking as a consolation prize. You couldn't afford to live in the city, but at least you could afford to park there.

Greg taught an urbanism lecture course at the University of Austin, and one day he invited me to sit in alongside several members of Austin's Shoupista community. The reformers talked about their work in the city, and when they were done, Anderson faced a skeptical crowd. Eighty percent of the university's forty thousand undergrads live off campus, and many do not live particularly close. They bristled at the university's $600 annual parking fee. Less parking, to them, meant a more gated campus, an extra fee on top of tuition. They couldn't afford to live in West Campus, the bustling student neighborhood abutting the state capitol building. The question Greg wanted them to ask was not "Why is it so hard to park?" but "Why is it so hard not to drive, to live in a place where you could choose not to care about the cost or availability of parking?"

But even if Greg is right about Austinites' true preferences, the reality is that in Austin, as in many American cities, income stratification and sky-high real estate prices have pushed working-class families out of town. It was a disaster that parking politics made it hard to build the housing those people needed close to the city center. But once they were on the periphery, the dream of affordable housing didn't belong to them anymore. The city didn't belong to them anymore. What remained was free parking. In a city where living without a car could be a privilege, those congested curbs had a kind of egalitarian force. It took time to find a spot when parking was free, but time was the one thing we'd all been given in equal measure.

This argument has some flaws. People in America's suburbs are still, on balance, richer than people in its cities. People who own cars are richer than people who don't, and the richer they are, the more cars they own. And the immediate externalities of all our driving remain significant and weigh most heavily on urbanites who live near the busiest roads. But the central claim remains something I have heard more and more over the course of my reporting: that reducing parking's availability, or increasing its price, is a penalty that falls on the backs of those who can least afford it.

I can understand how this claim is compelling if you cannot picture a world of better parking, where housing is affordable and easy to build, driving is optional, streets are pleasant public spaces for children and the elderly, and a parking spot is readily available when you need it. Most of us cannot, because we are so deep within the parking crater we cannot see beyond its edges. I think again of the woman in Boston who is afraid to go the grocery store. Wasting away, but keeping her parking spot.

Parking is access. But it is access of the most superficial sort, one that often papers over deeper inequities we're unwilling to address. Ample parking at the ball fields feels like a requirement because the roads are too dangerous for parents to let kids ride their bikes. Free parking near campus looks good for students who can't imagine living close enough to walk. Easy parking in wealthy neighborhoods is a lifeline for workers who will never be allowed to live nearby. And acres of parking downtown feels like a right to commuters and shoppers when the bus comes only once an hour. In each case, parking stands for a primitive kind of access that both overshadows and impedes a more profound and widely held right to the city.

Acknowledgments

This book would have been impossible without the work of local reporters. Liam Dillon, Ben Poston, and Julia Barajas at the *Los Angeles Times* published a terrific story on Ginger Hitzke's project in Solana Beach and brought it to my attention in the first place. Adam Gaffin at Universal Hub reported on the Boston woman who said she'd lost eleven pounds because she was afraid to lose her parking space. Journalists at the *Chicago Reader* filed freedom-of-information requests that revealed the machinations behind the parking meter deal. Journalists at *Streetsblog* NYC have chronicled the illegal parking malfeasance of the NYPD, and the city's small steps toward reform. Those are just four of the countless local publications whose work allowed me to find the stories that, I hope, bring this dry subject to life.

I am also in debt to the parking studies that came before mine: Eran Ben-Joseph's *Rethinking a Lot*, John Jakle and Keith Sculle's *Lots of Parking*, Sarah Marusek's *Politics and Parking*, Mark Childs' *Parking Spaces*, Kerry Segrave's *Parking Cars in America*, Michael Condon's *The Chicago Parking Meter Concession of 2008*, Catherine Miller's essay on parking in history, JB Jackson's essay on the garage, and Donald Shoup's *The High Cost of Free Parking*. Don Shoup deserves to be singled out here, for his kindness, generosity, and encouragement as I took on a topic he has made his own. Those authors' contributions to my thinking about parking and cities goes well beyond the points at which they are cited. Thanks also to the parking people whose work populates the endnotes section of this book. It rests on the foundation of their research and knowledge.

Other excellent histories that helped inform my perspective on the development of the American city include *Crabgrass Frontier* by Kenneth Jackson, *Building Suburbia* by Dolores Hayden, *Mall Maker* by Jeffrey Hardwick, *Down the Asphalt Path* by Clay McShane, *Voices of Decline* by Robert Beauregard, *The Drive-In, the Supermarket, and the Transformation of Commercial Space in Los Angeles* by Richard Longstreth, *The Big Roads* by Earl Swift, *Dingbat 2.0*, edited by Therman Grant and Joshua Stein, and *The Politics of Place: A History of Zoning in Chicago* by Dana Caspall and Joseph Schwieterman. The first place I ever read a critical word about parking lots was, of course, in the chapter on "border vacuums" in *The Death and Life of Great American Cities.*

I did the reporting during the coronavirus pandemic and I am especially grateful to everyone who took the time to share some of their time in person: Ginger Hitzke, José Trinidad Castañeda, Nathan Carter, John Hammerschlag, Mark Lawrence, Lori Droste, Michael Manville, Mott Smith, John Van Horn, Sam Schwartz, Jane Wilberding, Lindsay Bayley, Chrissy Mancini Nichols, Mark Vallianatos, Victor Pontis, Howard Yarus, Christophe Najdovski, Clay Grubb, Matt Parkerson, Susan Holgren, Greg Anderson, and others.

Thanks to the libraries that opened their doors and trusted me with their resources: the Newberry Library and the Illinois Institute of Technology in Chicago, the New York Public Library, and the Richelieu Art History Library in Paris. My work was similarly aided by the people who put me up in their homes as I did the reporting, including Amy Mendelson in Chicago, Peter Schultz in Los Angeles, Adriel Saporta and Anichya Gujral in San Francisco, and Nick Gruy and Meesha Savadkoohi in Houston.

I had the good fortune to have my interest in this weird subject supported by a number of colleagues past and present, especially Jonathan

Fischer at Slate, who has put up with my long, late drafts for more than six years and been a font of editorial wisdom and good cheer. Leon Neyfakh was the first person who thought this book would be a good idea. Dan Kois did the brave work of reading the first draft—poor guy. Jessica Winter gave me notes on the introduction, as did Peter Beck. Jared Hohlt, Lowen Liu, and Hillary Frey gave me the time I needed to get the thing done.

The whole team at Elyse Cheney Agency has been a terrific partner in this endeavor, and especially my agent, Alice Whitwham, whose constant attention to this project, since before a single word had been put on paper, has been a blessing. She also came up with the title.

At Penguin Press, thanks to Ann Godoff, Casey Blue James, Sarah Hutson, Sam Mitchell, Jamie Lescht, Lauren Lauzon, and everyone from the art and production teams who has worked on turning a Word document into a book. Thanks to Natalie Coleman, who wrangled my drafts and put up with my lateness, and especially to my editor, Will Heyward, who spent more hours with this manuscript than anyone but me and has read the same jokes many, many times. He knew when and where to push for more, and many of the book's finest moments reflect his terrific instincts.

Hilary Roberts and Eric Wechter gave this book a masterful copyedit and fixed countless mistakes. Alfred Twu produced its lovely illustrations, and was a joy to work with besides. They knew exactly how to put my words into art, and I'm very grateful. Sam Lee had the idea for a two-way arrow.

This book took almost four years to write, from the time I started the proposal to signing off on this text and the galley proofs, and it was a trying time. I am beyond grateful for my friends who shared their parking stories, provided feedback when I needed it, or simply asked, "How's it going?" My sister, Olivia, and my sibling, Mars, are the best a guy could ask for. My parents, meanwhile, were characteristically supportive and, uncharacteristically, hands off. This book is dedicated to them.

And thanks above all to Magda, whose belief in this book and its author never wavered, even when I wasn't so sure. There's no one I'd rather look for a spot with.

Notes

Introduction

x **"Thinking about parking seems":** Donald Shoup, *The High Cost of Free Parking*, updated ed. (New York: Routledge, 2011), xxiii.

xi **spit in their food:** Claudia Peschiutta, "California Looks to Curb Meter-Maid Assaults," NPR, August 14, 2007, npr.org/templates/story/story.php?storyId=12776134.

xii **LA County was adding:** Mikhail Chester et al., "Parking Infrastructure: A Constraint on or Opportunity for Urban Redevelopment? A Case Study of Los Angeles County Parking Supply and Growth," *Journal of the American Planning Association* 81, no. 4 (October 2015): 268–86.

xiii **In Seattle, for example:** Daniel Rowe, "Right Size Parking: Final Report," King County Metro Transit, August 2015, metro.kingcounty.gov/programs-projects/right-size-parking/pdf/rsp-final-report-8-2015.pdf.

xiii **drives up apartment rents:** Jesse London and Clark Williams-Derry, "Who Pays for Parking? How the Oversupply of Parking Undermines Housing Affordability," Sightline Institute, December 2013.

xii **In California and Arizona:** United States Government Accountability Office, "Low-Income Housing Tax Credit: Improved Data and Oversight Would Strengthen Cost Assessment and Fraud Risk Management," September 2018: 31, gao.gov/assets/gao-18-637.pdf.

xiii **twelve whole blocks:** Hayden Clarkin (@the_transit_guy), "If the Empire State Building had to adhere to Cupertino, CA's parking requirements, the surface parking lot would cover 12 city blocks or 2.541 million square feet!," Twitter, June 9, 2022, 4:51 p.m., twitter.com/the_transit_guy/status/1534910961055940609.

xiii **"Parking is power":** Andres Duany, interview with the author, February 10, 2022.

xiv **"We devote so much land":** Henry J. Cordes, "Chamber Eyes 'Big Moves' to Transform Omaha's Urban Core," *Omaha World-Herald*, March 27, 2022, omaha.com/news/chamber-eyes-big-moves-to-transform-omahas-urban-core/article_0f6d1b6e-ab97-11ec-88eb-172f1c0d58b1.html?fbclid=IwAR1yaG9EX5e3B-F0mpQHyHWJuUujz_EBKXSzyWBGa2ou-kd_-FyMNekE6hMf.

xv **The "parking problem" is as old:** Catherine G. Miller, *Carscape: A Parking Handbook* (Columbus, IN: Washington Street Press, 1988), 4–9.

xvi **King Kong–sized gorilla:** Bruce Russell, "Gargantua," *Los Angeles Times*, November 18, 1945.

xvii **"Like a bastard child":** Larry Cohen, *The Quirky World of Parking: Four Decades of Observations, One Parking Space at a Time* (self-published, 2021), 23.

xviii **"The only thing drivers know":** Dennis Cunning, email to the author, June 2, 2020.

CHAPTER 1: **Housing for Cars and Housing for People**

3 **"The quality of life in cities":** Pope Francis, *Laudato Si': On Care for Our Common Home* (Vatican City: The Holy See, 2015), sec. 153, vatican.va/content/francesco/en/encyclicals/documents/papa-francesco_20150524_enciclica-laudato-si.html.

4 **"It's like a plain pasta":** Mott Smith, interview with the author, February 21, 2020.

4 **"sunny coastal ambiance":** Brian Wiersema, "Emerging Solana Beach," *San Diego Union-Tribune*, June 7, 1984.

4 **Eviction notices went up:** Lee Romney, "Beyond Repair? Landlord to Evict, Not Fix Up Units," *Los Angeles Times*, November 19, 1992.

6 **"I think people take a bit":** Ginger Hitzke, interview with the author, October 17, 2020.

8 **More than 7 percent:** Chris Salviati, "Super Commuting Patterns at the County Level," *Apartment List*, accessed August 13, 2019, apartmentlist.com/research/super-commuting-at-the-county-level.

8 **In Texas, beaches are presumed:** Texas General Land Office, *Texas Beach Accessibility Guide* (Austin, TX: January 2011), 3–4, glo.texas.gov/coast/coastal-management/forms/files/texas-beach-accessibility-guide.pdf.

9 while Greenwich adults can buy: Town of Greenwich Department of Parks and Recreation, "Summer in Greenwich," 2021.

9 In Westport, Connecticut, residents: Keith M. Phaneuf, "New Haven Lawmaker Would Ban Exclusionary Beach Policies," *CT Mirror*, February 2, 2021, ctmirror.org/2021/02/02/new-haven-lawmaker-would-ban-exclusionary-beach-policies.

10 ten-year study of low-income: Carolina Reid, "The Costs of Affordable Housing Production: Insights from California's 9% Low-Income Housing Tax Credit Program," Terner Center for Housing Innovation, UC Berkeley, March 2020, ternercenter.berkeley.edu/uploads/LIHTC_Construction_Costs_March_2020.pdf.

11 Required parking costs the average: C. J. Gabbe and Gregory Pierce, "Hidden Costs and Deadweight Losses: Bundled Parking and Residential Rents in the Metropolitan United States," *Housing Policy Debate* 27, no. 2 (2017): 217–29, doi.org/10.1080/10511482.2016.1205647.

13 "Low-income people tend": Liam Dillon, Ben Poston, and Julia Barajas, "Affordable Housing Can Cost $1 Million in California. Coronavirus Could Make It Worse," *Los Angeles Times*, April 9, 2020, latimes.com/homeless-housing/story/2020-04-09/california-low-income-housing-expensive-apartment-coronavirus.

13 "Hispanic people typically drop": Karl Schwing, "San Diego Coast District Deputy Director's Report for September 2017," California Coastal Commission, September 6, 2017, documents.coastal.ca.gov/reports/2017/9/w12/w12-9-2017-report.pdf.

13 "The development plan calls": Marty Graham, "Guns Aimed at Solana Beach Cheap Housing," *San Diego Reader*, January 18, 2019, sandiegoreader.com/news/2019/jan/18/guns-aimed-solana-beach-cheap-housing.

13 "Back in 1971": Sherilyn Sarb, "San Diego Coast District Deputy Director's Report," California Coastal Commission, December 1, 2016, documents.coastal.ca.gov/reports/2016/12/w11-12-2016.pdf.

14 "block the ocean air": Sarb, "San Diego Coast District Deputy Director's Report."

14 four-hour meeting: Solana Beach City Council, Joint Regular Meeting, April 23, 2014, solanabeach.granicus.com/MediaPlayer.php?view_id=5&clip_id=1464.

16 "I think it's very easy": Kristina Houck, "HOA Suing Solana Beach After City Council OKs Affordable Housing Project," *Del Mar Times*, August 6, 2014, delmartimes.net/sddmt-hoa-suing-solana-beach-after-city-council-oks-2014aug06-story.html.

17 **the city had spent $5 million:** Jonathan Horn, "New Life Looms for Old Solana Beach Trailer Park Site," *San Diego Union-Tribune*, October 15, 2011, sandiegouniontribune.com/sdut-new-life-looms-old-solana-beach-trailer-park-site-2011oct15-story.html.

18 **Hitzke's three-story, ten-unit:** Dillon, Poston, and Barajas, "Affordable Housing Can Cost $1 Million in California."

18 **longing to return:** Dillon, Poston, and Barajas, "Affordable Housing Can Cost $1 Million in California."

CHAPTER 2: Fighting Over Parking Spaces

20 **That is what happened in Boston:** Tim Logan, "Neighbor Sues to Block Pine Street Inn Project in Jamaica Plain," *Boston Globe*, August 9, 2020, bostonglobe.com/2020/08/09/business/neighbor-sues-block-pine-street-inn-project-jamaica-plain.

20 **That is also what happened:** Donna Bryson, "Why We Can't Have Affordable Homes: Parking Problems Stalled 36 Homes for Some of the Poorest Residents," *Denverite*, July 27, 2020, denverite.com/2020/07/27/why-we-cant-have-affordable-things-parking-problems-stalled-36-homes-for-some-of-the-poorest-residents.

21 **More than fifty neighbors:** Jonathan D. Epstein, "PUSH Buffalo Apartment Project Gets Pushback on Parking," *Buffalo News*, June 24, 2020, buffalonews.com/news/local/push-buffalo-apartment-project-gets-pushback-on-parking/article_6741f745-ce7c-5f2f-b4be-5c38079c4085.html.

21 **Malthusian thinking about:** Alex Pareene, "The Indignity of Automobile Dependence," AP Substack, May 10, 2022, theap.substack.com/p/the-indignity-of-automobile-dependence.

21 **In one 2022 survey:** Manny Garcia, "Across 26 Metro Areas, Residents Largely Support Allowing Missing Middle Homes in Residential Neighborhoods," Zillow, April 11, 2022, zillow.com/research/modest-densification-zhar-30934.

22 **as "frontier law":** Sarah Marusek, *Politics of Parking: Rights, Identity, and Property* (London: Routledge, 2016), 16.

23 **"notes on parking activity":** Jonathan M. Katz, "In Chapel Hill, Suspect's Rage Went Beyond a Parking Dispute," *New York Times*, March 3, 2015.

23 **It turned out that he had:** Kathryn Van, "No Arrest in Fatal Shooting During Argument over Handicap Parking Space," *Tampa Bay Times*, July 24, 2018, tampabay.com/news/publicsafety/crime/No-arrest-in-fatal-shooting-during-argument-over-handicap-parking-space_170174041.

24 **"The issue speaks":** Michael A. Heller and James Salzman, *Mine: How the Hidden Rules of Ownership Control Our Lives* (New York: Anchor, 2021), 44.

25 **They wait 33 percent longer:** R. Barry Ruback and Daniel Juieng, "Territorial Defense in Parking Lots: Retaliation against Waiting Drivers," *Journal of Applied Social Psychology* 27, no. 9 (1997): 821–34.

25 **In July 2020, a man:** Jay Hamburger, "Park City Police Told of Parking Shortage as Person Wonders 'If He Should Just Leave Town,'" ParkRecord .com, July 20, 2021, parkrecord.com/news/park-city/park-city-police-told -of-parking-shortage-as-person-wonders-if-he-should-just-leave-town.

25 **In 1987, Mother Teresa:** Sam Roberts, "Fight City Hall? Nope, Not Even Mother Teresa," *New York Times*, September 17, 1990.

26 **"As he moved down the street":** Calvin Trillin, *Tepper Isn't Going Out* (New York: Random House, 2003), 15.

27 **In Arizona, parking in the shade:** Diane Boudreau, "Urban Ecology: A Shady Situation," *Chain Reaction* 4 (2003): 18–19, cited in Tom Vanderbilt, *Traffic: Why We Drive the Way We Do* (New York: Knopf, 2008).

27 **The neuroscientist Andrew Velkey:** Vanderbilt, *Traffic*, 144.

28 **But the U.S. Supreme Court overturned:** Michelle D. Miller, "Neighborhood Parking Programs: Are They Unconstitutionally Discriminatory?," *Boston College Environmental Affairs Law Review* 6, no. 3 (1978), lawdigitalcommons.bc.edu/cgi/viewcontent.cgi?article=1854& context=ealr.

28 **It costs just $50:** Ike Brannon, "Gerrymandered Parking," *City Journal*, September 21, 2021, city-journal.org/how-washington-dc-gerrymanders -parking.

28 **limited, tradable assets:** Matt Yglesias, "A Bold Agenda for DC Housing," *Slow Boring*, July 25, 2022, slowboring.com/p/a-bold-agenda-for-dc-housing.

29 **Their attitude, she said:** Susan Holgren, interview with the author, October 22, 2020.

CHAPTER 3: **The Travails of New York's Top Parking Attendant**

32 **in 1990, 147,000 cars:** Josh Barro, "Here's Why Stealing Cars Went Out of Fashion," *New York Times*, August 11, 2014, nytimes.com/2014/08/12/upshot /heres-why-stealing-cars-went-out-of-fashion.html.

32 **"like moths devouring":** Mark Childs, *Parking Spaces: A Design, Implementation, and Use Manual for Architects, Planners, and Engineers* (New York: McGraw-Hill, 1999), xxi.

33 **cost money on Sundays:** Michael Manville, "Parking Pricing," in *Parking: Issues and Policies*, ed. Corinne Mulley and Stephen Ison (Bingley, UK: Emerald, 2014), 137–55.

34 **"Never turn your back":** Ana Russi, interview with the author, March 14, 2021.

34 **"I don't pay any mind":** Nicholas Pileggi, "The War on Traffic," *New York*, July 23, 1984, 26–31.

34 **"You had traffic agents":** Russi interview.

35 **"If they're getting beaten":** Pileggi, "War on Traffic."

35 **the owner broke her nose:** "Hearing May 10 Set in Meter Maid Case," *New York Times*, April 26, 1967.

35 **After Neal got out:** Emanuel Perlmutter, "Meter Maids Out for a Second Day," *New York Times*, May 25, 1967.

35 **One parking officer was assaulted:** Douglas Martin, "Traffic Agents Battle for Respect," *New York Times*, September 24, 1993.

35 **"Why is a parking attendant":** John Van Horn, interview with the author, October 13, 2020.

36 **"the public streets":** "Wallander Opposes Lifting Parking Ban in Home Areas," *New York Times*, March 31, 1947.

36 **overnight parking was legalized:** Alex Dworkowitz, "How the Alternate Side Lives," *The Awl*, May 22, 2014, theawl.com/2014/05/how-the-alternate-side-lives.

36 **The moniker *maid*:** James Longhurst, "Street Privilege: New Histories of Parking and Urban Mobility," *The Metropole* (Blog), April 29, 2020, themetropole.blog/2020/04/29/street-privilege-new-histories-of-parking-and-urban-mobility.

36 **Police responded with a spree:** "Meter Maid Pays $10 Traffic Fines," *New York Times*, September 7, 1960.

36 **she had made "unreasonable noise":** C. Gerald Fraser, "City Meter Maids Are Plagued by the Public's Insults, Harassments and Assaults," *New York Times*, September 28, 1969.

37 **For the rest of his life:** "Rebroadcast: An Interview with Mike Cataneo and a Conversation about the Parking Ticket Heard Around the World," December 24, 2019, in *The Parking Podcast*, podcast, produced by Isaiah Mouw, MP3 audio, 19:34, parkingcast.com/blog/rebroadcast-an-interview-with-mike-cataneo-and-a-conversation-about-the-parking-ticket-heard-around-the-world.

37 **"most unpopular civil servant":** "Meter Maids Decry Assaults on Ranks by Irate Motorists," *New York Times*, October 5, 1975.

38 "lab-like situations": Elizabeth Brondolo, interview with the author, March 5, 2021.

38 Dr. Brondolo studied traffic agents: Elizabeth Brondolo et al., "Anger-Related Traits and Response to Interpersonal Conflict among New York City Traffic Agents," *Journal of Applied Social Psychology* 28, no. 22 (November 1998): 2089–118, onlinelibrary.wiley.com/doi/abs/10.1111/j.1559-1816.1998.tb01362.x.

38 "Positive aspects of traffic enforcement": Elizabeth Brondolo, *Agent Conflict Resolution Training* (New York: St. John's University and NYC Department of Transportation, 1995).

39 "People got so sad": Brondolo interview.

39 A 2001 survey of eight hundred: Chris Yigit, "It's Time to Address Parking Enforcement Officer Safety," *Parking Today*, March 2020, 26.

39 "Don't beat up the officer": John M. Glionna, "Parking-Ticket Rage Targets the Messenger," *Los Angeles Times*, January 25, 2007, latimes.com/archives/la-xpm-2007-jan-25-me-sfparking25-story.html.

39 disco balls, Barbie dolls: Bradley Berman, "The Disco Ball Is How You Know She Won't Give You a Parking Ticket," *New York Times*, September 16, 2021, nytimes.com/2021/09/16/business/meter-maid-cars-san-francisco.html.

40 *The Philadelphia Inquirer* called: Jon Hurdle, "City Finds a Reality Show Hard to Watch," *New York Times*, June 22, 2009, nytimes.com/2009/06/22/us/22philadelphia.html.

40 "one of the worst things": Julie Dixon, interview with the author, October 30, 2020.

40 siphons revenue into lucrative patronage positions: Laura McCrystal, "Philly's Parking Agency Still Overpays Executives and Has Too Many Political Patronage Jobs, Audit Finds," *Philadelphia Inquirer*, December 9, 2020, inquirer.com/politics/philadelphia/philadelphia-parking-authority-audit-20201209.html.

40 In 2022, immigrants from Bangladesh: Joseph Goldstein, "Bangladeshis Build Careers in New York Traffic," *New York Times*, November 28, 2013, nytimes.com/2013/11/29/nyregion/bangladeshis-build-careers-in-new-york-traffic.html.

41 "We don't use it": Alex Marshall, "Americans Like Free Parking. They Don't Realize It Doesn't Exist," *Governing*, December 17, 2020, governing.com/community/Americans-Like-Free-Parking-They-Dont-Realize-It-Doesnt-Exist.html.

41 "If you're willing to approach": Barry Tarshis, "The Parking Hassle: A System to Beat the System," *New York*, March 17, 1969, 60–62.

41 "like musical chairs": *Seinfeld*, season 3, episode 22, "The Parking Space," directed by Tom Cherones, written by Larry David, Jerry Seinfeld, and Greg Daniels, aired April 22, 1992, on NBC.

42 canvass all the parked cars: William H. Whyte, "How to Unclog Midtown Traffic," *New York*, December 12, 1977, 47–58.

42 "is about the greatest nuisance": William Phelps Eno, *The Parking Problem: A Library Research* (Saugatuck, CT: Eno Foundation for Highway Traffic Control, 1942), 42.

42 Between March and October 1977: Whyte, "How to Unclog Midtown Traffic."

42 A later study: Raymond Fisman and Edward Miguel, "Corruption, Norms, and Legal Enforcement: Evidence from Diplomatic Parking Tickets," *Journal of Political Economy* 115, no. 6 (2007): 1020–48, journals.uchicago.edu/doi/10.1086/527495.

44 "Our NO PARKING signs": Pileggi, "War on Traffic."

44 "The Soviets are outraged": Sam Schwartz and Richard Levine, "Don't Even Think of Parking Here," unpublished manuscript in author's collection, 3.

44 It was not until 2002: Fisman and Miguel, "Corruption, Norms, and Legal Enforcement."

45 "Parking is the key to urban": Calvin Trillin, *Tepper Isn't Going Out* (New York: Random House, 2003), 205.

45 Thieves occasionally smashed windows: Ginger Adams Otis, "Placard Sharks Hit Bravest," *New York Post*, February 10, 2008, nypost.com/2008/02/10/placard-sharks-hit-bravest.

45 By 2017, there were two thousand: Susan Edelman and Aaron Short, "Police Groups in Scheme to Let Doctors Park in Illegal Spots," *New York Post*, April 9, 2017, nypost.com/2017/04/09/police-groups-perpetuate-permit-scheme-letting-doctors-park-in-illegal-spots.

45 In a 2011 study: Transportation Alternatives, "Totally Bogus: A Study of Parking Permit Abuse in NYC," static1.squarespace.com/static/5cab9d9b65a707a9b36f4b6c/t/5f08c32f5a33675b8c20c3e6/1594409779490/Totally_Bogus.pdf.

45 "stealing city resources": James C. McKinley Jr., "Dozens Charged with Using Fake Parking Placards to Avoid Tickets," *New York Times*, October 3, 2017, nytimes.com/2017/10/03/nyregion/fake-parking-placards-new-york.html.

46 11 of 244 permits: Transportation Alternatives, "Totally Bogus."

46 **"state government in a nutshell":** John Kaehny, interview with the author, March 10, 2021.

47 **"People given an inordinate amount":** @PlacardAbuse [pseud.], interview with the author, July 3, 2020.

48 **"a stunning show of vitriol":** N. R. Kleinfeld and John Eligon, "Officers Jeer at Arraignment of 16 Colleagues in Ticket-Fixing Investigation," *New York Times*, October 28, 2011, nytimes.com/2011/10/29/nyregion/officers-unleash-anger-at-ticket-fixing-arraignments-in-the-bronx.html.

48 **"When he came to meet me":** Alan Feuer, "Traffic Graft, from the Bootlegger to the Mayor," *New York Times*, April 27, 2018, nytimes.com/2018/04/27/nyregion/tracking-graft-from-the-bootlegger-to-the-mayor.html.

48 **"As we've heard in countless":** Errol Louis, "Placard Abuse, a Gateway Drug: It's How Much Broader Municipal Corruption Begins," *New York Daily News*, January 28, 2019, nydailynews.com/opinion/ny-oped-placard-abuse-a-gateway-drug-20190107-story.html.

49 **"If we knew that public employees":** Errol Louis (@errollouis), "If we knew that public employees were routinely and daily stealing milk from supermarkets and taverns around the city—while cops not only looked the other way, but participated—nobody would shrug and say 'who cares?' Parking in NYC costs a lot more than a gallon of milk," Twitter, June 2, 2021, 3:20 p.m., twitter.com/errollouis/status/1399853446329733120.

49 **"If you get a parking ticket":** Amanda Eisenberg (@aeis17), "'If you get a parking ticket, don't worry we'll take care of it,' Steve Cohn quipped before he introduced Brooklyn DA Eric Gonzalez," Twitter, October 29, 2021, 6:01 a.m., twitter.com/aeis17/status/1454070870918434817.

49 **In 2020, thousands:** Jesse Coburn, "Ignored, Dismissed: How the NYPD Neglects Complaints about Driver Misconduct," *Streetsblog NYC*, October 21, 2021, nyc.streetsblog.org/2021/10/21/ignored-dismissed-how-the-nypd-neglects-311-complaints-about-driver-misconduct.

49 **"I tried for years":** David Meyer, "New Bill Would Pay New Yorkers to Rat Out Illegal Parkers, Including Placard Holders," *New York Post*, November 19, 2020, nypost.com/2020/11/19/new-bill-would-pay-new-yorkers-to-rat-out-illegal-car-parking.

50 **"Imagine if every cop":** David Meyer, "NYPD Union Mocks Proposal to Pay New Yorkers for Ratting Out Parking Violators," *New York Post*, November 20, 2020, nypost.com/2020/11/20/nypd-union-mocks-proposal-to-pay-nyers-to-rat-out-parking-violators.

CHAPTER 4: Destroying the City in Order to Save It

51 **"the most important single problem":** John C. Teaford, *The Metropolitan Revolution: The Rise of Post-Urban America* (New York: Columbia University Press, 2006), 46.

52 **"you can't go to town":** Clay McShane, *Down the Asphalt Path: The Automobile and the American City* (New York: Columbia University Press, 1995), 134.

52 **"What can you do":** Kerry Segrave, *Parking Cars in America, 1910–1945: A History* (Jefferson, NC: McFarland, 2012), loc. 490 of 2950, Kindle.

52 **"From a survey":** Segrave, *Parking Cars in America*, loc. 597.

53 **Chicago widened 112 miles:** Paul Barrett, *The Automobile and Urban Transit: The Formation of Public Policy in Chicago, 1900–1930* (Philadelphia: Temple University Press, 1983), 145.

53 **Countless rows of street trees:** John A. Jakle and Keith A. Sculle, *Lots of Parking: Land Use in a Car Culture* (Charlottesville: University of Virginia Press, 2005), 8.

53 **"Aside from the weather":** Jane Holtz Kay, "A Brief History of Parking," *Architecture*, February 2001, 77–79, usmodernist.org/AJ/A-2001-02.pdf.

53 **In Washington, DC, parked cars:** McShane, *Down the Asphalt Path*, 194.

53 **McClintock calculated that curbside:** Miller McClintock, *Metropolitan Street Traffic Survey* (Cambridge, MA: Albert Russel Erskine Bureau for Street Traffic Research at Harvard University, 1926), 146.

53 **on some afternoons streetcar operators:** Barrett, *Automobile and Urban Transit*, 63.

53 **Property owners responded immediately:** Mark Bottles, "Mass Politics and the Automobile in Los Angeles," in *The Car and the City: The Automobile the Built Environment, and Daily Urban Life*, ed. Martin Wachs and Margaret Crawford (Ann Arbor: University of Michigan Press, 1992), 198–200.

54 **There were rumors of a woman:** Eran Ben-Joseph, *Rethinking a Lot: The Design and Culture of Parking* (Cambridge, MA: MIT Press, 2012), 69.

54 **Streetcars sped up:** Barrett, *Automobile and Urban Transit*, 160.

54 **By 1940, more than 80 percent:** Jakle and Sculle, *Lots of Parking*, 31.

54 **In a third of two hundred:** Richard Schicker, "The Parking Irritant," *Nation*, May 9, 1959, 427–29.

54 **"Next to winning the Peace":** Jakle and Sculle, *Lots of Parking*, 135.

55 "greatest problems facing the city": "Wallander Opposes Lifting Parking Ban in Home Areas," *New York Times*, March 31, 1947.

55 "Henry Ford probably never": Gordon Cowan, "Minneapolis Business Provides New Parking Garages," *American City*, January 1952.

55 The assessed taxable values: Teaford, *Metropolitan Revolution*, 45.

55 The proportion of metropolitan: Teaford, *Metropolitan Revolution*, 72.

55 by 1970, more Americans: James Flink, "America Adopts the Automobile," in Wachs and Crawford, *Car and the City*, 97.

55 Retail suburbanized fastest: John Kain, "The Distribution and Movement of Jobs and Industry," in *Metropolitan Enigma*, ed. James Q. Wilson (New York: Doubleday, 1970), 1–43.

55 "dying stars, sending out": Robert A. Beauregard, *Voices of Decline: The Postwar Fate of U.S. Cities*, 2nd ed. (New York: Routledge, 2002), 94.

55 "The whole financial structure": Teaford, *Metropolitan Revolution*, 19.

56 "premature decentralization" was brought about: William Phelps Eno, *The Parking Problem: A Library Research* (Saugatuck, CT: Eno Foundation for Highway Traffic Control, 1942), 58.

57 a parking lot away: Julian Scheineson, "This Parking Garage Leaves Nothing to Chance," *American City*, March 1968.

58 He spent his evenings: Jeffrey Hardwick, *Mall Maker: Victor Gruen, Architect of an American Dream* (Philadelphia: University of Pennsylvania Press, 2010), 10.

58 After a personal request: Hardwick, *Mall Maker*, 22.

58 "where parking is less of a problem": Hardwick, *Mall Maker*, 75.

59 "This is not just the opening": Hardwick, *Mall Maker*, 128–30.

59 "Europeanization of America": Hardwick, *Mall Maker*, 133.

60 "The only progress": Hardwick, *Mall Maker*, 92.

60 "something of the Vienna Waltz": Hardwick, *Mall Maker*, 131.

60 "usually not willing": Hardwick, *Mall Maker*, 133.

60 "a pleasure-dome-with-parking": Hardwick, Mall Maker, 145.

61 "It is a plan that will": J. B. Thomas, "Statement by J.B. Thomas at a Presentation of the Gruen Plan," March 3, 1956, Fort Worth Public Library Archives, The Gruen Plan, box 1, folder 7, fortworthtexasarchives.org/digital/collection/p16084coll18/id/52/rec/1.

61 "pomp, drama and fanfare": Hardwick, *Mall Maker*, 170.

61 His official Fort Worth report: Hardwick, *Mall Maker*, 176.

61 "INSERT LOCAL DATA HERE": Hardwick, *Mall Maker*, 185.

61 "needs a lesson": "Downtown Needs a Lesson from the Suburbs," *BusinessWeek*, October 22, 1955, 64–66.

61 The Gruen Plan had four: "Tomorrow's Greater Fort Worth," 1955–56, Fort Worth Public Library Archives, The Gruen Plan, box 1, folder 3, fortworthtexasarchives.org/digital/collection/p16084coll18/id/50/rec/42.

62 "*new walking habits*": "Report on Parking Facilities for 'The Gruen Plan'," De Leuw, Cather, and Company, Chicago, September 1956, Fort Worth Public Library Archives, the Gruen Plan, box 1, folder 5, fortworthtexasarchives.org/digital/collection/p16084coll18/id/82/rec/23.

62 "most magic plan": Hardwick, *Mall Maker*, 181.

62 "fan letter" to Gruen: Hardwick, *Mall Maker*, 181.

63 "is the only unborn child": Wolf Von Eckardt, "The Urban Liberator: Victor Gruen and the Pedestrian Oasis," *Washington Post*, February 23, 1980.

63 Fewer than a third: Dave Amos, "Understanding the Legacy of Pedestrian Malls," *Journal of the American Planning Association* 86, no. 1 (2020): 11–24, doi.org/10.1080/01944363.2019.1656103.

63 "by parking lots, garages": Hardwick, *Mall Maker*, 198.

64 "American cities, with their comparatively": Hardwick, *Mall Maker*, 218.

64 "Autocratic fanatics have already": Ben-Joseph, *Rethinking a Lot*, 91.

64 The same year, he wrote: Victor Gruen and Herbert Askwith, "Plan to End Our Traffic Jam," *New York Times*, January 10, 1960.

65 "loosens the fabric": Victor Gruen, *The Heart of Our Cities: The Urban Crisis: Diagnosis and Cure* (New York: Simon and Schuster, 1964), 124.

65 "severe emotional shock": Hardwick, *Mall Maker*, 157

65 "the ugliness and discomfort": Hardwick, *Mall Maker*, 216

65 "gigantic shopping machine": Neil R. Peirce, "The Shopping Center and One Man's Shame," *Los Angeles Times*, October 22, 1978.

65 "premeditated murder of a city": Peirce, "The Shopping Center and One Man's Shame."

66 "I'm often called the father": Peirce, "The Shopping Center and One Man's Shame."

66 In Buffalo, a chamber of commerce: Teaford, *Metropolitan Revolution*, 120.

67 "the shopping centers of today": "Economies, Planning, and Prospects," *Architectural Record*, March, 1960, 211.

67 In 1951, Houston: "Parking Lots Owned by 465 Cities," *American City*, September 1952, 169.

67 Just 5 percent of parking spaces: Ben-Joseph, *Rethinking a Lot*, 76.

67 By 1968, two in three: *Parking Principles*, Highway Research Board (Washington, DC: National Academy of Sciences, 1970), 10.

67 "reaching crisis proportions": Federal City Council, "Parking in the Nation's Capital," Washington, DC, September 1964, 2.

67 "single largest use": United States Congress, House Committee on the District of Columbia, "Parking Facilities" (Washington, DC: US Government Printing Office, 1968), 186.

68 "We have never worked up": "Does Off-Street Parking Increase Land Valuations?," *American City*, July 1952.

68 "We are more interested": Segrave, *Parking Cars in America*, loc. 1180.

69 95 percent of U.S. cities: Erik Ferguson, "Zoning for Parking as Policy Process: A Historical Review," *Transport Reviews* 24, no. 2 (2004): 177–94.

69 "duller and deader": Jane Jacobs, *The Death and Life of Great American Cities* (New York: Vintage Books, 1968), 19.

69 7 percent each year: Schicker, "Parking Irritant."

CHAPTER 5: Paved Paradise

71 By square footage: Maria Cecilia P. Moura, Steven J. Smith, David B. Belzer, "120 Years of US Residential Housing Stock and Floor Space," *PLoS ONE* 10, no. 8 (2015): e0134135, doi.org/10.1371/journal.pone.0134135.

71 "maze of driveways": Christopher Alexander, Murray Silverstein, and Sara Ishikawa, *A Pattern Language: Towns, Buildings, Construction* (New York: Oxford University Press, 1977), 177.

72 The conventional wisdom in Chicago: "Mayor to Crash Gates at Park's Garage Debut," *Chicago Tribune*, August 26, 1954.

72 "until that terminal point": Earl Swift, *The Big Roads: The Untold Story of the Engineers, Visionaries and Trailblazers Who Created American Superhighways* (Boston: Houghton Mifflin Harcourt, 2011), 243.

72 "dumping a whole orphanage": Swift, *Big Roads*, 204.

72 "How many of you": Swift, *Big Roads*, 302.

73 "Destroying buildings and using valuable land": D. C. Hyde, "In Business Areas, Think in Terms of Mass Transit," *American City*, October 1952, 153.

73 arguing that *better transit*: H. S. Bingham, "City Transit Can Thrive Again," *American* City, January 1953.

73 "the bolstering effect": George Berkley, "Municipal Garages in Boston: A Cost-Benefit Analysis," *Traffic Quarterly* 19, no. 3 (1965): 213–28.

73 Even President Dwight D. Eisenhower: Swift, *Big Roads*, 250.

74 "insatiable appetite for space": John A. Jakle and Keith A. Sculle, *Lots of Parking: Land Use in a Car Culture* (Charlottesville: University of Virginia Press, 2005), 10.

74 even parking lots were being abandoned: Jakle and Sculle, *Lots of Parking*, 179.

74 Most studies put America's: Mikhail Chester et al., "Parking Infrastructure and the Environment," *Access*, Fall 2011.

74 Phoenix has 12.2 million parking spaces: Christopher G. Hoehne et al., "Valley of the Sun-Drenched Parking Space: The Growth, Extent, and Implications of Parking Infrastructure in Phoenix," *Cities* 89 (2019): 186–98, doi.org/10.1016/j.cities.2019.02.007.

74 In Silicon Valley, America's: C. J. Gabbe and Michael Manville, "The Opportunity Cost of Parking Requirements: Would Silicon Valley Be Richer if Its Parking Requirements Were Lower?," *Journal of Transport and Urban Land Use* 14, no. 1 (2021): 277–301.

74 There are 15 million: Mikhail Chester, Alysha Helmrich, and Rui Li, "Inventorying San Francisco Bay Area Parking Spaces: Technical Report Describing Objectives, Methods, and Results," *Mineta Transportation Institute Publications* (2022), doi.org/10.31979/mti.2022.2123.

75 Estimates range from 1.3 million: Low estimate from Eric Scharnhorst, "Quantified Parking: Comprehensive Inventories for Five US Cities," Research Institute for Housing America, 2018. High estimate from Polly Trottenberg; see Gersh Kuntzman, "Reporter's Notebook: Corey's a 'Master' Planner—and Other City Hall Takeaways," *Streetsblog NYC*, June 13, 2019, nyc.streetsblog.org/2019/06/13/reporters-notebook-coreys-a-master-planner-and-other-city-hall-takeaways.

75 441,541 curb spaces: Matthew Roth, "San Francisco First City in the Nation to Count Its Parking Spaces," *Streetsblog SF*, May 29, 2010, sf.streetsblog.org/2010/03/29/san-francisco-first-city-in-the-nation-to-count-its-parking-spaces.

75 Philadelphia has 2.2 million: Scharnhorst, "Quantified Parking."

76 "When I started measuring": Geoff Manaugh and Nicola Twilley, "The Philosophy of SimCity: An Interview with the Game's Lead Designer," *Atlantic*, May 9, 2013, theatlantic.com/technology/archive/2013/05/the-philosophy-of-simcity-an-interview-with-the-games-lead-designer/275724.

76 the production of cement: Johanna Lehne and Felix Preston, *Making Concrete Change: Innovation in Low-Carbon Cement and Concrete* (London: Chatham House, 2018), chathamhouse.org/2018/06/making-concrete-change-innovation-low-carbon-cement-and-concrete.

76 A second is the loss: T. E. Dahl, *Status and Trends of Wetlands in the Conterminous United States 2004–2009* (Washington, DC: U.S. Fish and Wildlife Service, 2011), 40.

76 **This transition is associated:** Benoît Geslin et al., "The Proportion of Impervious Surfaces at the Landscape Scale Structures Wild Bee Assemblages in a Densely Populated Region," *Ecology and Evolution* 6, no. 18 (September 2016): 6599–615, doi.org/10.1002/ece3.2374.

76 **prior to 1950:** Oliver Gillham, *The Limitless City: A Primer on the Urban Sprawl Debate* (Washington, DC: Island Press, 2002), 85.

77 **Various studies have estimated:** Annalise G. Blum et al., "Causal Effect of Impervious Cover on Annual Flood Magnitude for the United States," *Geophysical Research Letters* 47, no. 5 (March 2020): e2019GL086480, doi.org/10.1029/2019GL086480.

77 **Approximately 770 square miles:** C. R. Hakkenberg et al., "Characterizing Multi-decadal, Annual Land Cover Change Dynamics in Houston, TX Based on Automated Classification of Landsat Imagery," *International Journal of Remote Sensing* 40, no. 2 (2019): 693–718, doi.org/10.1080/01431161.2018.1516318.

77 **land becoming impervious:** "Watch Two Decades of Growth in Houston," Kinder Institute Research, November 21, 2017, kinder.rice.edu/2017/11/21/watch-two-decades-of-growth-in-houston.

77 **almost a third of its wetlands:** John S. Jacob, "Houston-Area Freshwater Wetland Loss, 1992–2010," Texas A&M AgriLife Extension, 2015, cdn-ext.agnet.tamu.edu/wp-content/uploads/2019/04/ERPT-001-more-flooding-fewer-fish-freshwater-wetland-loss-in-the-houston-area-1992-2010-1.pdf.

77 **runoff is up 204 percent:** "Another Flood," *Houston Chronicle*, January 8, 2017, houstonchronicle.com/opinion/editorials/article/Another-flood-10867145.php.

78 **by 2020 they had created:** Warren Campbell, "Western Kentucky University Stormwater Utility Survey 2020," Western Kentucky School of Engineering and Applied Sciences, March 13, 2020, digitalcommons.wku.edu/cgi/viewcontent.cgi?article=1002&context=seas_faculty_pubs.

78 **drivers in Texas alone:** Texas Department of Transportation, Environmental Affairs Division, "Technical Report: Statewide On-Road Greenhouse Gas Emissions Analysis and Climate Change Assessment," October 2018, ftp.txdot.gov/pub/txdot/get-involved/sat/loop-1604-from-sh16-i-35/091020-greenhouse-gas-report.pdf.

79 **car-centric environments:** Angie Schmitt, *Right of Way: Race, Class, and the Silent Epidemic of Pedestrian Deaths in America* (Washington, DC: Island Press, 2020).

79 **"key policy instrument":** Institution of Highways and Transportation

(2005), "Parking Strategies and Management, London," in *Parking Issues and Policies*, ed. Stephen Ison and Corrine Mulley (Bingley, UK: Emerald Group, 2014), 4.

79 **In 2017, per-capita car ownership:** Stacy C. Davis, Susan E. Williams, and Robert G. Boundy, *Transportation Energy Data Book*, ed. 35 (Oak Ridge, TN: Oak Ridge National Laboratory, October 2016), energy.gov/eere/vehicles/fact-962-january-30-2017-vehicles-capita-other-regions countries-compared-united-states.

79 **we also drove 60 percent:** Ari Kahan, "Annual Passenger Travel Tends to Increase with Income," U.S. Energy Information Administration, May 11, 2016, eia.gov/todayinenergy/detail.php?id=26192.

80 **One study from 2017:** INRIX Research, "Searching for Parking Costs Americans $73 Billion a Year," press release, July 12, 2017, inrix.com/press-releases/parking-pain-us.

80 **According to the U.S. Department of Energy:** Data retrieved from SLOPE: State and Local Planning for Emergency, a project of the National Renewable Energy Laboratory, in July 2020, eere.energy.gov/sled/#/results/sources?city=Orlando&abv=FL§ion=electricity¤tState=Florida&lat=28.5383355&lng=-81.3792365.

81 **"If we buy a new car":** *The Simpsons*, season 4, episode 9, "Mr. Plow," directed by Jim Reardon, written by Jon Vitti, aired November 19, 1992, on Fox.

81 **parking in America is free:** *Nationwide Personal Transportation Survey 1990*, cited in Donald Shoup, "An Opportunity to Reduce Minimum Parking Requirements," *Journal of the American Planning Association* 61, no. 1 (1995), doi.org/10.1080/01944369508975616.

81 **median cost of a new:** Raymond Smith, "Parking Structure Cost Outlook for 2020," WGI, no date, wginc.com/wp-content/uploads/2020/07/Parking-Construction-Cost-Outlook.pdf.

81 **$4,400 to supply parking:** Todd Litman, "Parking Costs," Victoria Transport Policy Institute, 13, vtpi.org/tca/tca0504.pdf.

81 **between $189 and $554 billion:** Mark Delucchi, "The Annualized Cost of Motor-Vehicle Use in the U.S., 1990–1991: Summary of Theory, Data, Methods, and Results," Institute of Transport Studies, University of California, Davis, 1998, 52.

82 **In 2015, a group of researchers:** Chris McCahill et al., "Effects of Parking Provision on Automobile Use in Cities: Inferring Causality," *Journal of the Transportation Research Board* 2543, no. 1 (2016): 159–65, doi.org/10.3141/2543-19.

82 **Parking built into houses:** Adam Millard-Ball et al., "What Do Residential Lotteries Show Us about Transportation Choices?," *Urban Studies* 59, no. 2 (2022): 434–52, doi.org/10.1177/0042098021995139.

82 **Though Jackson Heights residents:** Rachel Weinberger et al., "Residential Off-Street Parking Impacts on Car Ownership, Vehicle Miles Traveled, and Related Carbon Emissions New York City Case Study," *Journal of the Transportation Research Board* 2118, no. 1 (2009): 24–30, doi.org/10.3141/2118-04.

83 **"Anyone who purchases":** Rachel Weinberger, "Parking Mismanagement: An RX for Congestion," in *Parking and the City*, ed. Donald Shoup (New York: Routledge, 2018), 103.

83 **A separate study found:** Zhan Guo, "Residential Street Parking and Car Ownership: A Study of Households with Off-Street Parking in the New York City Region," *Journal of the American Planning Association* 79, no. 1 (2013): 32–48, doi.org/10.1080/01944363.2013.790100.

83 **Nationally, people who live:** Michael Manville, "Bundled Parking and Vehicle Ownership: Evidence from the American Housing Survey," *Journal of Transport and Land Use* 10, no. 1 (2017), doi.org/10.5198/jtlu.2016.730.

83 **surveyed lottery winners:** Adam Millard-Ball, Jeremy West, Nazanin Rezaei, and Garima Desai, "What Do Residential Lotteries Show Us about Transportation Choices?" *Urban Studies* 59, no. 2 (February 2022): 434–52, doi.org/10.1177/0042098021995139.

83 **When workers are forced:** Shoup, "An Opportunity to Reduce."

83 **expensive parking is the key determinant:** Daniel G. Chatman et al., *Making Effective Fixed-Guideway Transit Investments: Indicators of Success* (Washington, DC: National Academies Press, 2014), doi.org/10.17226/22355.

83 **fell by 17 percent:** Donald Shoup, "Evaluating the Effects of Cashing out Employer-Paid Parking: Eight Case Studies," *Transport Policy* 4, no. 4 (October 1997), 201–16, doi.org/10.1016/S0967-070X(97)00019-X.

83 **A particularly dramatic example:** David Gutman, "The Not-So-Secret Trick to Cutting Solo Car Commutes: Charge for Parking by the Day," *Seattle Times*, August 10, 2017, seattletimes.com/seattle-news/transportation/the-not-so-secret-trick-to-cutting-solo-car-commutes-charge-for-parking-by-the-day.

84 **parking is a kind of narcotic:** Victor Dover, quoted in Donald Shoup, *The High Cost of Free Parking*, updated ed. (New York: Routledge, 2011), 122.

84 **exposed to a parking crater:** Kelcie Ralph, "Is It Really Too Far? Overestimating Walk Time and Distances Reduces Walking," *Transportation*

Research Part F: Traffic Psychology and Behaviour 74 (October 2020), doi.org/10.1016/j.trf.2020.09.009.

85 **"parking is jammed":** Richard Willson, interview with the author, November 21, 2019.

85 **In a study of ten Southern California:** Shoup, *High Cost of Free Parking*, 82.

85 **"not available when I arrive":** David Fields, interview with the author, December 6, 2019.

85 **"parking was universally oversupplied":** Rachel Weinberger and Joshua Karlin-Resnick, "Parking in Mixed-Use US Districts: Oversupplied No Matter How You Slice the Pie," *Journal of the Transportation Research Board* 2537, no. 1 (2015), doi.org/10.3141/2537-19.

85 **Near hip South Congress Avenue:** Samuel King, "There's Plenty of Parking around South Congress, Study Finds. But Nobody Knows Where It Is," KUT 90.5, November 29, 2019, kut.org/transportation/2019-11-29/theres-plenty-of-parking-around-south-congress-study-finds-but-nobody-knows-where-it-is.

85 **In Albany, New York:** Caitlyn M. May, "Parking Study Shows No Parking Issue," *Albany Democrat-Herald*, November 13, 2019, democratherald.com/news/local/parking-study-shows-no-parking-issue/article_aa1dc144-5ef1-5830-a314-bbad4fe8d18b.html.

86 **In Paducah, Kentucky:** Shamarria Morrison, "City Parking Study Does Not Recommend Creating Additional Parking Downtown," WPSD Local 6, March 9, 2020, wpsdlocal6.com/news/city-parking-study-does-not-recommend-creating-additional-parking-downtown/article_210c5cac-625d-11ea-82a5-9358fc4eb87b.html.

86 **maximum parking occupancy:** Daniel Rowe, "Right Size Parking: Final Report," King County Metro Transit, August 2015, metro.kingcounty.gov/programs-projects/right-size-parking/pdf/rsp-final-report-8-2015.pdf.

86 **In Seattle, residential lots:** Jesse London and Clark Williams-Derry, "Who Pays for Parking? How the Oversupply of Parking Undermines Housing Affordability," Sightline Institute, December 2013.

86 **A study of more than two hundred:** Jonathan Rogers et al., "Estimating Parking Utilization in Multi-family Residential Buildings in Washington, D.C.," *Transportation Research Record Journal of the Transportation Research Board* 2568, no. 1, 72–82 (2016) doi:10.3141/2568-11.

86 **In Chicago, builders supply:** "Stalled Out: How Empty Parking Spaces Diminish Neighborhood Affordability," Center for Neighborhood Technology, 2016, cnt.org/sites/default/files/publications/CNT_Stalled%20Out_0.pdf.

86 **In Boston and its suburbs:** "Metro Boston Perfect Fit Parking Initiative: Phase II Report," Metropolitan Area Planning Council, 2019, perfectfit parking.mapc.org.

86 **Consider the parking-rich:** Norman Garrick, "Valuing Parking and the Land on Which It Stands," lecture, Compass Community Planning Association of Southwest Idaho, 2020.

87 **large body of research:** J. Morrall and D. Bolger, "The Relationship Between Downtown Parking Supply and Transit Use," *ITE Journal* 66, no. 2 (1996).

87 **In 1966, one transportation scholar:** Wilfred Owen, *The Metropolitan Transportation Problem* (Washington, DC: Brookings Institution, 1966), 70.

CHAPTER 6: How to Use Parking for Money Laundering, Tax Evasion, and Theft

91 **"Why should I pay":** *Seinfeld*, season 3, episode 22, "The Parking Space," directed by Tom Cherones, written by Larry David, Jerry Seinfeld, and Greg Daniels, aired April 22, 1992, on NBC.

92 **"Guys love parking":** Brian Iske, interview with the author, November 22, 2019.

92 **In the 1950s, architects dreamed:** Michael Brawne, "Parking Terminals," *Ekistics* 10, no. 61 (November 1960): 332–35, jstor.org/stable/43615944.

92 **"All muscle without clothing":** Fred A. Bernstein, "Come to Park: Stay for the Architecture," *New York Times*, December 1, 2009.

92 **Since 1990, the American Society:** Eran Ben-Joseph, *Rethinking a Lot: The Design and Culture of Parking* (Cambridge, MA: MIT Press, 2012), 4.

92 **artist Ed Ruscha:** Tom Vanderbilt, "Can Parking Lots Be Great?," *Slate*, March 31, 2012, slate.com/culture/2012/03/eran-ben-josephs-rethinking-a-lot-reviewed.html.

92 **That low opinion is shared:** Jordan Weissmann, "The Least Meaningful Job in America (According to PayScale)," *Slate*, July 22, 2015, slate.com/blogs/moneybox/2015/07/22/the_least_meaningful_job_in_america_according_to_payscale_it_involves_cars.html.

93 **"ragtag group of fractured poets":** *The Parking Lot Movie*, directed by Meghan Eckman (2010).

94 **"Parking is a cash business":** John Van Horn, *Death by Parking* (Los Angeles: self-published, 2017), 31.

94 **"People never understood":** Dennis Cunning, interview with the author, June 4, 2020.

94 "There's no attendant here": Ben Feigenbaum, interview with the author, December 9, 2019.

94 The union contract had a special: Cunning interview.

95 "one of the largest rip-offs": Linda Loyd, "11 Ex-Employees for Airport's Lots Convicted in Scam," *Philadelphia Inquirer*, May 21, 1997.

96 One cashier, Carol Eller: Bob Warner, "Former Parking Aide Tells Court of Scam," *Philadelphia Daily News*, March 28, 2000.

97 1,400 tickets a week: Bob Warner, "Cyber Whiz Paced $3.4M Scam," *Philadelphia Daily News*, March 29, 2000.

98 In 1995, the year after: Bob Warner, "2 Leaders Guilty in Airport Scam," *Philadelphia Daily News*, April 6, 2000.

98 One cashier testified: Linda Loyd, "Official Linked to Parking Scam at Phila. Airport," *Philadelphia Inquirer*, October 9, 1997.

98 "raised not to believe in banks": Bob Warner, "2 Deny Skimming Airport $$," *Philadelphia Daily News*, April 4, 2000.

98 "position of public or private trust": *United States v. Gricco*, 277 F.3d 339 (3d Cir. 2002).

99 store bootleg hooch: Connie Bruck, *Master of the Game: How Steve Ross Rode the Light Fantastic from Undertaker to Creator of the Largest Media Conglomerate in the World* (New York: Simon & Schuster, 2013), 27.

99 the message goes out to his friends, too: Bruck, *Master of the Game*, 43–44.

99 to pay bribes: Bruck, *Master of the Game*, 43–44.

99 In a 1970 feature: "Market Mystery," *Forbes*, June 1, 1970, 22–23.

99 Mayor Abe Beame, who succeeded: Lee Dembart, "Broad Parking Ban in Manhattan Begins as Mayor Yields to Ruling," *New York Times*, June 16, 1977.

100 twenty-five thousand spaces: Carter B. Horsley, "Plan Would Trip Parking Spaces," *New York Times*, August 16, 1981.

100 up 33 percent: Richard Levine, "Car Madness in Manhattan: Cure Sought," *New York Times*, October 11, 1987.

100 "Let's do something together": Leonard Boxer, interview with the author, June 16, 2020.

100 "If the Anglo-Saxons could come": Christopher Gray, "What Are Dakota and Montana Doing in New York?," *New York Times*, September 28, 1986.

100 Between 1982 and 1983: David Bird, "Parking Costs Mount with No End in Sight," *New York Times*, October 22, 1984.

100 they accounted for 80 percent: Emily Sacher, "New Parking Lots Can't Find Space," *Newsday*, October 21, 1985.

102 "I was running the garage": Cunning interview.

102 "shortage of brown paper bags": Clyde Wilson, interview with the author, June 16, 2020.

102 "wet cement poured down": Tom Robbins, "Taken for a Ride," *New York Daily News*, March 6, 1994.

102 "ever go near Charlie Salerno": Frederick B. Lacey, "Decision of the Independent Administrator, Investigations Officer vs. Victor Alfieri and Eugene Bennett," October 27, 1992, 29–31.

102 his own son offered: William K. Rashbuam, "Two Are Charged in Money-Laundering Scheme," *New York Times*, July 14, 2001, nytimes.com/2001/07/14/nyregion/two-are-charged-in-money-laundering-scheme.html.

103 It belongs to our brugad: Frederick B. Lacey, "Opinion of the Independent Administrator, Investigations Officer vs. Cirino 'Charles' Salerno and William Cutolo," August 20, 1990, 13–14.

103 "Speed collects money": Bruck, *Master of the Game*, 248.

103 "shakedown" funds from the local: Organized Crime: 25 Years after Valachi: Hearings before the Senate Permanent Subcommittee on Investigations of the Committee on Governmental Affairs, Day 5, 100th Cong. 883 (1988) (affidavit of Vincent Cafaro, New York, NY).

103 "a sweetheart" contract: Bruck, *Master of the Game, 249.*

103 "Katz told speed": Bruck, *Master of the Game*, 250.

104 "bad business deals": Bruck, *Master of the Game,* 253.

104 "He wasn't happy, of course": Bruck, *Master of the Game,* 253.

104 "hard to believe now": Doug Sarini, interview with the author, June 16, 2020.

104 "Have we had a poor reputation": Clyde Wilson, "Newcomers—Welcome to the Parking Business," *Parking Today*, November 2021, 40.

CHAPTER 7: A Trip to the Heart of the Commercial Parking Industry

106 "surprises and magical moments": Brian Dixon et al., "Parking at Disney World" [PowerPoint slides], presented at Disney World, Florida, October 21, 2019.

107 "Don't worry, I'm a professional": *Ferris Bueller's Day Off,* directed by John Hughes (1986).

107 "Manhattan's crazy, but it's an animal": Carl DePinto, in conversation with the author, October 21, 2019.

108 "There is so much": Christine Banning, "Welcome Address," speech at The Mobility Revolution: 2019 NPA Convention & Expo, Orlando, Florida, October 21, 2019.

109 "We'd never admit this": Jim Huger, interview with the author, October 22, 2019.

110 "Of the expansive list": Bella Miller, "Tickets, Towing and Tyranny: Duke Parking and Transportation," *Duke Chronicle*, November 13, 2019, dukechronicle.com/article/2019/11/duke-university-parking-tickets-unjust.

110 "making it really hard": Iris Liang, "'There's No Way to Win against Parking': Faculty, Staff Vent Frustrations against Parking and Transportation," *Duke Chronicle*, November 18, 2019, dukechronicle.com/article/2019/11/faculty-staff-frustrations-parking-and-transportation-duke-university.

110 "we are mostly hated": Carl DePinto, in conversation with the author, November 26, 2019.

110 "providing parking for faculty": "Former UC President Clark Kerr, a National Leader in Higher Education, Dies at 92," press release, UC Berkeley Public Affairs, December 2, 2003, berkeley.edu/news/media/releases/2003/12/02_kerr.shtml.

110 "a series of individual faculty": Clark Kerr, *The Uses of the University*, 5th ed. (Cambridge, MA: Harvard University Press, 2001), 15.

110 Students say parking rates: John A. Jakle and Keith A. Sculle, *Lots of Parking: Land Use in a Car Culture* (Charlottesville: University of Virginia Press, 2005), 216.

110 "institutional caste system": Kiriana Cowansage, email to the author, October 29, 2019.

111 "delayed my career": Cowansage, email to the author.

111 "It takes four years": Eran Ben-Joseph, *Rethinking a Lot: The Design and Culture of Parking* (Cambridge, MA: MIT Press, 2012), 4.

111 "On-site parking I got!": Ben Thomas, "Mayo Clinic On-Site Parking Reaction," YouTube video, December 3, 2015, 1:23, youtube.com/watch?v=KUkOupnpu_4.

112 "proud of that": Carl DePinto, in conversation with the author, October 21, 2019.

120 With SpotHero, one study: Joseph P. Schwieterman, C. Scott Smith, and Jessica Kupets, "Driving toward Efficiency: How SpotHero and Other Parking Booking Intermediaries Add Value to Off-Street Parking in Chicago," Chaddick Institute Policy Series, DePaul University, November 21, 2019.

CHAPTER 8: When Wall Street Bought Chicago's Parking Meters

123 selling off the city's garages: Chicago City Council, "Authorization for Execution of Intergovernmental Agreement with Chicago Park District and

Lease Agreement with Loop Parking, LLC for Chicago Downtown Parking System," *Journal of the Proceedings of the City Council of the City of Chicago, Illinois*, November 1, 2006.

123 "You couldn't go anywhere": Paul Volpe, interview, November 1, 2017, Richard M. Daley Oral Histories, University of Illinois–Chicago Digital Collection, collections.carli.illinois.edu/digital/collection/uic_rmdoh/id/18/rec/43.

123 When Daley offered him the job: Paul Volpe, interview.

124 In 2016, for example, the country's: Michael Maciag, "How Autonomous Vehicles Could Affect City Budgets," *Governing*, July 28, 2017, governing.com/gov-data/gov-how-autonomous-vehicles-could-effect-city-budgets.html.

124 off by more than a thousand: Michael Condon, *The Chicago Parking Meter Concession of 2008* (Chicago: Windy City Publishing, 2017), 4.

124 "strengthen our city finances": "Chicago Privatization Blitz Draws Critics," NPR, December 8, 2008, npr.org/templates/story/story.php?storyId=97973438.

124 "We've been working on this": Ben Joravsky and Mick Dumke, "FAIL, Part One: Chicago's Parking Meter Lease Deal," *Chicago Reader*, April 9, 2009, chicagoreader.com/news-politics/fail-part-one-chicagos-parking-meter-lease-deal.

125 His staff put together: Patryk Piwinski, "Chicago Metered Parking System Concession Agreement: An Analysis of the Long-Term Leasing of the Chicago Parking Meter System," files of the 32nd Ward Office, Alderman Scott Waguespack, City of Chicago.

125 "You know, I got the thing": Condon, *Chicago Parking Meter Concession*, 37.

126 "This money is not going": Condon, *Chicago Parking Meter Concession*, 49–53.

126 "How many of us read": Joravsky and Dumke, "FAIL: Part One."

127 "think outside the box": Joravsky and Dumke, "FAIL: Part One."

127 he told reporters who asked: Dan Blake, "Daley Takes Blame for Meters," *Chicago Tribune*, May 20, 2009.

129 Chicago's downtown resurgence: Adie Tomer and Lara Fishbane, "Big City Downtowns Are Booming, but Can Their Momentum Outlast the Coronavirus?," Brookings Institution, May 6, 2020, brookings.edu/research/big-city-downtowns-are-booming-but-can-their-momentum-outlast-the-coronavirus.

130 "exiles from Jerusalem": Nathan Carter, interview with the author, July 28, 2020.

130 "let me count the ways": Nathan Carter, interview with the author, September 22, 2020.

132 "live that out": Carter interview, July 28, 2020.

132 dropped a bombshell report: David Hoffmann, "Report of Inspector General's Findings and Recommendations: An Analysis of the Lease of the City's Parking Meters," Office of the Inspector General, City of Chicago, June 2, 2009. igchicago.org/wp-content/uploads/2011/03/Parking-Meter-Report.pdf.

132 amount to $9.58 billion: Darrell Preston, "Windfall for Investors, a Loss for the Windy City," *Bloomberg Businessweek*, August 16, 2020.

133 "between $650 million and $1.2 billion": F. Salmon, "Chicago's Good Parking Deal," Reuters, November 23, 2009, web.archive.org/web/20091128063520/blogs.reuters.com/felix-salmon/2009/11/23/chicagos-good-parking-deal. Accessed 27 July 2022.

134 Mayor Daley blustered: Dan Mihalopoulos and Dan Blake, "Daley Decries Meter Report," *Chicago Tribune*, June 3, 2009.

134 Bernard Stone slammed Hoffman's credentials: Mihapoulos and Blake, "Daley Decries Meter Report."

134 "Monday-morning quarterback": Mihapoulos and Blake, "Daley Decries Meter Report."

134 paying city mechanics: Fran Spielman, "Parking Meter Changeover Led to Windfall for City Mechanics," *Chicago Sun-Times*, March 31, 2010.

134 "extremely low rate": David Hoffmann, "Report of Inspector General's Findings and Recommendations: An Analysis of the Lease of the City's Parking Meters," Office of the Inspector General, City of Chicago, June 2, 2009, 26, igchicago.org/wp-content/uploads/2011/03/Parking-Meter-Report.pdf.

135 In 2007, Daley's administration: Ben Joravsky and Mick Dumke, "FAIL, Part Two: One Billion Dollars!," *Chicago Reader*, May 21, 2009, chicagoreader.com/news-politics/fail-part-two-one-billion-dollars.

135 "It's one thing to give": Marilyn Katz, interview, June 9, 2018, Richard M. Daley Oral Histories, University of Illinois–Chicago Digital Collection, collections.carli.illinois.edu/digital/collection/uic_rmdoh/id/129/rec/19.

136 "had amazing instincts": Paul Volpe, interview, November 1, 2017, Richard M. Daley Oral Histories, University of Illinois–Chicago Digital Collection, collections.carli.illinois.edu/digital/collection/uic_rmdoh/id/18/rec/43.

136 commissioner, Gabe Klein: Gabe Klein, interview with the author, December 6, 2019.

136 "We got scammed": Hal Dardick and Kristen Mack, "Meter Deal Isn't a Hit with Hopefuls," *Chicago Tribune*, November 1, 2010.

136 By the time Daley left: Dan Mihalapoulos, "Daley's Budget Guts Parking Meter Deal Funds," *Chicago News Cooperative,* October 13, 2010, web.archive.org/web/20120723080116/chicagonewscoop.org/daleys-budget-guts-parking-meter-deal-funds.

136 the firm that claimed: William Blair & Co., "Chicago Metered Parking System Long-Term Concession," January 2, 2011, web.archive.org/web/20110102161415/williamblair.com/documents/MeterTransaction.pdf.

137 "one of the dumbest": "Fool Me Once," editorial, *Chicago Tribune,* May 5, 2013.

138 "comps" were traded away: Stephanie Farmer, "Cities as Risk Managers: The Impact of Chicago's Parking Meter P3 on Municipal Governance and Transportation Planning," *Environment and Planning A: Economy and Space* 45, no. 9 (2014): 2168, doi.org/10.1068/a130048p.

138 Rush-hour parking bans: Mary Wisniewski, "More Rush-Hour Parking?," *Chicago Sun-Times*, April 10, 2010.

139 "If you violate that rule": Studs Terkel, *Working: People Talk about What They Do All Day and How They Feel about What They Do* (New York: Pantheon Books, 1974), 142.

139 Baltimore had some blocks: Jenni Bergal, "Parking Abuse Hampers Disabled Drivers," Pew Trusts, Stateline, November 13, 2014, pewtrusts.org/en/research-and-analysis/blogs/stateline/2014/11/13/parking-abuses-hamper-disabled-drivers.

139 San Francisco estimated: San Francisco Office of the Comptroller–City Service Auditor, "Parking Meter Collections and Citation Fines Equal 96 Percent of Expected Revenue, Excluding $31.1 Million in Foregone Revenue Given Various Legal Exemptions," November 13, 2014, accessibleparkingcoalition.org/wp-content/uploads/SFMTA-Parking-Meter-Revenue-Audit-Report.pdf.

140 disabled placard use in the Loop: John Kass, "For Blue-Card Scammers, the Jig Will Be Up Soon," *Chicago Tribune*, December 22, 2013.

141 revealed a new contract: Greg Hinz, "Emanuel Revises Chicago Parking Meter Deal, but How Good Is It Now?," *Crain's Chicago Business*, April 29, 2013, chicagobusiness.com/article/20130429/BLOGS02/130429788/chicago-parking-meter-deal-revised-but-is-it-better.

142 "CPM was like a vendor": Scott Waguespack, "Rahm's Parking Meters 2013—City Keeps Paying, CPM Keeps Getting More Revenue," files of the 32nd Ward Office, City of Chicago, April 2014.

142 the city defended: Mick Dumke, "Appellate Court: Chicago's Parking Meter Deal Is Lousy but We're Stuck with It," *Chicago Reader*, June 21, 2014, chicagoreader.com/Bleader/archives/2014/06/21/appellate-court-chicagos-parking-meter-deal-is-lousy-but-were-stuck-with-it.

142 **"It's bad parking policy":** Hal Dardick, "Advantage, Meter Firm," *Chicago Tribune*, May 24, 2013.

142 **Later, Arena got:** Fran Spielman, "Ald. John Arena under Fire for Demanding Parking Perk before Cubs-Sox Game," *Chicago Sun-Times*, May 21, 2018, chicago.suntimes.com/2018/5/21/18392802/ald-john-arena-under-fire-for-demanding-parking-perk-before-cubs-sox-game.

143 **"What it ends up setting":** Hal Dardick, "Free Sunday Parking Has Cost, Some Aldermen Say," *Chicago Tribune*, May 29, 2013.

143 **"raising of the rates":** Klein interview.

143 **make back its billion-dollar investment:** Fran Spielman, "Hated Parking Meter Deal Just Gets Worse," *Chicago Sun-Times*, August 3, 2020.

CHAPTER 9: The Professor of Parking Starts a Cult

147 **"I believe it's a wake-up call:** Mike Adamick, "Cheap Parking Costly for Cities," *Philadelphia Inquirer*, April 3, 2005.

148 **"He's an evangelical person":** Kevin Holliday, interview with the author, October 12, 2020.

148 **"blood on your hands":** "Mission Hills Residents Upset over Mayor Gloria's Decision to Remove over 20 Parking Spaces," KUSI News San Diego, February 22, 2021, kusi.com/mission-hills-residents-upset-over-mayor-glorias-decision-to-remove-over-20-parking-spaces.

148 **"My earliest memory":** Donald Shoup, interview with the author, February 20, 2020.

150 **In 1998, all of America's:** Donald Shoup, *The High Cost of Free Parking*, updated ed. (New York: Routledge, 2011), 208.

151 **Cities could require developers:** Eran Ben-Joseph, *Rethinking a Lot: The Design and Culture of Parking* (Cambridge, MA: MIT Press, 2012), 79.

151 **"a breathtaking combination":** Shoup, *High Cost of Free Parking, 46.*

152 **A typically prolix and arcane:** 2019 Detroit City Code, Detroit, Michigan, "Chapter 50 Zoning," Article XIV, Development Standards, Division 1, Off-street Parking, Loading, and Access, library.municode.com/mi/detroit/codes/code_of_ordinances?nodeId=n2019DECO_CH50ZO_ARTXIVDEST.

153 **Parking requirements for funeral parlors:** Shoup, *High Cost of Free Parking*, 78.

153 Memphis and Miami had: Seth Goodman, "The United States of Parking," in *Parking and the City*, ed. Donald Shoup (New York: Routledge, 2018), 109–24.

155 "People would come in": Daniel McKenna-Foster, interview with the author, October 2, 2020.

156 a study of Philadelphia grocery stores: Donald W. Maley and R. Weinberger, "Food Shopping in the Urban Environment: Parking Supply, Destination Choice, and Mode Choice," 2011, cited in Rachel Weinberger, "Three Faces of Parking: Emerging Trends in the U.S.," in *Parking: Issues and Policies*, ed. Corinne Mulley and Stephen Ison (Bingley, UK: Emerald, 2014), 254.

157 A similar survey on commercial parking: Christopher McCahill and Norman Garrick, "Parking Supply and Urban Impacts," in *Parking: Issues and Policies*, ed. Corinne Mulley and Stephen Ison (Bingley, UK: Emerald, 2014), 33–56.

157 "some patrons will not be able": Donald Shoup, "Cashing Out Employer-Paid Parking: An Opportunity to Reduce Minimum Parking Requirements," *Journal of the American Planning Association* (Winter 1995): 14–28.

157 "Religious leaders advise": Shoup, *High Cost of Free Parking*, 138.

158 At Arizona State University: Rachel Leingang, "Want Really Cheap Parking at ASU? The Church of Jesus Christ of Latter-Day Saints Can Help," *Arizona Republic*, September 30, 2019.

158 The ITE's 1997 data: Shoup, *High Cost of Free Parking*, 43.

158 A study of Portsmouth: Andres Duany et al., *Suburban Nation: The Rise of Sprawl and the Decline of the American Dream* (New York: Macmillan, 2010), 22.

158 A 2013 study found: Jerry Walters, Brian Bochner, and Reid Ewing, "Getting Trip Generation Right: Eliminating the Bias Against Mixed Use Development," PAS Memo, American Planning Association, May–June 2013, planning.org/publications/document/9139902.

158 Another study found the ITE: Kelly Clifton, Kristina M. Currans, and Christopher D. Muhs, "Adjusting ITE's Trip Generation Handbook for Urban Context," *Journal of Transport and Land Use* 8, no. 1 (2015): 5–29, doi.org/10.5198/jtlu.2015.378.

159 "cycle of automobile dependency": Todd Litman, "Breaking the Cycle of Automobile Dependency," *Planetizen*, June 3, 2019, planetizen.com/blogs/104620-breaking-cycle-automobile-dependency.

159 "It's all volunteer!": Randy McCourt, interview with the author, December 14, 2020.

159 "Free parking has become": Shoup, *Parking and the City*, 10.

159 Bruce Belmore renounced: Bruce Belmore, "President's Message," *ITE Journal: A Community of Transportation Professionals*, February 2019, 4.

161 "On the unmetered side": John A. Jakle and Keith A Sculle, *Lots of Parking: Land Use in a Car Culture* (Charlottesville: University of Virginia Press, 2005), 39–40.

162 "One had to see it": Kerry Segrave, *Parking Cars in America, 1910–1945: A History* (Jefferson, NC: McFarland, 2012), loc. 2099 of 2950, Kindle.

162 "This is just a combination": Cynthia Crossen, "When Parallel Parking Was New and Meters Seemed Un-American," *Wall Street Journal*, July 30, 2007, wsj.com/articles/SB118574808780081653.

162 cowboys in Paso Robles: Katherine Edgerly and David Skophammer, "The Customer Experience Parking Transformation," *Parking Today*, April 2020, 30.

163 In a small city where: Highway Research Board, *Parking Principles* (Washington, DC: National Academy of Sciences, 1970), 10.

163 In a review of this practice: United States Department of Justice, Civil Rights Division, "Investigation of the Ferguson Police Department," March 4, 2015, justice.gov/sites/default/files/opa/press-releases/attachments/2015/03/04/ferguson_police_department_report.pdf.

164 When meter systems are working: Shoup, "Free Parking or Free Markets," in *Parking and the City*, 338.

164 A 1960s study of parking prices: Shoup, *High Cost of Free Parking*, 314.

164 In 1983, Don and Pat: Shoup, *High Cost of Free Parking*, 314.

165 "reserve army of the unparked": Shoup, *High Cost of Free Parking*, 354.

167 took all of thirty minutes: Bill Fulton, "Parking Management That Actually Manages Parking," *Fulton4Ventura* (blog), September 14, 2010, fulton4ventura.blogspot.com/2010/09/parking-management-that-actually.html.

167 Most parking in most U.S. cities: Michael Manville, "Parking Pricing," in *Parking: Issues and Policies*, ed. Corinne Mulley and Stephen Ison (Bingley, UK: Emerald, 2014), 137–55.

168 "Parking," Mayor Dianne Feinstein: Robert Lindsey, "The Rush These Days Is Hardly for Gold, *New York Times*, January 15, 1988.

169 Between July 2011 and January 2013: Gregory Pierce and Donald Shoup, "SF*park*: Pricing Parking by Demand," *Access* 43 (Fall 2013): 20–28, accessmagazine.org/wp-content/uploads/sites/7/2015/10/SFpark.pdf.

169 The prices have continued: Michael Manville and Daniel G. Chatman, "Theory Versus Implementation in Congestion-Priced Parking: An Evaluation of SF*park*, 2011–2012," *Research in Transportation Economics* 44, no. 1 (June 2014): 1–9.

169 **Price changes reduced the time:** Jay Primus, "Charging the Right Prices for On-Street Parking," in Shoup, *Parking and the City*, 334.

169 **Garage revenues rose:** Pierce and Shoup, "SF*park*."

169 **2,500 miles *a day*:** Primus, "Charging the Right Prices," 334.

170 **In 2016, the Obama administration:** The White House, "Housing Development Toolkit," September 2016, obamawhitehouse.archives.gov/sites/whitehouse.gov/files/images/Housing_Development_Toolkit%20f.2.pdf.

CHAPTER 10: **Parkitecture**

172 **the Palmetto Room:** Devin T. Frick, *Bullock's Department Store* (Mount Pleasant, SC: Arcadia Publishing, 2015).

173 **In 1955, the DBMA:** "Phillip Corrin to Head Downtown Parking Plan," *Los Angeles Times*, October 24, 1955.

173 **By 1957, downtown interests:** "Parking and Traffic Still Unaffected," *Los Angeles Times*, December 6, 1957.

173 **a downtown parking map:** "Parking Map of Downtown," *Los Angeles Times*, November 27, 1958.

175 **"two theme parks, a beach, and a sign":** Allison B. Cohen, "Buying into LA," *Los Angeles Times*, April 13 2003.

178 **"The measure of time":** Joel Garreau, *Edge City* (New York: Anchor Books, 1991), 124.

178 **Valley of High Parking Requirements:** Payton Chung, interview with the author, January 23, 2020.

179 **"You can't buy just one":** Katelyn Stangl, "Parking? Lots! Parking over the Minimum in Los Angeles," UCLA Institute of Transportation Studies, June 2019, doi.org/doi:10.17610/T65P41.

180 **the production of buildings:** U.S. Census Bureau and U.S. Department of Housing and Urban Development, "New Privately-Owned Housing Units Completed: Units in Buildings with 2–4 Units," FRED Economic Data, Federal Reserve Bank of St. Louis, fred.stlouisfed.org/series/COMPU24USA.

181 **"I had some architect":** Mott Smith, interview with the author, February 20, 2020.

181 **were like "dark energy":** Donald Shoup, Introduction, in *Parking and the City*, 18.

181 **"The A&P parking lot":** Robert Venturi and Denise Scott Brown, "A Significance for A&P Parking Lots or Learning from Las Vegas," *Architectural Forum*, March 1968, 36–43, usmodernist.org/AF/AF-1968-03.pdf.

182 **The architect, Turan Duda:** Erin Edgemon, "First Look: Why the New 405 Colorado Tower Looks So Different," *Austin Business Journal*, July 13, 2020, bizjournals.com/austin/news/2020/07/13/first-look-austin-405-colorado-tower.html.

183 **The policy effectively killed:** Stefanos Polyzoides, Roger Sherwood, and James Tice, *Courtyard Housing in Los Angeles: A Typological Analysis* (Berkeley: UC Press, 1982).

183 **In 1964, LA increased:** Steven A. Treffers, "The Embodiment of Speculation and Regulation: The Rise and Fall of the Dingbat Apartment," in *Dingbat 2.0: The Iconic Los Angeles Apartment as Projection of a Metropolis* (Los Angeles: Dopplehouse, 2016), 71–74.

184 **the sculptures vanished:** Susan Orlean, *The Library Book* (New York: Simon & Schuster, 2018), 237.

185 **seemed to mostly hate:** Chase Scheinbaum, "L.A.'s Small Lot Homes: Destroying Low-Rent Housing, Restoring the American Dream, or Both?," KCET, February 9, 2015, kcet.org/agenda/las-small-lot-homes-destroying-low-rent-housing-restoring-the-american-dream-or-both.

185 **"You think architects design buildings":** Daniel Dunham, interview with the author, March 11, 2020.

186 **Admission to this temple:** Michael Cieply, "At the Movie Museum, Like the Rest of LA, It's All about the Parking," Deadline, October 7, 2021, deadline.com/2021/10/movie-museum-like-rest-of-la-about-parking-1234851165.

187 **"a blood sport":** Marisa Gerber, "Want to Park in Koreatown? Get Ready for a Blood Sport," *Los Angeles Times*, May 28, 2019, latimes.com/local/lanow/la-me-ln-koreatown-parking-ktown-black-car-silver-car-20190528-story.html.

188 **Los Angeles was the least affordable:** National Association of Home Builders, "Housing Opportunity Index," 4th Quarter 2019. (Los Angeles–Long Beach–Glendale ranks last of 238 American metros, with 11.3 percent of homes classified as "affordable" for the median income.)

188 **"We had to make chicken salad":** Carol Schatz, interview with the author, June 22, 2020.

189 **"Without the ordinance":** Izek Shomof, interview with the author, July 15, 2020.

189 **A partner said:** Robert A. Jones, "Once More with Enthusiasm," *Los Angeles Times Magazine*, October 1999, 11–14.

190 running out of money: Jones, "Once More with Enthusiasm."

190 New York Goober: Ed Leibowitz, "How Developer Tom Gilmore's Wild Idea Launched the Downtown Loft Craze," *Los Angeles Magazine*, July 1, 2004, lamag.com/longform/how-developer-tom-gilmores-wild-idea-launched-the-downtown-loft-craze.

190 "a real city": Frances Anderton, "Swank Plans in Skid Row Los Angeles," *New York Times*, January 25, 2001.

190 "Show me the city": Leibowitz, "How Developer Tom Gilmore's Wild Idea Launched the Downtown Loft Craze."

190 "ashamed of our downtown": Jones, "Once More with Enthusiasm."

191 "We would do anything": Jones, "Once More with Enthusiasm."

191 "Transportation was ultimately": "Tom Gilmore: A CSQ&A with the Downtown Developer," *C-Suite Quarterly*, March 31, 2015, csq.com/2015/03/tom-gilmore-a-csq-and-a-with-the-downtown-developer/#.Yb9mHi1h1hA.

191 "The city looks like hell": Tom Gilmore, interview with the author, October 15, 2020.

192 That first year, Disney Hall: Donald Shoup, *High Cost of Free Parking*, updated ed. (New York: Routledge, 2011), 160.

194 historic conversions, in new buildings: Downtown Center Business Improvement District, "Downtown Los Angeles Housing Information," 1st Quarter 2009, web.archive.org/web/20110719141954/downtownla.com/pdfs/econ_residential/1Q09HousingBook.pdf.

194 "the most influential person": KGNOW, "The Woman That Revitalized Downtown Los Angeles, Carol Schatz Square Dedication 5.3.18," May 7, 2018, YouTube video, 19:14, youtube.com/watch?v=6WhseBANiys.

CHAPTER 11: The Shoupistas Take City Hall

198 "single greatest killer": Andres Duany et al., *Suburban Nation: The Rise of Sprawl and the Decline of the American Dream* (New York: Macmillan, 2010), 163.

198 "Everything we were trying to do": Chrissy Mancini Nichols, interview with the author, January 24, 2020.

199 "They all need help": Chrissy Mancini Nichols, interview with the author, February 27, 2020.

199 eighty-two thousand parcels: Metropolitan Planning Council, "The City of Chicago's Proposed 2015 TOD Ordinance: Estimated Impacts on Development Area and Economic Benefits," July 2015, Chicago, Illinois, metro planning.org/uploads/cms/documents/2015_tod_ordinance_impacts_mpc_analysis.pdf.

200 The share of large buildings: Borna Khoshand, "Parking Minimums Hold Developers Back: Examining the Impact of TOD Ordinances," *Streetsblog Chicago*, January 26, 2021, chi.streetsblog.org/2021/01/26/parking-minimums-are-holding-developers-back-examining-the-impact-of-chicagos-tod-ordinances.

200 "The joke is": Paul Sajovec, interview with the author, October 13, 2020.

201 "opened my eyes": Lindsay Bayley, interview with the author, July 14, 2020.

202 "In Florida, parking will wipe out": Jane Wilberding, interview with the author, July 24, 2020

204 "blighting time bomb": Joseph P. Schwieterman and Dana M. Caspall, *The Politics of Place: A History of Zoning in Chicago* (Chicago: Lake Claremont Press, 2005), 62.

205 The four-plus-one boom ended: Joseph P. Schwieterman and Dana M. Caspall, *The Politics of Place: A History of Zoning in Chicago* (Chicago: Lake Claremont Press, 2005), 45.

205 "Rigid enforcement of the 2½ parking": *United States v. City of Parma*, 494 F. Supp. 1049 (N.D. Ohio 1980).

205 Consider some of the contemporary: Amy Dain, "The State of Zoning for Multi-family Housing in Greater Boston," Massachusetts Smart Growth Alliance, June 2019, ma-smartgrowth.org/wp-content/uploads/2019/06/03/FINAL_Multi-Family_Housing_Report.pdf.

206 But in the first study: Daniel Baldwin Hess and Jeffrey Rehler, "Minus Minimums: Development Response to the Removal of Minimum Parking Requirements in Buffalo (NY)," *Journal of the American Planning Association* 87, no. 3 (2021): 396–408, doi.org/10.1080/01944363.2020.1864225.

206 In Seattle, developers taking advantage: C. J. Gabbe, Gregory Pierce, and Gordon Clowers, "Parking Policy: The Effects of Residential Minimum Parking Requirements in Seattle," *Land Use Policy* 91 (February 2020): 104053, doi.org/10.1016/j.landusepol.2019.104053.

206 the California statehouse quietly abolished: Michael Andersen, "Oregon Nears Green Light for Big Parking Reform," *Sightline*, May 21, 2022, sightline.org/2022/05/21/oregon-nears-green-light-for-big-parking-reform.

206 "That has been proven": Kate Sweeney, "Atlanta Looks for Solutions to City's Parking Lot Deserts," WABE, May 26, 2016, wabe.org/atlanta-looks-solutions-city-s-parking-lot-deserts.

206 "There's a really direct connection": David Hyde, "Should Seattle Declare War on Parking to Fight Climate Change?," KUOW, January 18, 2018, kuow.org/stories/should-seattle-declare-war-parking-fight-climate-change.

207 **"A gateway drug to parking":** Tony Jordan, interview with the author, February 26, 2020.

207 **"articulate, thoughtful, and wrong":** John Van Horn, "The Money Comes from Only One Place," *Parking Today*, January 19, 2021, parkingtoday.com/blog/2021/01/the-money-comes-from-only-one-place.

207 **Portland had been an early adopter:** Donald Shoup, "On-Street Parking Management Versus Off-Street Parking Requirements," in *Parking and the City*, ed. Donald Shoup (New York: Routledge, 2018), 228.

208 **In 2021, the city's largest preschool:** Tony Jordan, "Parking over Preschool," *The Parking Minute* (blog), June 1, 2021, theparkingminute.com/parking-over-preschool.

208 **"We'll do it for free":** Cary Westerbeck, interview with the author, June 22, 2020.

210 **"Blind people shouldn't have":** Patrick Siegman, "Should Blind People in Berkeley Be Required to Buy Parking Spaces?," *Streetsblog Cal*, January 25, 2021, cal.streetsblog.org/2021/01/25/should-blind-people-in-berkeley-be-required-to-buy-parking-spaces.

212 **the simple logic:** Office of the Governor of California (@CAGovernor), "CA is making housing cheaper & easier to build by eliminating parking requirements for new housing near transit and daily destinations like jobs, grocery stores, & schools. Thanks to the work of @laurafriedman43, we're prioritizing people and the planet over cars." Twitter, 4:54 p.m. September 22, 2022. twitter.com/CAgovernor/status/1573098564976508928.

212 **grateful for longevity:** Jared Brey, "Why California's Parking Reform Matters for Housing and Climate," Governing, September 7, 2022, governing.com/community/why-californias-parking-reform-matters-for-housing-and-climate.

CHAPTER 12: The Market: Parking after Minimums

214 **she couldn't even get their support:** Martha Roskowski, "Ideas to Accelerate Parking Reform in the United States," Institute for Transportation & Development Policy, 2021.

215 **On a Saturday before Christmas:** Kyle Gebhart, "Parking Oversupply in East Harlem: Analysis of Parking Occupancy and Mode Usage at East River Plaza in New York City," paper presented at the 92nd Annual

Meeting of the Transportation Research Board, Washington, DC, January 2013, trid.trb.org/view/1243080.

215 **issuing $237 million:** Jim O'Grady, "After Hundreds of Millions of Dollars of Public Subsidies, Barely Used Yankees Parking Garages Face Financial Collapse," WNYC, May 9, 2011, wnyc.org/story/285001-barely-used-yankees-parking-garages-face-financial-collapse.

215 **owed the city:** Gabriel Sandoval, "Yankee Stadium Parking Lot Woes Block Soccer Field Goal, Cost Taxpayers Millions," *The City*, December 7, 2020, thecity.nyc/2020/12/7/22159981/yankee-stadium-parking-lot-woes-block-soccer-field-goal.

215 **Zoning required 1,700 spaces:** Michael Neibauer, "DC Pays Off DC USA Garage 15 Years ahead of Schedule," *Washington Business Journal*, February 13, 2014, bizjournals.com/washington/breaking_ground/2014/02/dc-pays-off-dcusa-garage-15-years.html.

215 **"Every time we re-evaluate":** Roskowski, "Ideas to Accelerate Parking Reform."

215 **"May your dreams always be bigger":** Casey Rackham, "17 Jokes about Trader Joe's Parking Lots That You'll 100% Relate To," *BuzzFeed*, July 29, 2019, buzzfeed.com/caseyrackham/trader-joes-parking-lots.

216 **nearly $10,000 a year:** Ellen Edmonds, "Sticker Shock: Owning a New Vehicle Costs Nearly $10,000 Annually," AAA Newsroom, August 19, 2021, newsroom.aaa.com/2021/08/sticker-shock-owning-a-new-vehicle-costs-nearly-10000-annually.

216 **dealers now make more:** Ben Eisen and Adrienne Roberts, "The Seven-Year Auto Loan: America's Middle Class Can't Afford Its Cars," *Wall Street Journal*, October 1, 2019, wsj.com/articles/the-seven-year-auto-loan-americas-middle-class-cant-afford-their-cars-11569941215.

217 **"new move" for Charlotte:** Sarah Rabil, "Latta's Growing Pains," *Charlotte Observer*, July 26, 2006.

219 **"They don't share their parking":** Clay Grubb, interview with the author, July 20, 2020.

219 **"If my firm, Grubb Properties":** Clay Grubb, "How to Save Renters $15 Million with One Easy Change," *Charlotte Observer*, September 14, 2018.

222 **"To further put that":** David Cunningham, interview with the author, March 9, 2020.

222 **If the garage was underground:** Rider Levett Bucknall, "Quarterly Construction Cost Report, Third Quarter (2012)," cited in Donald Shoup, "The High Cost of Minimum Parking Requirements," in *Parking: Issues and Policies*, ed. Corinne Mulley and Stephen Ison (Bingley, UK: Emerald, 2014), 92.

224 **"post-car real estate developer":** "Post-Car Real Estate Developer, Culdesac, Announces First Car-Free Neighborhood Built from Scratch in the U.S.," press release, November 19, 2019, businesswire.com/news/home/20191119005568/en.

225 **"Our concept could be":** Jeff Berens, interview with the author, November 21, 2019.

226 **Journeys to work:** Adie Tomer, Joseph Kane, and Jennifer S. Vey, "Connecting People and Places: Exploring New Measures of Travel Behavior," Brookings Institution, October 2020, brookings.edu/interactives/connecting-people-and-places-exploring-new-measures-of-travel-behavior.

226 **half a mile of a retail cluster:** Andres Sevstuk, *Street Commerce: Creating Vibrant Urban Sidewalks* (Philadelphia: University of Pennsylvania Press, 2020), 23.

CHAPTER 13: **How Americans Wound Up Living in the Garage**

227 **After COVID-19, that figure:** Richard Fry, Jeffrey S. Passel, and D'Vera Cohn, "A Majority of Young Adults in the U.S. Live with Their Parents for the First Time since the Great Depression," Pew Research Center, September 4, 2020, pewresearch.org/fact-tank/2020/09/04/a-majority-of-young-adults-in-the-u-s-live-with-their-parents-for-the-first-time-since-the-great-depression.

229 **In 2008, a white city council:** Gustavo Arellano, "Save the Murals," *Los Angeles Times*, April 16, 2008.

230 **"All of them want":** José Trinidad Castañeda, interview with the author, February 20, 2020.

232 **Thomas Pynchon wrote:** Thomas Pynchon, *The Crying of Lot 49* (New York: Harper Perennial, 2014), 14.

233 **"When you think about the housing":** Dana Cuff, interview with the author, January 31, 2020.

233 **In Los Angeles, however:** Stephanie Chavez and James Quinn, "Substandard Housing: Garages: Immigrants In, Cars Out," *Los Angeles Times*, May 24, 1987.

234 **"It's not only that we've doubled":** Jared Brey, "Dana Cuff on Backyard Houses, an Architect's Role in Affordable Housing, and Spatial Justice in L.A.," *Next City*, October 8, 2019, nextcity.org/daily/entry/dana-cuff-on-backyard-houses-an-architects-role-in-affordable-housing.

234 **big-city ADU permits:** Karen Chapple et al., "Reaching California's ADU Potential: Progress to Date and the Need for ADU Finance," Terner Center for Housing Innovation, UC Berkeley, August 2020, 8, ternercenter.berkeley .edu/wp-content/uploads/pdfs/Reaching_Californias_ADU_Potential _2020.pdf.

234 **Citywide ADU permits rose:** City of Los Angeles Department of City Planning, Housing Progress Report: July–September, 2018, accessed December 19, 2021, planning.lacity.org/odocument/7b7f2d26-d4a2-428b-8c19 -0e846fd443a4.

235 **At least one in ten:** City of Los Angeles Department of City Planning, Housing Progress Report, October–December, 2018, planning.lacity.org /odocument/42cb2634-2885-4c33-9ff4-31c8f33c34d1#:~:text=In %202018%2C%20the%20City%20of,projects%20that%20required %20planning%20approvals.

235 **"size and dignity":** J. B. Jackson, "The Domestication of the Garage," *Places Journal*, February 2019, placesjournal.org/article/j-b-jackson-the -domestication-of-the-garage. Originally published in *Landscape* 20, no. 2 (1976).

236 **He had tried to put:** Olivia Erlanger and Luis Ortega Govela, *Garage* (Cambridge, MA: MIT Press, 2018), 32.

236 **"Putting a garage in a house":** Drummond Buckley, "A Garage in the House," in *The Car and the City: The Automobile, the Built Environment, and Daily Urban Life*, ed. Martin Wachs and Margaret Crawford (Ann Arbor: University of Michigan Press, 1992), 133.

236 **As late as 1936:** Buckley, "A Garage in the House," 138.

236 **"the ruin of the backyard":** Jackson, "Domestication of the Garage."

236 **"a utilitarian space":** Buckley, "A Garage in the House," 126.

237 **This was the function:** James Howard Kunstler, *The Geography of Nowhere: The Rise and Decline of America's Man-Made Landscape* (New York: Free Press, 1994), 151.

237 **"Toad at his best":** Quoted in Clay McShane, *Down the Asphalt Path: The Automobile and the American City* (New York: Columbia University Press, 1995), 145.

237 **"the increase in motor-traffic":** Buckley, "A Garage in the House," 127.

238 **"charm and sanctuary":** Buckley, "A Garage in the House," 129.

238 **electric garage door openers:** David Gebhard, "The Suburban House and the Automobile," in *The Car and the City*, 106–23.

239 **a "slack-jawed" mien:** Kunstler, *Geography of Nowhere*, 11.

239 **from front porch to back seat:** Beth Bailey, *From Front Porch to Back Seat: Courtship in Twentieth-Century America* (Baltimore, MD: Johns Hopkins University Press, 1989).

239 "stork's nest on the chimney": Jackson, "Domestication of the Garage."

240 "Basically, we want a house": Timothy Egan, "In Portland, Houses Are Friendly. Or Else," *New York Times*, April 20, 2000.

241 By data-mining real estate: Sam Khater and Kristine Yao, "Granny Flats, Garage Apartments, In-Law Suites: Identifying Accessory Dwelling Units from Real Estate Listing Descriptions Using Text Mining," Freddie Mac, July 16, 2020, freddiemac.com/research/insight/20200716-identifying-accessory-dwelling-units-from-real-estate.

241 ADUs offer a much-needed alternative: Magda Maaoui, "A Granny Flat of One's Own? The Households That Build Accessory-Dwelling Units in Seattle's King County," *Berkeley Planning Journal* 30, no. 1 (2018), dx.doi.org/10.5070/BP330137884.

241 In some of Cuff's fieldwork: Alysia Bennett, Dana Cuff, and Gus Wendel, "Backyard Housing Boom: New Markets for Affordable Housing and the Role of Digital Technology," *Technology | Architecture + Design* 3, no. 1 (2019): 76–88, doi.org/10.1080/24751448.2019.1571831.

241 One project looking at home sales: V. Mukhija, "Outlaw In-Laws: Informal Second Units and the Stealth Reinvention of Single-Family Housing," in *The Informal American City: Beyond Taco Trucks and Day Lab*, ed. V. Mukhija and A. Loukaitou-Sideris (Cambridge, MA: MIT Press, 2014), 39–58.

241 the *Los Angeles Times* estimated: Chavez and Quinn, "Substandard Housing."

243 Long Beach City College created: Jaysha Patel, "Long Beach City College Creates Program That Will Let Homeless Students Sleep in Cars on Campus," ABC 7, November 4, 2021, abc7.com/long-beach-city-college-homeless-students-parking-pilot-program-sleeping-in-cars/11191128.

244 "not the way I wanted it to go": José Trinidad Castañeda, interview with the author July 24, 2020.

CHAPTER 14: **Planting Gardens in the Gutter**

248 In East New York, an accomplice: Michael Stern, "Rival Ice Cream Vender Held in Mister Softee Holdup Case," *New York Times,* July 26, 1969.

249 "A route is money": Sabrina Tavernise and Howard O. Stier, "Ice Cream Truck Feud Leaves 2 Badly Hurt," *New York Times,* March 30, 2004, nytimes.com/2004/03/30/nyregion/ice-cream-truck-feud-leaves-2-badly-hurt.html.

249 "You used to get a wanderer": Maria Campanella, interview with the author, March 4, 2021.

249 "You will never see": Andy Newman and Emily S. Rueb, "A Renegade Muscles In on Mister Softee's Turf," *New York Times,* May 30, 2016, nytimes.com/2016/05/31/nyregion/a-king-of-ice-cream-a-renegade-upstart-and-a-simmering-turf-war.html.

250 a sting it called Operation Meltdown: Summons, *City of New York v. Athanasios Fotinakopoulos et al.* (N.Y. Sup. Ct. 2019) (No. 450802/19), courthousenews.com/wp-content/uploads/2019/06/ice-cream-comp.pdf.

250 The first taco truck: Jesus Sanchez, "King Taco Got Start in Old Ice Cream Van," *Los Angeles Times,* November 16, 1987, latimes.com/archives/la-xpm-1987-11-16-fi-14263-story.html.

251 Chicago forbade food trucks: George Will, "Surely Chicago Has Bigger Things to Worry About Than a Cupcake Truck," *Washington Post,* August 14, 2019, washingtonpost.com/opinions/surely-chicago-has-bigger-things-to-worry-about-than-a-cupcake-truck/2019/08/14/1bc6d268-bde4-11e9-9b73-fd3c65ef8f9c_story.html?wpisrc=nl_ideas&wpmm=1.

251 found "unscripted fragments": Benjamin Schneider, "How Parking Day Went Global," *Bloomberg,* September 15, 2017, bloomberg.com/news/articles/2017-09-15/a-brief-history-of-park-ing-day?sref=C3P1bRLC.

252 "Asphalt and paving-stone trapezoids": Valeria Luiselli, *Sidewalks* (Minneapolis: Coffee House Press, 2014), 71.

252 "A short time ago": Aaron Naparstek, "City Launches 'Public Plaza Initiative' at DUMBO Pocket Park," *Streetsblog NYC,* August 10, 2007, nyc.streetsblog.org/2007/08/10/city-launches-public-plaza-initiative-at-dumbo-pocket-park.

252 "It is a New York City traffic principle": Janette Sadik-Khan and Seth Solomonow, *Streetfight: Handbook for an Urban Revolution* (New York: Penguin Books, 2016), 189.

253 She rode on the seat: Sadik-Khan and Solomonow, *Streetfight,* 27.

253 The number of cars entering: New York City Department of Transportation, New York City Mobility Report, October, 2016, nyc.gov/html/dot/downloads/pdf/mobility-report-2016-screen-optimized.pdf.

254 William Whyte's 1974 survey: Richard Rein, *American Urbanist: How William H. Whyte's Unconventional Wisdom Reshaped Public Life* (Washington, DC: Island Press, 2022), 189.

255 "Why would so many people choose": Sadik-Khan and Solomonow, *Streetfight,* 86.

255 commercial rents tripled: Sadik-Khan and Solomonow, *Streetfight,* 95.

256 drivers seemed to view: See, e.g., Courtland Milloy, "Bicyclist Bullies Try to Rule the Road in D.C.," *Washington Post,* July 8, 2014, washingtonpost.com

/local/bicyclist-bullies-try-to-rule-the-road-in-dc/2014/07/08/f7843560-06e3-11e4-bbf1-cc51275e7f8f_story.html?itid=lk_inline_manual_2.

256 Anthony Weiner said in 2013: Andrew Kaczynski, "Anthony Weiner Pulls Out F-Bombs to Rip Bike Lanes," August 13, 2013, buzzfeednews.com/article/andrewkaczynski/anthony-weiner-pulls-out-f-bombs-to-rip-bike-lanes.

256 shouldn't discuss at dinner parties: Andrea Bernstein, "Chriss Quinn: Don't Talk About Bike Lanes at Dinner Parties," WNYC, January 11, 2013, wnyc.org/story/284074-chris-quinn-dont-talk-about-bike-lanes-at-dinner-parties.

257 "all-powerful enterprise": Erik Wemple, "WSJ Editorializer: "The Bike Lobby Is an All-Powerful Enterprise," *Washington Post*, June 3, 2013, washingtonpost.com/blogs/erik-wemple/wp/2013/06/03/wsj-editorializer-the-bike-lobby-is-an-all-powerful-enterprise.

258 In September 2021, the shared bikes: Citi Bike, "Ridership Records and Improving the Rider Experience," May 2021, ride.citibikenyc.com/blog/ridershiprecords.

258 "A millennium from now": Sadik-Khan and Solomonow, *Streetfight*, 215.

259 One box truck: How's My Driving NY (@HowsMyDrivingNY), "Known fines for #NY_86921ME: $127,055.00 | Fined $22,020.00 | Reduced $86,610.00 | Paid $18,425.00 | Outstanding," Twitter, September 24, 2019, 11:20 a.m., twitter.com/HowsMyDrivingNY/status/1176562123117404162.

259 timely or efficient manner: USPS Help (@USPSHelp), "I heard back from the local PO and this is what was communicated: Parking is extremely limited in Manhattan. If our Carriers searched for parking spaces that did not interfere at times with bike lanes we could never deliver the mail timely and efficiently. &ARL," Twitter, March 8, 2018, 1:12 p.m., twitter.com/USPSHelp/status/971856288689766400.

259 Just four companies: Matthew Haag and Winnie Hu, "1.5 Million Packages a Day: The Internet Brings Chaos to N.Y. Streets," *New York Times*, October 27, 2019.

260 On Santa Monica Boulevard: Ryland Lu, "Pushed from the Curb: Optimizing Curb Space for Use by Ride-Sourcing Vehicles," paper presented at the 98th Annual Meeting of the Transportation Research Board, Washington, DC, January 2019, trid.trb.org/view/1573377.

260 A study of 2,900 trips: Eric Jaffe, "Delivery Vehicles Waste a Lot of Time Searching for Parking. Cities Can Fix That," *City Monitor*, August 19, 2020, web.archive.org/web/20201104232030/citymonitor.ai/transport/delivery-vehicles-parking-traffic-loading-zone-study-5231.

262 "I have been in the middle": Howard Yaruss, email to the author, December 23, 2020.

263 **"Guess how many loading zones we have":** Howard Yaruss, interview with the author, January 14, 2021.

265 **At the public meetings:** Public meetings of the New York City Community Board 7 Transportation Committee, October–December, 2019.

265 **called Yaruss out by name:** Public meetings of the New York City Community Board.

266 **we gave public space away:** Public meetings of the New York City Community Board.

CHAPTER 15: The New World

268 **In Virginia Beach, megachurch parishioners:** Casey Cep, "How a Megachurch Adapted to Social Distancing," *New Yorker*, April 18, 2020, newyorker .com/culture/photo-booth/honk-twice-for-hallelujah-what-church -looks-like-in-the-parking-lot.

268 **"There's always a lot of people":** Jessica Farrish, "From Church Pews to the Parking Lot," *Register-Herald*, April 18, 2020, register-herald.com /health/from-church-pews-to-the-parking-lot/article_feb93218-5214 -5a8f-9e22-c31b3121c1ca.html.

268 **"I love that we just broke":** Kevin Cole, "Car-Horn Hallelujahs 'Broke Satan's Eardrums' at King of Kings Parking Lot Easter Service," *Omaha World-Herald*, April 12, 2020, omaha.com/news/local/car-horn-hallelujahs -broke-satans-eardrums-at-king-of-kings-parking-lot-easter-service/article _6e14f2f0-ab45-516c-901a-983d0d1f44b7.html.

269 ***The Onion* joked that LA:** "L.A. Designates Open-Air Dining Areas along 101 Freeway Median," *Onion*, July 28, 2020, theonion.com/l-a-designates -open-air-dining-areas-along-101-freeway-1844531667.

269 **Yelp reported a boost:** Laura Bliss, "Where Covid's Car-Free Streets Boosted Business," *Bloomberg*, May 11, 2021, bloomberg.com/news/articles /2021-05-11/the-business-case-for-car-free-streets.

271 **"Of course, that's more important":** *The Brian Lehrer Show*, "Mayoral Campaign Update; Vaccine Volunteers; Long Island Police Hiring Practices Under Scrutiny; Ask the Mayor," aired May 28, 2021, WNYC, wnyc .org/story/the-brian-lehrer-show-2021-05-28.

271 **restaurants had taken just 8,550:** David Meyer and Kevin Sheehan, "NYC Gave Up 8,550 Parking Spots for al Fresco Dining amid COVID," *New York Post*, May 23, 2021, nypost.com/2021/05/23/nyc-gave-up-8550 -parking-spots-for-outdoor-dining-amid-covid.

271 The idea was "amazing": Steven Nessen (@s_nessen), "Mayoral forum discusses@ShabazzStuart 'the gentleman' as Eric Adams calls him, says his bike parking system Oonee is 'amazing' should be 'throughout the entire city and we should expand it… Love the idea,'" Twitter, March 2, 2021, 4:54 p.m., twitter.com/s_nessen/status/1366552386521731072.

271 Sanitation Commissioner Kathryn Garcia: Gersh Kuntzman, "EXCLUSIVE: City Takes Major Steps to Get Garbage Off the Sidewalk," *Streetsblog NYC*, March 11, 2021, nyc.streetsblog.org/2020/03/11/exclusive-city-takes-major-steps-to-get-garbage-off-the-sidewalk.

271 "Priority No. 1 is repurposing": Eve Kessler, "DECISION 2021: The Next Mayor Will Monetize Free Parking," *Streetsblog NYC*, December 15, 2020, nyc.streetsblog.org/2020/12/15/decision-2021-the-next-mayor-will-monetize-free-parking.

272 The future Manhattan borough president: Dave Colon, "Manhattan BP Candidate Seeks to Curb Sidewalk Package Warehousing Issue," *Streetsblog NYC*, April 13, 2021, nyc.streetsblog.org/2021/04/13/manhattan-bp-candidate-seeks-to-curb-sidewalk-package-warehousing-issue.

272 In a 2021 report, Transportation Alternatives: Transportation Alternatives, "NYC 25x25: A Challenge to New York City's Leaders to Give Streets Back to People," 2021, nyc25x25.org.

274 "No other major city": Zhan Guo and Shuai Ren, "From Minimum to Maximum: The Impact of Parking Standard Reform on Residential Parking Supply in London from 2004–2010," *Urban Studies* 50, no. 6 (2013): 1183–200.

274 the city recalculated: Athlyn Cathcart-Keays, "Oslo's Car Ban Sounded Simple Enough. Then the Backlash Began," *Guardian*, June 13, 2017, theguardian.com/cities/2017/jun/13/oslo-ban-cars-backlash-parking.

275 "They're like vacuum cleaners": Christophe Najdovski, interview with the author, January 8, 2020.

CONCLUSION

278 "We have these pods": Anna Wiener, "Our Ghost-Kitchen Future," *New Yorker*, June 28, 2020, newyorker.com/news/letter-from-silicon-valley/our-ghost-kitchen-future.

278 "are we prey": John Van Horn, "Suddenly We Have a Unicorn—Now What?," *Parking Today*, December 12, 2018, parkingtoday.com/blog/2018/12/suddenly-we-have-a-unicorn-now-what.

282 "pile of shit": Greg Anderson, interview with the author, August 13, 2020.

Index

Italicized page numbers indicate material in photographs or illustrations.